THE LIFE AND
TIMES OF
ARCHBISHOP
JAMES USSHER

J. A. CARR

THE LIFE AND TIMES OF ARCHBISHOP USSHER

AN INTRIGUING LOOK AT THE MAN BEHIND
THE ANNALS OF THE WORLD

First printing, January 2006

ISBN-13: 978-0-89051-467-2
ISBN-10: 0-89051-467-4
Library of Congress Number: 2005936558

Cover by Bryan Miller

For more information on this topic:
www.nlpg.com/annals.asp

Please visit our website for other great titles:
www.masterbooks.net

For information regarding author interviews, please contact the publicity department at (870) 438-5288.

Printed in the United States of America

Master
Books
A Division of New Leaf Publishing Group

CONTENTS

Scribe's Prologue 7

Chronology of James Ussher's Life 13

Introduction 17

I. Introductory 19

II. Ireland at the Close of the Sixteenth Century 33

III. Early Education of Ussher; The Founding of
Trinity College 49

IV. Student Life; The Young Controversialist;
Puritanism in Trinity College 61

V. Ussher and the Roman Catholics 73

VI. Ussher's First Essays in Literature 85

VII. The Irish Articles of 1615; Correspondence 93

VIII. Ussher, a Court Preacher; Bishop of Meath 101

IX. Ussher's Advice to Preachers; A Provincial
Visitation; Theological Opinions 111

X. The Answer to a Jesuit 123

XI. Books and Manuscripts; Archbishop of Armagh;
The Question of Toleration 135

XII. The Provostship of Bedell; Use of the Irish
Language in Public Worship; Religious
Dissensions; Gottescalcus 149

XIII. Archbishop Ussher and Bishop Bedell; The Story
       of the Irish Bible... 165

XIV. Archbishop Ussher and Laud; Correspondence;
       The Nature of Sacramental Grace;
       Appointments to the Provostship of Trinity
       College 179

 XV. Archbishop Ussher's Personal Appearance and
       Character; Private Life in Drogheda;
       "Religion of the Ancient Irish" 191

XVI. Ussher and the Presbyterians; The Question of
       Episcopacy; An Eirenicon 209

XVII. Lord Strafford and the Church of Ireland;
       Question of Precedence between Armagh and
       Dublin; Articles of the Church of England
       and New Canons Adopted by the Irish
       Convocation 221

XVIII. Frest Literary Labours; "The Antiquities of the
       British Churches"; The Epistles of St. Ignatius 237

XIX. Ussher in England; Death of Strafford;
       Revolutionary Changes in Church and State 251

 XX. Ussher in London; Straitened Means; Cromwell
       and Ussher; The Death of Charles I 265

XXI. Persecution of the Church; Ussher's Fresh
       Literary Labours; Correspondence; Declining
       Health and Death; History of His Books
       and Library; Conclusion 273

       Appendix: Articles of Religion 289

Scribe's Prologue

J ames Ussher was a man of history, a man of honor, and a highly respected churchman and scholar in his day. He defined history before him, influenced his own time, and changed the future. Yet today, he is a man of mystery — a man so very misrepresented and so misunderstood. Unfortunately, there have been, and still are, those who misrepresent him.

After spending much time working on Ussher's *Annals of the World*, I was very disappointed in the reactions of not only unbelievers, but of the Christian community as well, to a work which really defines, through history, that the Bible is not that complicated (neither is its theology — only pride makes it so). It is a work that demonstrates a young earth history from its Genesis; a work that demonstrates the Church's mission of presenting to an unbelieving world what God has done, and what our "responsible" response should be.

I wanted to know more about Ussher. God, in His providence, helped me find a book about James Ussher, a book published in 1895 that details the *The Life and Times of James Ussher*. It was written by a churchman of Ireland, a historian, and a man sympathetic to one man's life's journey, the trials of his times, and the contributions of James Ussher.

I found this book in a college library, but was only allowed to read it in the library. I took the opportunity to photocopy the entire book and scan it into a word document. It was time consuming, but from the beginning I was shown its relevance.

This book, well written in old English style and documented to the extreme, details not only the life of James Ussher, but also the development of the Reformed movement of the 1600s, just after John Calvin died: a battleground of words, theologies, axes, and bullets. James Ussher was very much a part of the movement. He helped to define it, while at the same time he attempted to mediate and correct the opposing parties.

Maybe this is why James Ussher has been called the "Forgotten Archbishop." Mediation can be a thankless business, where the stubborn opposing parties do not appreciate peacemaking efforts. I would think that the Church, if anyone, would understand these efforts! Even the author of this 1895 book misunderstood Ussher's position on Calvinism, or was influenced by others who have interpreted John Calvin. Is it gratitude and freedom (in whom) and is it obedience and allegiance (to what)?

So who were the opposing parties? They were the Roman Church still in denial about its need for reformation; a sharply divided Reformation movement busily defining what reformed meant; the British Isles going through tremendous social upheaval; and a political system that did not yet quite understand the real meaning of "separation of church and state."

However, James Ussher's efforts were not in vain. His work (or contribution) on the Articles of Religion (1615), and his influence on the Westminster Confession (1648), really should "moderate" the Reformed movement, if the extremes are eliminated. These two documents, when viewed in tandem (the latter being a shadow of the former), though necessarily Calvinistic in nature, do have free will advocacies (the "God-given" free will of "reasonable" creatures is not violated — see Articles, Items 11 and 21 and Confession III, 1 and IV, 2). A contradiction? Or a reconciliation: free will is and at the same time it is not; both seem true; but only God is capable of dividing mankind by the difference. How arrogant and typical of us to assume that we must come down on one side or the other.

Of equally great contribution (and irritation to a skeptical world and the church in general) is James Ussher's *Annals of the World*. It put to death any notion of the devil's "evolution theory." The Bible's short time period, 6000+ years (4004 B.C. to now), combined with creation science's proofs that there really is no other valid alternative, should help us focus on the Bible's real message:

Romans 10

1. Brethren, my heart's desire and prayer to God for Israel is, that they might be saved.

2. For I bear them record that they have a zeal of God, but not according to knowledge.

3. For they being ignorant of God's righteousness, and going about to establish their own righteousness, have not submitted themselves unto the righteousness of God.

4. For Christ is the end of the law for righteousness to every one that believeth.

5. For Moses describeth the righteousness which is of the law, That the man which doeth those things shall live by them.

6. But the righteousness which is of faith speaketh on this wise, Say not in thine heart, Who shall ascend into heaven? (that is, to bring Christ down from above:)

7. Or, Who shall descend into the deep? (that is, to bring up Christ again from the dead.)

8. But what saith it? The word is nigh thee, even in thy mouth, and in thy heart: that is, the word of faith, which we preach;

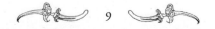

9. That if thou shalt confess with thy mouth the Lord Jesus, and shalt believe in thine heart that God hath raised him from the dead, thou shalt be saved.

10. For with the heart man believeth unto righteousness; and with the mouth confession is made unto salvation.

11. For the scripture saith, Whosoever believeth on him shall not be ashamed.

12. For there is no difference between the Jew and the Greek: for the same Lord over all is rich unto all that call upon him.

13. For whosoever shall call upon the name of the Lord shall be saved.

So, who was James Ussher? Was he a man of war? No, he did all he could to prevent it. Was he a man of peace? No, there is no permanent peace until our death in Christ. Was he a "Calvinist," or was he an "Arminian"? Did he believe that all peoples are potentially salvageable, or did he believe that only some must be? Was he a "Churchman" or a "Congregationalist"? Did he believe in "infant baptism" or "believer's baptism"? Did he wrestle with "New Testament prophecy," or did he rest in the "Old Testament fulfillment"? Was he a creationist, or was he some type of evolutionist?

If we examine James Ussher's life and times, we see that he was just a man who wanted to establish a church that would win the hearts and minds of all peoples for Jesus Christ, and provide a proper sanctifying environment by teaching the whole counsel of God. This would be a church full of what John Calvin would call "responsible citizens" — a church in which we all long in our hearts to be a participant — a church most needed in a world of political, social, and spiritual turmoil.

His life came at a critical point in Church history, a new beginning nestled between the enlightenment of people's minds from the superstition of lost centuries past and a time when all people would now have access to the truth of God's Word.

Was this truth too much for us to handle, and is the Church doomed to failure as Old Testament Israel demonstrated? Do we have a "split" kingdom that makes us vulnerable to our enemies? Do we actually believe that God did not give us all the tools to fulfill our mission of glorifying God while living peacefully in the "land"? Ancient Israel did not have the fulfillment of God's Word in Christ — we do. Ancient Israel, time and time again, suffered through the consequences of pride and unbelief — are we?

James Ussher was truly a man of God and a man for all times.

Scribe and concerned Christian,
Bruce Szwast

CHRONOLOGY OF JAMES USSHER'S LIFE

Elizabeth I made Queen 1558

"39" Articles Completed 1563

John Calvin Dies 1564

William Shakespeare born 1564

Elizabeth I excommunicated by Pope Pius V 1570

Ussher born .... Jan. 4, 1581

Spanish Armada 1588

Enters Trinity College as one of its first students .... Jan. 9, 1593

Controversy with Fitzsymons 1598

Graduates M.A. 1600

Ordained the same day Deacon and Priest .... Dec. 1601

First visit to England for the purpose of purchasing books ... 1603
James I made king 1603

Second visit (books) 1606

Regius Professor of Divinity and Chancellor of
St. Patrick's Cathedral 1607

English settlers to Virginia 1607

Third visit (books) 1609

KJV Bible 1611

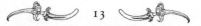

13

Fourth visit (books)... 1612

Publishes his first book — *De Continua Successione, etc.*..... 1613

Marries Phoebe Challoner 1614

Effort to impose Calvinistic Articles on the
    Church of Ireland 1615

    Shakespeare dies... 1616

Synod of Dort...................................... 1618–19

Fifth visit to England (books)................................. 1619

Birth of his daughter and only child 1620

    Plymouth Colony founded 1620

Consecrated Bishop of Meath 1621

Publishes his *Religion Anciently Professed, etc.*...................... 1622

Made a Privy Councillor 1623

Preaches before the king at Wanstead.................... 1624

Publishes his *Answers to a Jesuit* 1625

    King Charles I made king................................... 1625

Death of his mother... 1625

Appointed to the Primacy 1626

Publishes in Dublin his *Gottescalcus* 1631

Publishes in London the 2nd edition of his *Religion
    Anciently Professed by the Irish and British* 1631

Presides over Convocation...................................... 1634

Publishes *Immanuel*... 1638

Publishes his *Antiquities, etc.* in Dublin............................ 1639

Visits England again and never returns to Ireland 1640

Preaches before the English Parliament 1640

Resides at Oxford.. 1642

    Eng. Civil War begins... 1642

Assigned for his support the temporalities of the
    See of Carlisle... 1643

Publishes his *St. Ignatius*.. 1644

Invited to take his seat in the Westminster
    Assembly, refuses... 1644

Leaves Oxford for Cardiff 1645

Leaves Cardiff for London 1646

Elected Preacher at Lincoln's Inn...................................... 1647

Has an interview with Charles I in the Isle of Wight 1648

And with Cromwell 1649

    Charles I beheaded 1649

Publishes his *Annaels* 1650-1654

Meets with Cromwell.. 1653

    Charles II made king in Scotland............................ 1650

    Charles II flees to Europe 1651

    Cromwell declared Lord Protectorate...................... 1653

    Charles II restored 1660

Publishes his last book on the Septuagint......................... 1655

Dies in Lady Peterborough's house at Reigate
    and buried in Westminster Abbey ....March 21, 1656

INTRODUCTION

This writer's apology for this book will be found in the fact that there exists no accessible and popular *Life of Archbishop Ussher*. Anyone seeking to become acquainted with the principal events of his life will naturally have recourse to the most modern biography, that of Dr. Elrington, Regius Professor of Divinity in the University of Dublin, and published in 1848; but while the learning and research exhibited in this volume are undoubted, it must be acknowledged that the work itself is not conceived in a popular style, and the continuous narrative, unbroken into chapters, becomes tedious. Sufficient advantage, moreover, has not been taken of Ussher's voluminous correspondence, which is so helpful in giving the reader a proper idea of the times he lived in, the character of the man, and the friendships he formed, and is also so useful in affording an index to much of his literary work. Besides, Dr. Elrington's *Life of Ussher* was never intended, as he says himself, to be an independent publication, and is really only the introduction to an edition of the archbishop's works, extending to 17 volumes.

When we pass from Elrington's biography, we must go back to the close of the 17th century, and have to deal with the *Lives* by Parr and Bernard, both full, indeed, of interesting information, but antiquated in style, confined to old and scarce editions, and obtainable, for the most part, only in public libraries. The *Lives* by Smith and Dillingham are in the Latin tongue, and are therefore not of general service. Aiken's *Life* is written with an animus that deprives it of value. *The Ussher Memoirs*, however, compiled by the Rev. W. Ball Wright cast much light on the history of the Ussher family in its wide and important ramifications. The present volume is an effort to place the Irish Primate before the reader as he was, in his day a great ecclesiastic, a profound scholar, and a much-tried churchman. The writer has availed himself of all the sources of information he could command, and if he draws renewed attention to the life and work of a great Irishman, he will have found his best reward.

It is not necessary to mention in detail the works consulted in the preparation of the volume, as they are sufficiently enumerated in the footnotes. It may be observed that the edition of Ware's works uniformly referred to be that by Harris, published in Dublin in two volumes in 1764. Wood's Athena Oxonienses is that edited by Bliss, in three volumes. It is now known that the interesting sketches of Ussher that appeared (with portrait) in the *Dublin University Magazine* in 1841 were written by the late Bishop Fitzgerald (see the memoir prefixed to his Ecclesiastical Lectures, i, p. 16).

Some trouble has been taken to remove an undeserved slur on the memory of Archbishop Ussher, and to prove from contemporary literature that he did not counsel the death of Strafford. A vindicating of the Irish Church policy of Laud and Strafford will also be found in these pages.

It may be added that some trouble has been taken with the Ussher chronology, and an effort has been made to fix correctly the principal events of his life.

CHAPTER I

INTRODUCTORY

James Ussher, the greatest luminary, as he has been justly called, of the Church of Ireland was born in the year 1581. It was a memorable time. Queen Elizabeth was struggling hard to make her seat secure on the throne of England. The Roman Catholic reaction of Queen Mary's time had not yet died out. Jesuit Fathers Campion and Parsons, formerly Fellows of Oxford Colleges, were still preaching in Smithfield. Francis Drake had just returned from his wonderful voyage to the remotest parts of the earth, and was feting his Sovereign on board the little craft in which he had accomplished his daring enterprise. Bacon was even then cultivating those seeds of thought that were destined in due course to revolutionise alike the principles of science and theology.

Shakespeare was nourishing his mighty intellect, and dreaming immortal dramas.[1] Abroad, Spain was contemplating the proud design of the Armada, and collecting together her warships. In Ireland, things were in a very troubled condition. The country, never thoroughly conquered, was chafing under English

---

1. "Venus and Adonis" was entered upon the Stationers' Register in 1592, and "King Richard II" in 1597, but they had been probably written some time previously. — See Dowden's *Shakespeare*, p. 33.

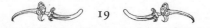

rule, and premeditating another uprising. Not far from the town of Fermoy, within the shelter of Kilcolman Castle, Spenser, "always idle among the cool shades of the green alders by the Mulla's shore," as it seemed to his friend Walter Raleigh, would shortly be completing the first three books of the *Faerie Queen*.[2]

It was in the January of this year that there was born in the city of Dublin a child who was to bear the honoured name of James Ussher, and become, in after years, one of the greatest scholars of his day in the Christian Church.[3]

In the year of grace 1581, the city of Dublin presented an aspect very different from that it bears now. Around the castle, then, as now, the symbol and the centre of English authority, there gathered, with few exceptions, blocks of ill-built and irregular houses, most of them wood, and many of them roofed with thatch,[4] which stretched themselves down the hill on which the castle stands, to the Liberties and Cathedral Church of St. Patrick. On the other side of the castle, the River Liffey extended its yellow waters almost to the foot of the sister Cathedral of the Holy Trinity, the survivor and memorial of the Danish conquest, and beneath whose walls the small vessels, which then did service as merchant ships between the two countries, deposited their freightage. The river was noted from earliest times for the turbid colour of its waters, which gave its name to the city of *Duibh linn-nigra therma*, or the Blackpool.[5] A small harbour existed at the mouth of the Poddle River, and was protected by the city ditch of that time.

---

2. A part of the poem was certainly written previous to 1584. See Hale's *Life of Spenser*, p. xxxii–iv. in Globe edition of the *Works of Spenser*.

3. "An eminent New Year's gift to the benefit of the whole Church of God." — Bernard's *Life of Ussher*, p. 19. Called James, after his grandfather, James Stanihurst.

4. See preface to Gilbert's *Calendar of Ancient Records of Dublin*, iii, p. xxix.

5. Halliday's *Scandinavian Kingdom of Dublin*, p. 23.

About the centre of the city, as it then stood, in the parish of St. Nicholas, James Ussher was born on the 4th of January, 1581. The house, No. 57 High Street, now a grocer's shop, is still pointed out as occupying the site of the original house where he was born.[6] It was at the time an important part of the city of Dublin. Here the first books published in Ireland were issued from the press, and here the first newspapers were started. The booksellers of that day flourished in St. Nicholas Street, Castle Street, and, Skinner's Row. In St. Nicholas Street was printed one of the first volumes of which there is any record in Irish history, being a copy of the *Articles of Religion* with the following title: "A brefe declaration of certain principall Articles of Religion set out by order and authoritie, as well of the Right Honourable Sir Henry Sidney, Knight of the most noble Order, Lord President of the Council in the Principalities of Wales and Marches of the same, and General Deputie of this realm of Ireland, as by Tharchebyshops and Byshopes and other of Her Majesties High Commissioners for causes ecclesiastical in the same realme,

---

6. This is the only house in High Street that stands in the parish of St. Nicholas. It faces the present Synod Hall of the Church of Ireland. Having been born here, Ussher (who was one of nine children, having had two brothers and six sisters) was probably baptised in St. Nicholas Church, but there is no record of the event, and the church has long since disappeared. The neighbourhood was then a fashionable one. Stanihurst, in his description of Dublin in 1577, says of the adjoining parish of St. Audoen: "The parish of this church is accounted the best in Dublin for that the greater number of the aldermen and the worships of the citie are demurrant within that parish." — *Calendar of Ancient Records of Dublin*, ii, p. 544–5. Some of the houses were fine enough to receive the Lord-Deputy of the day. Thus we read how Sir William Russell removed on the night of March 1st, 1597, from the castle to lie at Mr. Ussher's house at the Bridgefoot (so called when there was only one bridge in Dublin) to make room for the new deputy, Lord Burg, "against he should receive the sword." — Carew MSS. of above date. The Liffey then flowed round Ussher's house at the Bridgefoot. The gardens extended along the banks of the river, where Lord Moira's house (now the Mendicity Institution) afterwards stood. The banks were then planted with trees.

imprynted at Dublin by Humfrey Powel the 20th of January, 1566."[7]

Here also the first Irish newspaper saw the light under the title of *Pue's Occurrences.*

The first mention of the family of Ussher occurs in the reign of Henry the First, when we find one Richard le Ussher possessed of a house in Winchester. A Robert Ussher is witness to a deed in the reign of Edward the Third. We find a family of the name settled in Yorkshire in 1377. The descendants of Primate Henry Ussher quartered the arms of the Yorkshire Usshers, and many of their Christian names correspond with

---

7. See Arber's *Stat. Reg.* under above date. The only copy of these articles believed to be in existence may be found in the library of Trinity College (Class DD. gg. 65). The first volume printed in Dublin appeared in 1551 from the press of the above Humfrey Powel. It was Edward VI's first Prayer-book. It has the following title-page: "The Boke of Common Praier and the administracion of the Sacraments and other Rites and Ceremonies of the Churche after the use of the churche of England, Anno Dom. M.C.L.I." This volume, which was a folio of some 140 pages, was printed in black letter and in a superior style. What is believed to be a solitary copy may be seen in Trinity College, Dublin (Class BB., A. 3). Humfrey Powel, who lived in London in 1548, above the Holborn Conduit, migrated to Ireland in 1551, and was the first to introduce the art of printing into that country. His name appears in the Charter, 1556, as a Fellow of the Stationers' Company. — See Arber's *Register, the Irish Builder* for 1887, Ball's *History of the Reformed Church of Ireland*, p. 46 (note), Killen's *Ecclesiastical History*, Vol. 1, p. 377 (note). The name was a common one then among the printers. Arber records no less than eighteen. The persistence of names in the printer's art is remarkable. Thus we have almost from the beginning, Pickerings, Rivingtons, Newberys, &c. The first book printed in the Irish language was an Alphabet and Catechism translated from Latin and English "with the privilege of the great Queen," who gave the type for the purpose, and published by John Ussher (Alderman), in his house at Bridgefoot, Dublin, June 20, 1571. The first Irish version of the New Testament was printed by Sir William Ussher "at the Town of the Ford of the Hurdles" (Ath-Cliath, an old name for Dublin), by John Francke, 1602, from the text of William O'Donnell, afterwards Archbishop of Tuam.

those of the Yorkshire clan. The name is also to be found in Scotland, and there is a tradition that James Ussher's family and that of the Scotch Usshers sprang from a common stock. John Ussher of Topfield, near Melrose, was a friend of Sir Walter Scott.[8] The name appears in Ireland as early as 1281 under the form of Usher, and in 1288 as De Usher.

The Ussher family appears to have been an influential clan in the city of Dublin at the opening of the sixteenth century, where they held a large amount of property. In 1517, Christopher Ussher had the lease of a house in "the Fishe Street in Dublin," and Nos. 3, 16, and 17, in the same street, were in the possession of the family at the close of the century. Ussher himself lived in No. 17 in 1593 when he became a Scholar of Trinity College. In later years, when he had attained to the Primacy, his country house in Dublin stood outside the city boundaries on Hoggan Green, opposite to Trinity College, and probably on the site of the present Bank of Ireland. In the Dublin Assembly Rolls, Easter 1632, there is this entry: "A lease made to Archbishop James Usher, Primate, of a plot of ground, walled about facing his house on Hoggan green, for 99 years, containing the ditch west end 10 yards, and from north to south 30 yards, at 5s. sterling."[9] Ussher's name is still largely preserved in the nomenclature of the streets of Dublin. Thus we have "Usher's Quay," "Usher's Island," "Usher's Street," "Usher's Court," "Usher's Lane," &c. The family must have been a prominent and influential one in the olden time to extend its name after this fashion.

It is said that the founder of the Irish family of Ussher originally bore the name of Neville, but that coming over to Ireland with King John in 1185 in the capacity of an usher in the Royal

---

8. Ball Wright's *Memoirs of the Ussher Families*, p. 3.

9. The house on Hoggan Green had belonged to Lord Caulfield. Ussher desired to build and reside there, "in regard to the affection he bore to the city, having been born and bred there." — Gilbert's *Cal. Anc. Records*, iii, p. 260.

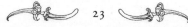

household, he changed his name for that of his office.[10] James Ussher's father was one of the six Clerks in Chancery, while his mother, Margaret, was the daughter of James Stanihurst, Recorder of the City of Dublin and Speaker of the House of Commons for three successive Parliaments. Ussher thus came into the world with all the prestige that belongs to high social position. Stanihurst seems to have been a person fully alive to the importance of changing with the times. He was Speaker in Queen Mary's reign, and afterwards in that of Elizabeth. The probability is that he was always in heart a Roman Catholic.

His brother Richard was a strong Roman Catholic controversialist. It must be said to his credit that Stanihurst was one of the first to move in Parliament the matter of founding a National University for Ireland. James Ussher[11] was essentially a city man, and there is evidence that he took much pride in his native place and was full of admiration for it surroundings. Very early in his life, while he was still a student, he writes a Latin epistle to the learned Camden, who was then accumulating material for his great work on the antiquities of Britain in which he describes the city of Dublin. This is the picture he draws of the city and suburbs as they were known to him at the close of the sixteenth century. He calls it "the city of his birth," and he

10. "The coat-of-arms which was in use by the father and uncles of the great Primate-viz., a chevron ermine between three batons or, on a ground azure, and the crest, a mailed hand and arm holding a baton are testimony of the tradition being founded on some such fact." — Ball Wright's *Ussher Memoirs*, p. vii. The Ussher arms may still be seen on the front of a house formerly occupied by Adam Ussher. No. 3 Lord Edward Street, and formerly No. 3 Fishamble Street.— *Irish Builder,* 1888, p. 23.

11. A controversy has always gone on as to the correct way of spelling Ussher's name, whether with one or two s's. In Ware's work, the double s uniformly found. It is also found in the MSS of the day and it is printed so in the title of his *Annals*, London, 1658. Elrington uniformly observes this spelling. Some branches of the family, however, use only one s. Archbishop Henry Ussher in his will spelt his name "Uscher." We have the Irish spelling "Uiser," in Arber's *Stat. Reg.* under June 1571.

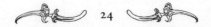

describes is as "full of people (as well he might, considering how it was hemmed in at the time by its surrounding walls, rendering it difficult enough to accommodate the increasing population); it is most beautifully situated; it's river and the neighbouring sea are full of fish" (the "Dublin Bay herring" was even then prized as a well-known luxury).

It is also noted for its commercial enterprise. The city itself is enclosed by green fields — all outside the end of Dame Street, Nicholas Street, and Castle Street, being then open country to the south and east, and beyond were oak groves and hazel woods with preserves of game for the amusement of the citizens. "I may say," he writes, "that the city, enjoys a particularly beautiful and salubrious situation. The mountains rise on the south, and a level country stretches away to the west. On the east is the sea, and looking to the north the River Liffey is seen pursuing its way seawards, where it affords a fine harbour for ships." He also speaks of the "Keys," by which the course of the river is confined. The city is surrounded by strong walls built of stone and with six gates leading into the open country.[12] Stanihurst, in his description of Dublin in 1577, enumerates eight gates as follows: "Whitefriers, Saint Kevin his Gate, Hogs Gate, Dammes Gate, Poule Gate, Newgate, Wintavern Gate, Saint Audoen his Gate, hard by the Church, going down by the Cooke Street."[13]

In his *Ecclesiastical Anitiquities*, composed later in life, Ussher dilates with evident pleasure of the two Cathedrals. He writes with the eye of an antiquarian and a Churchman. "Dublin," he says, "has two Cathedral Churches — one without walls of the city known by the name of St. Patrick's (it will be observed that the St. Patrick's Cathedral was then outside of the city), the other in the midst of the city, and dedicated to the Holy Trinity, within the bounds whereof the Archbishop of Dublin was hereto seated,

---

12. For much of his description Ussher evidently drew on Jocelin's *Life of St. Patrick*. — See Camden's *Ireland*, p. 92.

13. See *Calendar of Ancient Records of Dublin*, ii, appendix 1.

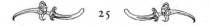

we learn from Giraldus. Within the limits of the Church of St. Patrick, not far from the belfry, we see the well (lately enclosed) at which the new converts of Dublin were baptised by St. Patrick, near the city to the south. The other Cathedral, consecrated to the name of the Holy Trinity, commonly called Christ Church. The arches or vaults were built by the Danes before the coming of St. Patrick, and at that time Christ Church was not founded nor built as it stands now. So it was that St. Patrick celebrated Mass in one of the vaults which is called to this day 'St. Patrick's Vault.' " Elsewhere, we find Ussher again enlarging on the features of the two Cathedrals, whose noble proportions seemed to have filled him with pride.

St. Patrick's is a spacious church, noted for its carved work, its tesselated pavement, and its fine tower. He also speaks of the wealth of silver and gold that had been lavished on Christ Church Cathedral.[14]

We have already alluded to the ancestry of the Ussher family. We may observe that Archbishop Ussher, always interested in archeological and historical questions, drew up a pedigree of his family, dating from Arlandus Ussher, who was Bailiff of Dublin in 1460, and afterwards Mayor, and who was one of the merchant princes of his day. Sir William Betham enlarged on this genealogical table, and traces the Ussher family onwards, showing the connection with the noble families of Wellesley, Mornington, Wellington, Cowley, and Kildare. Among other noted families connected with the Usshers are the Carberys, Plunketts of Dunsany, Newcomens, Warings, Osbornes, Colleys, &c.

In addition to the great James Ussher, Archbishop of Armagh, there were his uncle and predecessor in the see, Henry

---

14. Ussher's *Works*, xv, p. 10–14. Camden seems to have availed himself of Ussher's knowledge in his *Ireland*, p. 93. In. 1607, Camden himself was in Dublin collecting materials for his *Britannia*. It would be an interesting and suggestive study to trace the fate of the silver and gold ornamentations and plate of our cathedral churches. The old Norman Cathedral of Waterford, for example, was rich in such.

Ussher, Luke Ussher, afterwards Archdeacon of Armagh, Robert Ussher, Bishop of Kildare, and other noted ecclesiastics. In secular life there were also distinguished members of the family filling the offices of Mayor, Sheriff, and Alderman of the city of Dublin.[15] And in other walks of life this family likewise distinguished itself in later times. For example, we have the Rev. Henry Ussher, D.D., and Senior Fellow of Trinity College, Dublin, first Astronomer Royal of Ireland, who died in 1790; and Sir Thomas Ussher, who died in 1862, was Rear-Admiral of the Blue. John Ussher, another of the family, filled the honourable position of Maser in Chancery in 1730. The connection of the Welsey or Wellesley family with the Usshers will be of interest. Mary Ussher, the sixth child of Sir William Ussher, of Bridgefoot, County Dublin, Knt., married Henry Cowley, or Colley, of Dangan, County of Westmeath, and Castlecarbery, County of Kildare, in 1674. Richard Colley, their son, took the name and property of his cousin, Garret Wesley, and was created Lord Mornington. He married the eldest daughter of Dr. Sale, Registrar of the Diocese of Dublin, and their eldest son was created Earl of Mornington.

He married the eldest daughter of Lord Dungannon, and their eldest son was Richard, afterwards Marquis Wellesley, their second son William, afterwards Earl of Mornington, and their third son, Arthur Wellesley, afterwards the famous Duke of Wellington.

Coming back now to James Ussher, an interesting question suggests itself as to where this great scholar and divine, who shed such lustre on his native land, and whose learning acquired a fame for itself far beyond our insular precincts, obtained his early education. Ten years before Ussher was born a statute of Queen Elizabeth required a free school to be established in every diocese in Ireland. The masters were to be "Englishmen, or of good birth." But independently of that statute, the Dublin Corporation had

---

15. See Gilbert's *Calendars*, Vols. ii and iii, Passim.

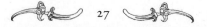

established a free school for the sons of its citizens, and in that school it would appear that Ussher received his earliest education.[16] We find in the records of the City of Dublin, recently published under the learned editorship of Mr. J.T. Gilbert, an order for payment of the salary of one James Fullerton for the year 1588 of £20, due to him for fee and diet.[17]

The entry runs as follows: "Order: James Fullerton, schoolmaster, to have twenty pounds sterling for teaching the children of the citizens for this year. He shall use all diligence, take nothing from the children, and have liberty to teach scholars from the country for so much as he may reasonably agree upon with them." James Fullerton and James Hamilton the latter afterwards ennobled by James I. As Viscount Clandeboy, an ancestor of the present Marquis of Dufferin and Ava, had come over from Scotland to take charge of the school.[18] There Ussher was entered as a pupil when eight years of age. Among later pupils in the same were Theophilus Tate, D.D., F.T.C.D., John Churchill, afterwards the great Duke of Marlborough, and Bishop Foy, F.T.C.D., who afterwards founded a scholastic establishment in the city of Waterford.[19] Can we identify at the present time the site of this interesting academy?

The present Bishop of Cashel, Dr. Day, in a lecture on Ussher, mentions a tradition that the school in a room over the

---

16. The first schoolmaster was David Duke, who had a salary of £10 a year, and 12d. (Irish) per quarter for every child of a free citizen. — *Calendar of Ancient Records of Dublin*, ii, p. 181.

17. Ditto, p. 245.

18. James Hamilton, "one of the greatest scholars and hopeful wits of his time," was the eldest son of the Rev. Hans Hamilton, Vicar of Dunlop, Ayrshire. In his estate at Killelagh he built "ane very strong castle, the lyke is not in the North." — See *Dictionary of National Biography*, xxiv, p. 178.

19. The Rev. W.G. Carroll, in articles on the school in the *Freeman's Journal* (1875 and 1877), preserved in the MS. Room, College, Dublin. See also Gilbert's *Calendar of Ancient Records of Dublin*, ii, p. 245, 249.

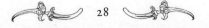

south aisle of St. Patrick's Cathedral, possibly the present robing room;[20] but this tradition appears to have no proper support. There seems to be little reason for doubting that the school stood in a locality at the rear of the present Synod House in Christ Church Place, and gave its name to the narrow street in which it was situated. "School House Lane" is marked in the old maps of the City of Dublin. It was a narrow passage that ran down to the river from the High Street at the back of St. Owen's, now St. Audoen's Church, to the west of the site now occupied by the Synod House, and where formerly stood the Old Church of St. Michael's, on St. Michael's Hill.[21]

In 1859, Ussher took his place here as a pupil under the tutelage of the above-mentioned Scotchmen, who were graduates of the University of Glasgow, and had been pupils of the celebrated Andrew Melville, Principal of Glasgow, and afterwards of St. Andrew's University. When the newly founded University of Dublin was opened for students, a few years later, these two men were the first elected Fellows of the new College. Scarcely a trace of this ancient schoolhouse now remains, as it was only the investigations of the late Rev. W.G. Carrol in the

---

20. See *Archbishop Ussher: His Life and Character*, by Rev. Maurice L. Day, *Lectures to Young Men*. 1861, p. 293–4. Canon Leeper was also under the impression that Ussher received his education in St. Patrick's Free School. — See his *Hist. Handbook to the Cathedral*, p. 71.

21. "The schoolhouse, of which some walls still remain, stood on the eastern side of School House Lane, which is extremely narrow, and runs north from High Street to Cook Street. The schoolhouse only fell about 1846. The great and learned Archbishop Ussher had been educated at this school." — *The Life of the Duke of Marlborough*, by Viscount Wolseley, I, p. 29. Lord Wolseley, it may be observed, is also allied by marriage of an ancestor with the Archbishop's branch of the Ussher family. — See Ball Wright's *Memoirs*, p. 153. A daughter of Adam Ussher, second son of Sir William Ussher, married Daniel Molyneux, Ulster King of Arms, in 1597. Their third son was ancestor of Sir Capel Molynenx, whose granddaughter married Sir Richard Wolseley, ancestor of the present Viscount.

Dublin Assembly Rolls that a few years ago unearthed the fact of its existence and site.[22]

Ussher's daily walk to and from his studies was not a very prolonged one. The boy had only to leave his father's home, and quietly stroll down, his satchel on his back, between rows of cage work houses,[23] from the High Street, to School House Lane, on the opposite side of which, in a recess on the right-hand side stood the school buildings.

It is an interesting reflection that if in the earliest ages of the Christian faith Ireland gave to Scotland such teachers as St. Columba, Scotland, in her turn, provided at the close of the sixteenth century the teachers who were in a large measure to direct the studies and fashion the mind of a youth who in later days was to revive the ancient fame of his country for learned and pious studies, and earn for himself, even at the hands of one of his rival religionists, the title of *acatholicorum doctissimus*. When Trinity College was opened in 1593, James Ussher was elected one of its first Scholars. He afterwards became a Fellow, was the first Professor of Divinity, collected the first books for the Library, and was subsequently raised to the Bishopric of Meath and, finally, to the Primacy. It is the story of the life of this great Irish Churchman and scholar we propose to tell in the following pages.

In order to fix Ussher's place in that wonderful galaxy of writers and literary workmen that were then making the age famous, we may observe that Bodley, the founder of the library,

---

22. "Here it was," says, Bishop Reeves, "that the building stood where, in the lad James Ussher, the light was kindled which shed such lustre on his native land as to draw the eyes of learned Europe towards it, and for a generation, restore to Ireland her ancient pre-eminence in sacred literature." — Bishop Reeves' Preface to Carroll's *Succession of Clergy in St. Bride's Parish*, p. 1.

23. For an account of the old Irish half-timbered houses, see article by Dr. Frazer in *Journal R.S.A.*, i, p. 367–369; Harris's *History of Dublin*, p. 76–81; Petrie's article in *Dublin Penny Journal*, I, p. 268–270.

was thirty-seven in the year Ussher was born; Camden, the learned antiquarian and one of his earliest correspondents, thirty; Spenser and Raleigh, twenty-nine; Hooker, twenty-eight; Bacon, twenty; Shakespeare, seventeen; Andrewes and Cotton, eleven; Laud, eight; Jonson and Hall, seven; Selden, three.

The first three books of Spenser's *Faerie Queen* were published when Ussher was fifteen, and Bacon's *Essays*, the first part of the *Ecclesiastical Polity*, and Jonson's *Every Man in His Humour* in the following year. It does not appear that Ussher ever met Hooker, but he was evidently well acquainted with his great work; nor does he mention Shakespeare in any of his correspondence. Ussher may be regarded as the sole Irish representative of that golden era of literary energy that characterized the close of Elizabeth's reign and extended to those of her two successors.[24] The times in Ireland were against his producing any great work of constructive theology; he was too taken up with the everlasting Roman controversy, but his *Religion of the Ancient Irish* will perpetuate his name as a student in ecclesiastical history, and his labours on the *Ignatian Epistles* establish his position in the first rank critical scholars.

---

24. See, for a literary estimate of Ussher, *Carte's Ormonde*, I, p. 77.

CHAPTER II

IRELAND AT THE CLOSE OF THE SIXTEENTH CENTURY

Before we continue our story, let us glance at the Ireland into which Ussher found himself born in 1581. Let us first say something more about his native city as it was then and for some time later, and supplement, in some degree, the picture we have already given from the pen of Ussher himself. Dublin, as we have already seen, was then a small place hemmed in on every side by its walls. The adult population at the close of the century could not have been more than 8,000 souls; in 1644, four years after Ussher had left Ireland for good, the adult city population was counted at 5,551 Protestants and 2,608 Roman Catholics.[1] The city was lighted at this time with lanterns and candles set in every fifth house.

The city gates were closed at nightfall by beat of a drum and the tolling of the bells of St. Andrew's Church. The keys were then carried off to the mayor, and particular watch was kept on "the Irish" and all "masterless people." Armed watchmen under

---

1. Gilbert's *Ancient Records,* iii, p. xxxi. The religious requirements of the people were met by nine churches and the two cathedrals.

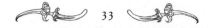

captains patrolled the city every hour.[2] During the raging of the plague in 1604–05, it was ordered that "for the better purging of the air" every inhabitant "should burn a faggot at his door on the nights of Mondays, Wednesdays, and Saturdays."

The city was governed by a mayor and alderman, and the records of the time show that the municipal hospitality was on a profuse scale. From early morn till dewy eve and later, the wine barrels were tapped and the ruddy juices flowed copiously. The days of temperance and Sunday closing had not yet come, and the wines were choice clarets, sack, malmsey, and muscadel. Civic order was strictly observed; and the aldermen and the officers appeared according to their several ranks in scarlet, violet, and Turkey gowns. They were proud of their "yoong London" as they called it, and aped the latest London fashions. Campion, of St. John's College, Oxford, visited the city in 1571, and gave it as his opinion that "for state and change and bountiful hospitality the mayoralty of Dublin exceeded any city in England except London."

But there is another side to this picture. The city was undoubtedly not clean: neither was it sober. It was "dirty Dublin" in Ussher's day. The official who did duty as the city scavenger in 1617 was, strange to say, a widow — Kate Strong, who seems to have enjoyed a vested interest in her office. Like other civic officers, she took an oath to do her duty, but failed in the obligation. She "scarce kept the way from the Castle to the church clean, or that from the mayor's house to the church, and, neglected the rest of the city, which she cleaned but sparingly, and very seldom." "The more that she was followed the worse she grew, and kept the streets the fouler," the pigs that ran about the streets freely did not make things better. Bailiffs were told off to kill them with pikes and throw their dead bodies into carts. The "unringed swyne" did much damage on Hoggan Green, and hindered the increase of fish in the strand. Others were frequently issued not to allow "doong" to accumulate in the thoroughfares.

---

2. Gilbert's *Ancient Records,* iii, p. xiv.–vi.

It was also one of the "car-drivingest" cities in the kingdom, a reputation it still maintains. The carmen of that day, we learn, rode up and down the streets upon their cars and car horses, with such speed that they endangered the lives of the citizens, especially in the crowded parts about Wood Quay and Merchant Quay.

The numerous brewers' carts were also a great nuisance. To control the carmen who "pestered" the streets, it was ordered that they should wear badges, with the arms of the city, "after the London fashion."[3]

The excessive number of taverns in the city was a third feature. They were resorted to by "vagabonds, bad livers, and idle persons, to the infamy and disgrace of the Government." By an order of the Lord-Deputy and Council in 1586–87, no keeper of an inn or tavern was to admit a Fellow, student, or scholar of Trinity College, without the written permission of the Provost. For having violated this order, Eliza Jones, an alehouse keeper, was fined £40, and obliged to stand doing penance on a market-cross from 9 to 10 A.M., bearing on her head with the ominous inscription: "for harbouring a collegian contrary to the Act of State."[4] We have said there was no Sunday closing. We read in the pages of an author[5] who published *A New Description of Ireland in 1610*, that "during the time of divine service and in the time of the sermon forenoon and afternoon, every filthy ale-house was thronged full of company."

It was a profitable business this sale of strong drink. "There is no merchandise so vendible; it is the very marrow of the commonwealth in Dublin; the whole profit of the town stands upon ale-houses and selling of ale. There are whole streets of taverns." The brewers were principally women. "The better sort, such as the aldermen's wives, are those that brew; every householder's

---

3. Gilbert's *Anc. Records,* iii, p. xv; xxiii–iv.

4. Ibid., p. xii–xiii. Oxford suffered from the same state of things. See Hutton's *Laud,* p. 117.

5. Barnabe Rich, who was in Dublin in 1594 when Ussher was thirteen years of age. — *Calendar of State Papers.*

wife is a brewer." The moral character of the sellers of strong drink is not painted in the brightest of colours; their charges are denounced as "exorbitant."[6]

Hospitality, as we have seen, was on an extensive scale; there is evidence that the leading citizens frequently entertained the Lord-Deputy and in return were entertained by him. Some of the houses must have been large and comfortable.

The suburbs of the city, as it was then, are now leading streets and squares. A long lane now represented by Georges Street, led into the open country; and the same may be said of Grafton Street. St. Stephen's Green was an extensive sheep-walk,[7] and in the winter was, with the adjoining fields, shot over for snipe. Further afield was Cullen's wood, a favourite roystering place, but always with a look-out for the enemy — the wild mountain men who came down now and again to harry the citizens in the midst of their sports.[8] Beyond were the mountains, the haunts of the O'Byrnes and the O'Tooles, clothed with thick forests and pierced with inaccessible glens — perfect *terra incognita,* unknown and dreaded. On the north side of the city, across the river, there stretched into the country vast hazel woods. This side of the city was more protected as being included within the Pale.

Was there any intellectual society in Dublin at this period, or was it all rough and coarse living? There are proofs that letters were not altogether neglected. Spenser, who lived in Ireland for eighteen years in all, and wrote there his great poem, had a house in the city where he lived off and on for six years. Here, too, for a time, lived Walter Raleigh, the "Captain of the Guard," and hither came Camden intent upon antiquarian research.

A city that numbered among its inhabitants the Usshers and Stanihursts of the day, must have had some intellectual

---

6. Rich's *New Desc. of Ireland,* ch. Xvii, p. 69–74. Strafford in his day proposed to tax the Dublin brewers. Gardiner's *Hist. of Eng.,* viii, p. 39.

7. Gilbert's *Calendar of Ancient Records,* iii, p. 145.

8. See Stanihurst's *Description of Dublin* in 1577.

life. Fortunately, we have a picturesque account of a gathering of thoughtful men to discuss high problems of philosophy, which took place about 1589 at the cottage of a Mr. Ludowick Bryskett, the friend of Spenser and himself a poet, near Dublin, and which historic gathering was the original of all the literary clubs and philosophical societies that have sprung up since in the city. Hither came Dr. Long, the Primate, Sir Robert Dillon, the Chief Justice, Captain Norris, and Warham St. Leger, Thomas Smith, the mayor and city apothecary, and not least, Edmund Spenser. The subject of their discussion turned chiefly on "the ethic part or moral philosophy," and Spenser unfolded the principle of his great poem. A meeting like this shows culture was not altogether neglected in the Dublin of that day.[9]

When we turn from the city to the country at large, we find it in a transition state, slowly passing from a condition of barbarism into one of parative civilisation. The old order was by degrees giving place to the new, but the pangs of political and religious childbirth were acute. Ireland did not give up her free and easy ways, nor surrender her tribal rights without a struggle. The Irish chiefs viewed with jealousy and apprehension the growing power of the English colony. Two dangerous conspiracies had already

---

9. Bsryskett's essay was published in 1606, under the title "A Discourse of Civil Life, containing the Ethike Part of Moral Philosophy." It was really a translation from the Italian of Giraldo's philosophic treatise. In the introduction is found the interesting passage describing the literary and philosophic gatherings at his cottage. The author was an Italian, probably, from Florence. He matriculated in Trinity College, Cambridge in 1559. In 1571, he was Clerk of the Council in Ireland under Sir Henry Sidney. In 1577, we find him Clerk of the Chancery in Ireland, Keeper of the Signet, in which office he was succeeded by Spenser, whom he taught Greek; Spenser addressed a sonnet to him from Dublin, July 18, 1586. In 1584, Bryskett was made a burgher of Dublin, "on condition of not using any occupation which would be hurtful to any corporation of the city." — Gilbert's *Calendar of Ancient Records,* ii, p. xiii and 194; Hales's *Life of Spenser,* prefixed to Globe edition of Spenser's *Works,* p. xxxii–iv; *Calendar of State Papers,* 1576–81.

threatened the stability of the Queen's Government, and were being put down with the usual amount of severity. As a child, Ussher must have gazed with an inward horror at three heads rotting over gates of Dublin Castle. They were the heads of the two Desmonds and Fitzmaurice, their cousin.[10] These frequent outbreaks and summary acts of vengeance left the country, as might be supposed, in a deplorable condition.

Even the Pale afforded little protection to the isolated English and Protestant settlers.[11] Dublin itself was insecure. Those who dwelt "even within the sight of the smoke of the city" were not subject to the laws.[12] No man could venture "half a quarter of a mile" out of Cork without danger of his life.[13] It can be well understood how insecure in country parts must have been the lives and properties of all well-disposed persons. Nor were the seas safe. Spanish ships were continually hovering about the southern and western coasts and threatening descents.

Twenty years before Ussher was born, Sir Henry Sydney had made a vice regal progress through all Ireland, and, in a letter to the Queen, he gave a graphic account of what he saw and heard. Let us see what he says of the Pale and its immediate neighbourhood — supposed to be the most civilised part of Ireland. Louth was impoverished by the continual passage of soldiers to the north. Meath was "cursedly scorched on the outside." Westmeath was "spoiled and wasted by the rebels."

Kildare was "greatly impoverished by thieves and the O'Mores." Carlow was "more than half wasted." Wexford was

---

10. See Froude's *History of England,* xi, p. 249: also Gilbert's *Calendar* ii, p. 20, where notice is taken of a similar and later exhibition of savage vengeance. The Castle was in this respect, the Temple Bar of Dublin.

11. "In the Pale a very large proportion of the population were Papists and malcontents." — Carew *MSS.,* 1589–1600, p. 106.

12. Sir George Carew to Heneage, November 1590.

13. St. Leger to Burleigh, January 1580. Cork was then a small place, "but one street not half a quarter of a mile in length."

in like condition. King's County was "spoiled and wasted by the decay of English tenants."[14] If these things were done in a green tree, what was done in the dry? "This country," writes St. Leger to Perrot, April 22, 1582, "is so ruined as it is near unpeopled by the murders and spoils done by the traitors on the one side, and by the killing and spoiling on the other side, together with the great mortality in town and country, which is such as the like has never been seen." "That part of Ireland" says another authority, "which is nearest to England is most civilised; the other part is brutal." "The inhabitants live in wooden huts, covered with straw. A large part of them herd with their cattle in the fields."[15] Andrew Trollope, writing to Walsingham, September 12, 1581, gives an astonishing picture of the degraded and miserable condition of the peasantry: "The Irishe men, except [in] walled houses, are not Christyans, cyvell or humane creatours, but heathen, or rather savage and brute bestes.

"Many of them, as well women as men, goe, commonly all naked, saveing onely a loose mantle hanging aboute them. If they can gett no stolen fleshe, they eat, if they can get them, leek blades, or a three leaved grasse which they call shamrocks, and for want thereof carryon and grasse in the fields, with such butter as is loathsome to descrybe."[16] Camden and Spenser have been taken to task for drawing what have been condemned as extravagant pictures of the miseries and wickedness of Irish life at this time, but they are fully justified by the sober State Papers of the period.[17]

14. See Brewer's *Introduction to the Carew MSS., 1589–1600, p. lxxii–iii.*

15. Theiner's *Monumenta,* p. 521.

16. *Calendar of State Papers,* of above date.

17. A MS. of Ussher's in the Library of T.C.D. distinguishes the three kinds of Irish that held the country in his time. (1) The ancient Irish. (2) The mixed, descended from Irish mothers, and who in language habit, and custom conformed to the Irish. (3) The English Irished, who, hold not Irish customs or language — the merchants and traders of towns, and some knights and gentlemen of East Meath and about Dublin and in the Pale. — See Hogan's *Irishmen of the Sixteenth Century,* p. 355.

If such was the political and social condition of the country, its religious condition was no better. The manner of working out the Reformation in Ireland gave a blow for the time to any religion that remained in the country. The seizure of the abbey lands and the demolition of monasteries gave a shock to all ecclesiastical property. The churches were in ruins, and bishops and chieftains contended for the spoil.

The begging friars, who alone preserved a spark of spiritual feeling in the land, were hunted and scattered.[18] The religious houses with their inmates disappeared, and there was nothing to take their place. "Nothing is more common, nothing is more frequently reiterated by the deputies or by others who joined in their hostings or circuits, than passionate outcries at the ruinous condition of the churches, not only in regions beyond the Pale, but within the very heart of it."[19] We find one official writing to another: "There are here so many children dispensed withal to enjoy the livings of the Church, so many laymen, as they are commonly termed, suffered to hold benefices, without cure, so many clergymen tolerated to have the profit of three or four pastoral dignitaries, who being themselves unlearned are not meet men though thought willing, to teach and instruct others, as whoso beholdeth it must not choose but make it known."[20]

---

18. "These preachers, little better than outcasts themselves, still kept up in their own rude way the feeble sparks of religion. They were the true priests of the native Irish population. Brewer's *Introduction to the Carew MSS.,* 1589–1600, p. xv.

19. Brewer, p. ix.

20. William Johnes to Walsingham, July 14, 1584. This sounds incredible; but it was so. Even bishoprics were held by laymen. — See Kelly's *Dissertations,* p. 370. We find Spenser writing, in 1598 (Ussher being then in his seventeenth year): "The Irish priestes, who now enjoye the Churche livings there, are, in a manner meere laymen, go lyke laymen, live lyke laymen, and followe all kinde of husbandrye and other worldly affayres as thother Irish men doe. They neither reade scriptures, nor preache to the people, nor minister the sacrament of communion, but the baptism they doe, for they christen yet after the popish fashion, and

40

We find the Primate, Dr. Long, writing in 1585: "Many souls daily perish whose cure are committed to boys and to open wolves."[21] The country clergy, testifies another, are "idols and cyphers." The whole Episcopal system had broken down. It was proposed to give bishoprics to soldiers as a means of restoring peace in the country.[22] While some of the bishoprics, as, for example, those of Ross and Kilfenora, were held by laymen, we find a boy student at Oxford, Maurice O'Brien, put in possession of the temporalities of Killaloe, the excuse made being that it was a good thing to propitiate a powerful Irish clan like the O'Briens, and that if the bishopric were not given to him, no other would be suffered to hold it.

The majority of the bishops who held their sees during the reigns of Edward, Mary, and Elizabeth could scarcely have had strong religious convictions of any kind. They changed with the changing times; now they were Protestants, now they were Roman Catholics. But this state of things could not last, and by degrees the two churches emerged from the ecclesiastical chaos. At the close of Elizabeth's reign we come on what may be called the watershed of Irish Church history. A line drawn due north and south through the centre of Ireland will roughly divide the island for our purpose. To the east of this division a considerable minority of the population, representing chiefly the English settlers, were members of the Reformed Church. This Protestant population was further increased by the immigration of Scotch settlers into the northeast corner.

---

with popish ministration." Archbishop Loftus, in 1594, presented his nephew, a layman, to the archdeaconry of Glendalogh. — Elrington's *Life of Ussher,* p. 114. Spenser himself seems to have held a Church dignity in Elphin. — See *Calendar of State Papers,* December 1586.

21. Archbishop Long to Perrot, in 1585. Even the sacrament and baptism seems to have been intermitted in many places, and the people suffered to lapse into a condition of absolute heathenism. Sir H. Sydney to Elizabeth. — Brewer's *Introduction to Carew MSS.,* p. lxxx.

22. Sir Edward Waterhouse to Walshingham, June 14, 1574.

On the western side of this line the vast majority of the people, however shaken they may have been for a time, at length settled down into what they called "the old religion."[23]

Very much the same story is to be told of the clergy. For a time, the priests wavered, conformed, said the Reformed Liturgy, and retained their churches. But the Bull of Pius the Fifth, followed as it was by the counter-reformation of the Jesuits, forced their hand, and by degrees they returned to their old ways. The bishops as a rule took the oath of allegiance, but many of them in their hearts remained Roman Catholics. A remarkable

---

23. Throughout these conflicting changes, the Episcopal succession remained as a matter of course with the Reformed, that is to say, the State Church. Some of the bishops were deposed by Mary, chiefly on the ground that they were married men; two were deposed by Elizabeth for refusing the oath of supremacy, but the succession went on uninterruptedly. In the same way, the cathedrals and parish churches were held by those who, at least outwardly, conformed to the new order. It was no more necessary in Ireland than in England to pass Acts of Parliament, transferring the Church property. "There was no moment," says Professor Freeman, "when the State, as many people fancy, took the Church property from one religious body and gave it to another. . . . The general taking from one religious body and giving to another, which many people fancy took place under Henry VIII or Elizabeth, simply never happened at all." — *Disestablishment and Disendowment*, p. 17, 20. These words are equally true of the Church of Ireland. When the Jesuit counter-reformation had begun to tell, and the majority of the people had ceased to be "Church papists" as they were called, the Pope saw his way to introduce by degrees a new hierarchy from abroad, and this was the origin of the present Roman Catholic Episcopate in Ireland. Things went exactly on all-fours in the two Churches. The bishops in England and Ireland alike continued to discharge their Episcopal functions during the reigns of Edward VI, Mary, and Elizabeth, or else were deposed, but the unbroken continuity of the Episcopate remained. Unnecessary anxiety seems to be manifested by Irish Roman Catholic writers to prove that their Church retains the old Episcopal succession, seeing that, according to its authorities, there can be no higher Episcopal grace than that which flows from St. Peter through the Popes. This is a succession untroubled by the interference of princes. — See remarks by Brewer, *Carew MSS.*, 1589–1600, p. 1.

proof of this may be found in Sir Henry Sydney's account of his progress through the country. He tells us how "the bishopps of the province of Cashel and Theweme [Thomond], albeit they were Papists, submitted themselves unto the Queen's Majesty, and unto me, her Deputy, acknowledging that they had all their patrimony of the Queen's Majesty, and desired humbly that they might (by her Highness) be inducted into their Ecclesiastical prelacie."[24] It was only by degrees that this class of bishops was weeded out, and that chiefly by the introduction of men of English and Scottish descent and education.

It has constantly been brought as a charge against the Government that they put English and Scotch divines into Irish bishoprics; but they had no alternative. The supply of Irish bishops was not forthcoming. There was no university or college to educate them. "The Cleargye there, (except some few grave fathers which are in high place about the state and some fewe others which are lately planted in theyr Newe Colledge) are generally badd, licentious, and most disordered."[25] On the other

---

24. See *Ulster Archeological Journal,* where this interesting paper of Sydney's is given at length, iii, p. 312. It would be a mistake to confound the oath of supremacy with conformity. It was only in later days, after the Reformation, that the supremacy of the Pope was made an *articulus stantis et cadentis ecclesiae.* As a matter of fact, English kings assumed the title of "Vicars of Christ" before it was taken by the Bishops of Rome. No new thing was introduced when Henry VIII was declared to be the Supreme Head of the Church alike in England and Ireland. It was not required that a man should be a Protestant to maintain that the Pope had no right to tithes or to nominate bishops in the Queen's dominions. In these respects, Mary was every whit as strong a Protestant as her sister. She clung to the title "Defender of the Faith," and would allow of no provisoes from the Roman Court, and maintained, at least till towards the end of her reign, her royal title as "Supreme Head over the Church in all things temporal." — See *Carew MSS.,* 1589–1600, *Introduction,* p. xxi; Collier's *Records,* lxviii; and *Ecclesiastical History,* vi, p. 38: Perry's *Church History,* ii, p. 223, note; Denny's *Anglican Orders and Jurisdiction.* p. 153–9.

25. Spenser's *View of the Present State of Ireland,* p. 647 (Globe edition).

hand, many of the English clergymen who came over to Ireland were little better. "The most parte of such English as come over thither of themselves, are either unlearned, or men of some badd note for which they have forsaken England."[26] We find the, Queen herself observing this state of things and complaining of the small number of persons of the clerical calling in Ireland who "were able to teach especially in the functions of a bishop."[27] All the schools and places of learning up to this time had been in the hands of the Roman Catholics, and in addition, teachers of the nonconforming clergy were largely recruited from foreign universities. It was only by degrees that the recently established college "near Dublin" could supply the want.

We can thus understand how the political and social demoralisation of the times found its counterpart in a disorganised and distracted Church.[28] Many of the bishops who accepted the new order of things and outwardly conformed, were altogether unworthy of their positions. One of these was the notorious Miles Magrath, "that wicked bishop" (as Strafford calls him, in a letter to Laud), and who lived well into the times of Ussher. Originally an Irish Franciscan, in the earlier part of Elizabeth's reign he is found the Roman Catholic Bishop of Down and Connor. He then conformed, and, strange to say, proved a special favourite with the Queen, visiting her Court frequently. He became Bishop of Clogher in 1570, and subsequently Archbishop of Cashel. After having held the archbishopric of Cashel and bishopric of Emly for thirty-six years, the two cathedrals were found in ruins.[29]

---

26. Spenser.

27. Morrin's *Calendars,* ii, p. 31.

28. We must not forget that the Church of England at the same period was passing through a very similar state of chaos, though the ultimate result was different. — See for a condensed account, Green's *History of the English People,* ii, p. 306–308.

29. Captain Bodley, brother of the founder of the Bodleian Library, writing to Sir Henry Sydney, describes Cashel Cathedral as he saw it in Magrath's

Twenty-six livings were held by his sons or near relations, and in nearly every case there was no provision for divine worship. The Archbishop himself held more than twenty-six livings, and received the profits "without order taken for the service of the Church." In the two dioceses there, was not one preacher or good minister to teach the people their duty. In addition to the above sees, Magrath managed to get possession likewise of the bishoprics of Waterford and Lismore.[30] No wonder, when men of this type were misrepresenting the Reformation in Ireland, if Protestantism speedily decayed, so that a bishop like Lyon of Cork could complain in 1595 that, whereas he once had a congregation of a thousand when he preached, he had not now five, and that his communicants had declined in proportion.

Lyon had then been thirteen years a bishop.[31] Writing again, July 6, 1596, Lyon says, "The best name that they (the Roman Catholics) give unto the divine service appointed by Her Majesty in the Church of England and Ireland (sic) is the Devil's Service, and the professors thereof devils; and when they meet one of the profession they will cross themselves after the Popish manner. . . . I have provided books for every church through my diocese,

---

time, as "no better than a hog-stye." — *Carew MSS.,* 1601, p. 12, 13. The same writer, in an account of a journey he made into Ulster in 1603, charges the Archbishop with the vice of drunkenness. "The Bishop of Cashel and others, men and women, pour usquebaugh down their throats by day and by night — *Ulster Journal of Archaeology,* ii, p. 85. Bryan O'Rourke, Prince of Breffney, when about to be executed at Tyburn for treason, refused the Archbishop's ministrations on the ground that he was a bad man. Magrath carried off much of his ill-gotten spoil to England. Fenton reports to Burleigh, May 26, 1593, that the Archbishop had suddenly departed out of Ireland "with great sums of money, besides plate and jewels." — *Calendar of State Papers.*

30. See Ware's *Bishops,* I, p. 485–6; *State Papers,* 1607; *Regal Visitation* of 1615. Sir John Davies, writing to Cecil, February 20, 1624, says Magrath "held twenty-seven livings besides his four bishoprics, Cashel, Emly, Waterford, and Lismore."

31. Lyon to Burleigh, September 23, 1593 — *Calendar of State Papers.*

as Bibles, New Testaments, Common Books, both English and Latin, and the Injunctions, but none will come to the church at all, not so much as the country churls."[32] It is almost a bootless labour for any man to preach in the country but in Dublin for want of hearers."[33] "Nothing in truth could exceed the general squalor, wretchedness, and poverty, with all their kindred evils, under which the Protestant Church of Ireland thus laboured in all respects. The wonder is that the Reformation ever succeeded, that there should be an Irish Protestant Church at all."[34]

Magrath's simony and rapacity and evil example did incalculable harm to Irish Protestantism."[35]

Unfortunately, also, Irish Protestantism assumed a form that was least likely to recommend it to the people. It lent itself to an extreme Puritan type, and thereby offered but little attraction to the warm, imaginative Celtic mind.[36] The abject condition in which the parish churches were allowed to remain, in itself was a repellent. Spenser, who lived in Ireland for eighteen years, notices this. He speaks of the churches "so unhandsomely patched and thatched. Men doe even shunne the places for the uncomeliness thereof." He wisely recommends that "order should be taken to have them builte in some better forme, according to the churches in England, for the outward shewe (assure your selfe) doth greatly drawe the rude people to the

---

32. Bishop Lyon to Lord Hunsden — *Calendar of State Papers.*

33. Loftus to Lord Burleigh, September 22, 1590 — *Calendar of State Papers.*

34. Brewer's *Introduction;* Carew MSS., 1589–1600, p. xxxix.

35. Bagwell's article on Magrath, *Dictionary of National Biography,* xxxv, p. 327. "The people of his dioceses scarcely knew if there was a God." — Davies to Cecil, February 20, 1604. See also what King — a strong Protestant authority — says on the subject. — *Church History,* Supp. Vol., p. 1223–4.

36. See on the impressionableness of the Irish Celt, Gardner's *Hist. of England,* I, p. 389; and Ball's *Reformed Church of Ireland,* p. 352 and note.

reverencing and frequenting thereof, whatever some of our late too nice fooles saye — 'there is nothing in the seemlye forme and comely ordere of the churche.' "[37]

It must be remembered, however, as some extenuation for such a state of things, that it was not one which the Reformed Church created. It found it so. It was its misfortune, not its fault, that it came in for the sad heritage of dismantled cathedrals and decayed churches.[38]

Thus have we reviewed the general condition of the country as Ussher grew up into manhood. The Roman Catholic Church was straining every nerve to recover her lost position, and under the guise of religion was fostering with assiduity all efforts made to overthrow the Queen's authority.[39]

One Deputy after another was seeking to cope with the tremendous difficulty of governing the country and extending the blessings of religion and civilisation. They met with but indifferent

---

37. Spenser's *View* &c, p.680 (Globe edition).

38. Nothing proves more clearly the renewed and vigorous life of the Irish Church at the present time than the zeal with which it has of late gone about repairing its waste places. Within the past quarter of a century it has restored and otherwise improved nearly all its ancient cathedral churches, while two of them have been rebuilt from their foundations. In the north, the cathedrals of Derry and Armagh; in the west, of Tuam, KillaIoe, and Limerick; in the east, of St. Patrick's, Christ Church, St. Lazarian, St. Canice, and Holy Trinity, Waterford; in the south, of St. Colman and St. Finbarre, all testify to this zeal for the houses of God in the land. The parish churches have likewise shared in this general desire for re-edification and adornment, and some of them have been rebuilt in a sumptuous style by private liberality.

39. The questions of religious belief and of civil allegiance are inextricably connected at this period, and it is as impossible for us as it was for Elizabeth to treat them as really separate." — Bagwell's *Ireland under the Tudors,* iii, p. 460–1. As a proof of this we may refer to the fact that on February I3, 1596, Cornelius Ryan, Papal Bishop of Killahoe, is found advising the Pope to "separate Ireland from England for ever," and hand it over to Tyrone — *Calendar of State Papers.*

success; they were hampered and countermanded from London by persons who did not realise the gravity and difficulty of the problem. The English Government never knew its own mind for long and perpetually vacillated and halted between indulgence on one side and severity on the other. Ireland was the grave then, as since, of more than one noble reputation. Lord Sussex, Sir Henry Sydney, Lord Grey de Wilton, Sir John Perrot, and others went down before the apparently insoluble problem. Still withal the country and its people had a strange fascination for English governors. No Englishman ever tasted the bitter-sweet of the Irish Deputyship but sighed and prayed to leave it, and then sighed and prayed to return to it. They were political moths, and Ireland was the candle in which they singed their wings and sometimes lost their lives.[40]

It is curious how rarely we find Ussher, in voluminous correspondence, referring to the general condition of Ireland. He seldom alludes to politics at all, except when his official position required it. He leaves that to his correspondents. The fact is that throughout his life Ussher was, above everything else, a student. He made little pretensions to that statecraft for which some of his contemporaries were distinguished. He loved his books; he lived, in a large measure, the life of a recluse; his vision was bounded by the walls of his splendid library; here he wrought, and the fruit of his toil may still be found in tomes from which successive generations of students have gathered fresh spoils.

---

40. See Brewer's *Introduction to Carew MSS.*, p. xxviii, and the graphic picture drawn by Dean Church of the condition of Ireland at this time in his *Spenser*, ch. iii, "Spenser in Ireland." It was not always easy, however, to get English statesmen to undertake the troublesome and oftentimes dangerous task of governing Ireland. In 1579, Mendoza, writing to the King of Spain, mentions that Elizabeth had offered the viceroyalty to several nobles who had refused it — *Spanish State Papers*. There has been the same difficulty in our own day.

CHAPTER III

EARLY EDUCATION OF USSHER; THE FOUNDING OF TRINITY COLLEGE

The early education of Ussher had been committed to his two blind aunts, who were most careful to instruct him in the Holy Scriptures.[1] The reason for this is plain. Ussher was surrounded by Roman Catholic relatives, who laid more than one trap to catch him. His mother became a Roman Catholic after her husband's death. It was even reported that he himself, shortly before his death, joined the Church of Rome, though there is not a shadow of foundation for the statement.[2]

---

1. Parr's *Life of Ussher,* p. 2. Richard Parr, the biographer of Ussher, son of the Rev. Richard Parr, was born in Fermoy, county of Cork, in 1617. He was educated in the parish school of Castlelyons, and when eighteen years of age entered Exeter College, Oxford, as a servitor. In 1643, Ussher met him there, and made him his chaplain. He accompanied the Archbishop to London, married a rich widow, and became vicar of Reigate. He died at Camberwell in 1691, aged seventy-four. Ware's *Writers of Ireland,* p. 314; Wood's *Ath. Oxon.,* iv, p. 341–2.

2. From his death-bed he wrote to Rome to open negotiations for the purpose of being received back into the bosom of that very Catholic Church

The memory of these two ladies must have been phenomenal, as they are said to have remembered what was once repeated to them "They were able," says Dr. Parr, "on a sudden to repeat any part of the Bible."

Like other remarkable men, Ussher in his earliest years turned to poetry, but eventually put it aside, "as not suitable to the great end of his more resolved serious and profitable studies. Yet he always loved a good poem that was well and chastely writ."[3] There is also reason for thinking he had a taste for music.[4]

According to Dr. Bernard, one of his biographers, Ussher was led to serious thoughts when ten years of age, by hearing a sermon preached on Romans xii, I. St. Augustine's *Confessions* had a great influence over him, and we are told he wept while he read them. A MS. essay on the Sabbath by one Master Perkins, gave him early in life a strong Sabbatarian bias. His spiritual experience was fed during solitary walks by the banks of the Dodder,

---

which he had so willfully maligned." *Archbishops of Dublin,* by Dr. Moran, p. 312 (note); see *infra.* The report had been circulated even earlier that he had "turned a papist," but, says one of his biographers (Dr. Bernard), "it fell out to be at the same time or immediately after he had, in two learned sermons, given his judgment at large that the Papacy was meant by Babylon in the 17th and 18th of the Revelation which in the return of his answer to the report he did affirm, and was his judgment to his last." — Bernard's *Judgment of the late Archbishop of Armagh,* p. 144. Ussher's view was also that of Bedell, in a sermon on Rev. xviii, 4, preached in 1634, before the Lord-Deputy and Parliament. It is the prevailing opinion of the Anglican divines of the sixteenth-seventeenth century, as may be seen from the writings of Jewell, Hooper, Whitgift, Andrewes, Bilson, Hall, Davenant, &c.

3. Parr's *Life of Ussher*, p. 3.

4. Elrington's *Life of Ussher*, p. 321, note. See also Bernard's *Life of Ussher*, p. 26. Nicholas Bernard was educated in Cambridge and coming over to Ireland was ordained by Ussher, who made him chaplain, and got him preferred to the Deanery of Ardagh. He eventually became chaplain and almoner to Oliver Cromwell (Ware's *Writers of Ireland*, p. 342). He died incumbent of the rich living of Whitchurch in 1661.

a river which then poured its clear waters through sequestered valleys on the south side of Dublin.[5]

One of his earliest published letters, addressed to his uncle, Richard Stanihurst, but undated, gives us an account of his youthful studies. It shows the strong bias that had already set in, in favour of theological and antiquarian pursuits. "The principal part of my study at this time is spent in perusing the writings of the Fathers, or observing out of them the doctrine of the ancient Church. . . . Besides my main studies, I have always used as a kind of recreation, to spend some time gathering together the scattered antiquities of our nation," and he inquires after a MS, *Life of St. Patrick*, at Lovain.[6]

In the next letter published, and addressed to Camden, he is again interested in the writings of St. Patrick, and notes the birth of the Irish apostle as having taken place in Clydesdale, "by the place which is now called Kirkpatrick." In the same letter (dated 1606) he takes notice of the "new county of Wicklow, and the new city of the Derrie lately erected by his Majesty."[7] When thirteen years of age, Ussher entered the newly created University of Dublin, the year of his matriculation being 1593. He received his first communion the following year.[8]

Let us here glance at some of the efforts that were made from time to time to found a national University in Ireland. In the early days of her Christian history, Ireland was well supplied

---

5. The river along whose banks Ussher thus wandered is identified by Dawson Massy, *Secret History of Romanisim,* p. 505.

6. Ussher's *Works,* xv, p. 3, 4.

7. Ibid., p. 17.

8. Ussher was the first scholar entered into Trinity College, Dublin. "It was so ordained upon design by the government of it observing the pregnancy and forwardness of him, that it might be a future honour to it, to have it on record in the frontispiece of their admission book." — Bernard's *Life of Ussher,* p. 25. Ussher himself says he was *inter primos in illam admissos. — Dublin University Calendar,* 1877, pt. 2, p. 192.

with schools of learning; her colleges were to be found in every part of the land.

The University of Armagh, said to have been founded by St. Patrick, was certainly an establishment of great antiquity. Theological schools existed at Clonard, Ross, Lismore, Clonfert, Bangor, and other places. The invasion of the Ostmen, who had no love or respect for learning, scattered these institutions, and for several centuries the country appears to have relapsed into a state of barbarism. We owe the first attempt to establish anything like a national University in Ireland to the intention of its promoters to bind the country more closely to the Anglo-Papal dominion. In 1311, John de Leeke (or Lech), Archbishop of Dublin, obtained a Bull from Clement V for the foundation of "a university of scholars" in Dublin. Clement in his Bull states: "Desiring that out of the said land men skillful in learning and faithful in the sciences may proceed, who may be able by fruitful doctrines to sprinkle the said land like a watered garden to the exaltation of the Catholic faith, the honour of Mother Church, and the profit of the faithful, we do by our apostolic authority ordain that in that said city of Dublin a university of scholars be established."[9]

This project fell through at the time, but was revived a few years later (February 10th, 1320), when a school of the kind was opened under a patent granted by Edward III to Alexander de Bicknor, Archbishop of Dublin, and the chapters of St. Patrick's and of Christ Church Cathedrals, and with the sanction of Pope John XXII. The University was to be under the government of a Chancellor, who must be a Doctor of Divinity or of the Common Law, and would have spiritual jurisdiction over the masters and scholars. A Regent in Divinity was to be appointed

9. Alan's *Liber Niger*, 2, f. 75–6; Ware, ii, p. 242; Monck Mason's *St. Patrick's Cathedral*, appendix ix–x. In the preface to the Bull the Pope notices that there would be less difficulty in founding a University in Ireland as many doctors of divinity were to be found in that country. The original Bull was destroyed by a fire in Christ Church Cathedral. Alan's copy is printed by Ware. — See *Works*, ii, p. 242–3.

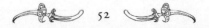

who should read lectures on the Holy Scriptures in St. Patrick's Cathedral "without challenge or contradiction from any person whatsoever." Three Doctors of Divinity were forthwith appointed — William Hardite, Henry Cogry, and Edmund Bernardine; and William Rodiant, Archdeacon of Dublin, was appointed Doctor of the Common Law.[10] This University, which seems to have possessed no buildings, languished for lack of funds. In 1358, Edward III gave it some further encouragement, and an additional Divinity Lecture was established. The needed protection was granted to students coming up to Dublin from the country, who stated that they could not proceed to Oxford on account of their poverty and the dangers of the way.[11]

A further effort was made to revive the college in the reign of Henry VII, the Archbishops and clergy contributing various sums toward its maintenance.

In 1465, an effort was made to establish a University in Drogheda during the session of a Parliament held there. It was to be founded after the model of the University of Oxford. The Duke of Clarence was Lord-Lieutenant at the time, with the Earl of Desmond as his deputy. The statute of foundation was as follows: "At the request of the Commons, because there is no University or general study in Ireland, which is a work that would advance knowledge, riches, and good government, and also prevent riot, ill-government, and extortion in the said land, it is ordained and established and confirmed by authority of Parliament, that there be an university in the town of Drogheda wherein there may be made bachelors, masters, and doctors in any science and faculty in like manner as in the University of Oxford, which may also have, occupy, and enjoy, all manner of liberties, privileges, laws, and laudable customs, that the said University of Oxford doth occupy or enjoy, so

---

10. See Alan's *Liber Niger;* Ware, as above, also, I, p. 330; Stubbs' *History of the University of Dublin,* p. 1–3; Monck Mason's *St. Patrick,* appendix, x–xi.

11. *Rot. Pat.,* 32, ed. 3rd; Ware, ii, p. 244.

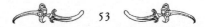

that it be not prejudicial to the mayor, sheriffs, or commonalty of the said town of Drogheda."[12]

This project also fell through for want of proper endowment. Then another scheme seems to have been taken up by George Browne, first Protestant Archbishop of Dublin in 1547. His plan was to endow "a faire and lardge colledge" out of the revenues of St. Patrick's Cathedral to be called Christ Church College. It was further to be supported by the income from the benefices of Trim, Armulghan, Rathewere, Callan, Durigarvan, and the Wardenship of Youghal.[13] It was not till 1568, however, that anything was done of such a definite nature as to promise success. In that year, Queen Elizabeth deputed certain officers to go over to Ireland and see if a national University could not be established. A Parliament was summoned for the purpose in Dublin, and the question was discussed in the presence of the Lord-Deputy, Sir H. Sydney.[14]

These efforts also failed, and then Sir John Perrot, in 1584, proposed the foundation of two Universities in Dublin to be endowed out of the revenues of St. Patrick's Cathedral. The church itself was to be turned into a court-house, and the canons' houses into inns for the Judges.[15] This plan was strenuously opposed by Archbishop Loftus, apparently from fear lest it might lead to an investigation into the way in which he had enriched himself and his family out of the income of the

12. Ware, ii, p. 245. The foundation statute, which is in French, may be seen in the Chancery Records, Edward IV, *An.* 5, cap. 46. A copy is also preserved in the Library T.C.D, (Class E; 3, 18).

13. See Shirley's *Original Letters,* p. 5–14.

14. A proposal was before the Government in 1579 to found a University at Clonfert, on account of its central position, "for that the runnagates of that nation which, under the pretence of study in the universities beyond the seas, do return freight with superstition and treason, are the very instruments to stir up our subjects to rebellion," — See Morrin's *Cal. Of Patent and Close Rolls of Chancery in Ireland,* ii, p. 22.

15. Perrot to Walshingham, August 21,1584; *Calendar of State Papers.*

Church.[16] The Archbishop succeeded in getting Sir John Perrot recalled. He died suddenly in the Tower of London in the following year.[17]

Although the plans thus put forward of founding a University in connection with St. Patrick's Cathedral fell through at the time, the idea survived of a connection between that ancient ecclesiastical and a national University, as is proved by the fact that the Trinity College Commencements were held within the precincts of the Cathedral up to 1732, when they were stopped by the Lords Chief Justices in consequence of riots between Town and Gown.[18]

The anomaly, and injury to the best interests of the country in leaving it for centuries without the benefit of a national University, especially in the case of an island once famous for its schools of learning, continued to press on the minds of those who desired to see Ireland lifted out of the slough of moral and intellectual degeneracy in which it was plunged. It was therefore constantly and urgently brought under the notice of the Sovereign.

---

16. Ware's *Bishops,* p. 353; Elrington's *Life of Ussher,* p. 6 (note); see contra Monck Mason's *St. Patrick's Cathedral* and *Dublin University Calendar,* 1833. The revenue of St. Patrick's Cathedral was then 4,000 marks per annum, which, it was understood, would endow the colleges with £1000 a year each. — See also Shirley's *Letters,* as above.

17. Cox's *History of Ireland,* vol. I, p. 387. This scheme for establishing a University out of the revenues of St. Patrick's had also been opposed by Archbishop Curwin. — *Calendar of State Papers,* January 21, 1564. Loftus and Perrot had quarrelled fiercely over this business, and the Archbishop threatened to resign if it ("Perrot's College") was carried out (March 18, 1585). A temporary reconciliation was effected on Easter Day, 1586, when they received the communion together, but the old "bickerings" soon broke out again. Perrot swore he would not be crossed, and threatened to be the utter enemy of Loftus; but it was the old story of the earthen jar and the iron pot.

18. St. Patrick's Cathedral has served many purposes in its day. At one period it was used as a common hall for the Four Courts, and under Cromwell for courts-martial.

A great wave of enlightenment was passing over England; the question was, Was Ireland to remain outside its influence?

Attention was now directed to the revenues of some of the suppressed monasteries, and Archbishop Loftus eventually prevailed on the mayor and citizens of Dublin, some of whom were Roman Catholics, to grant "the late ambit and precinct" of the dissolved monastery of All Hallows, Hoggan Green (now College Green).[19] Previously to this, the Speaker, Stanihurst, grandfather of James Ussher, had moved in the matter of setting up grammar schools in Ireland, where "babes from their cradle should be inured under learned schoolmasters with a pure English tongue, habite, fashion and discipline"; and then he goes on to urge the foundation of "an University here at home." Stanihurst was himself a man of literary tastes and patron of learning. Campion, in his *History* acknowledges his indebtedness to him. "This book" he says, "could never have so grown except for such familiar societe and daily table-talk with the worshipful Recorder, who beside all curtesie of hospitality and a thousand loving turns not here to be recited, both by word and written documents, and by the benefit of his own library, nourished most effectually his endeavor."[20]

In pursuance of instructions towards the above object, Henry Ussher, Archdeacon of Dublin and uncle of James Ussher, had petitioned the Queen to grant a charter, mortmain, licence, and royal warrant for the new College, all of which were granted on December 29th, 1591, with permission to enjoy lands to the annual amount of £400.[21] At Easter, Archbishop Loftus, with his clergy, met the mayor (Thomas Smith), aldermen, and commons

---

19. Hoggan Green derived its name, not from the hogs that roamed over it, but from a Scandinavian word, signifying a mound. — See Halliday's *Scandinavian Kingdom of Dublin,* p. 196. Hoggan Green was, in its day, the Tyburn of Dublin.

20. Campion's preface to "the loving Reader, from, Drogheda, June 9, 1571."

21. The warrant was received by Archdeacon Ussher on January 13, 1592. — *Calendar of State Papers* (1588–92), p. 455.

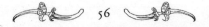

of Dublin, at the Tholsel in High Street, and there made a speech to them, setting forth the advantage of having such a nursery of learning founded, and how well the Queen would take it if they bestowed the old decayed monastery of All Hallows for the purpose.[22] The site which was then handed over embraced "about twenty-eight acres, of which twelve acres were meadow, nine pasture, and seven orchards. On the north towards the river there was a boggy strip of ground, covered by the water at high tide, and on the south it was bounded by the path leading to St. Patrick's Well, near the present Lincoln Place.

On the east it was bounded by lands formerly belonging to the Abbey of the Blessed Virgin, but then in the tenure of John Dougan; the modern Westland Row would constitute this boundary."[23]

In this spot was established "the College of the Sacred and Undivided Trinity near Dublin," as its title runs to the present day, although the institution may now be said to lie almost in the heart of the city — the one great national institution which has flourished and grown with years in a country where all besides has worn the aspect of change and uncertainty. The names of the following citizens deserve to be placed on record as nominated, along with others, to receive benevolences "towards the fynishing of the bylding nowe in doinge": Mr. Gyles Allen, Mr. Walter Ball, Mr. James Bellewe, John Terrell, Matthewe Handcok, John Marshall, and Ralfe Sancky."[24]

The original foundation consisted of one Provost, and of three Fellows, and three scholars in the name of more respectively. One of the three Fellows was Henry Ussher, who worked hard to get the royal charter, and who afterwards became Archdeacon of Dublin, and finally Archbishop of Armagh. The

22. See Hearne's preface to Camden's *Annals,* p. lvii; Stubb's *Hist. Univ. Dub.,* app., ii.

23. Dr. Stubbs' *History of the University of Dublin,* p. 6.

24. *Calendar of Ancient Records of Dublin,* ii, p. 253.

first Chancellor was Sir William Cecil, Lord Burleigh. Among the first students enrolled as we have already seen, was James Ussher, admitted January 9th, 1593.

The first public Commencements took place on Shrove Tuesday, February 1601, and twelve years later, in the month of August, a great Commencement was held, when the "Acts" were performed in the high choir of St. Patrick's Cathedral, because "the college rooms were very small." Five Doctors of Divinity were then made, one of them being James Ussher. A procession, we are told, was made through the city in very stately order, the Doctors, as enjoined, habited every one in his scarlet robes and hood, the Masters and Bachelors being likewise properly attired, and all presenting "a beautiful view to the sight of all men." Apparently Ussher valued such academical display. "I remember," writes Dr. Bernard, "one passage in his speech at a public Commencement, that the hoods and other distinctive ornaments used by several graduates in our universities were in use in Basil's and Nazianzen's time, so not Popish, as some have apprehended."[25] In after years, when a bishop, Ussher, as has been noted by some of his biographers, was particular about wearing his episcopal robes, and "was much for the distinctive habit of the clergy-cassocks, gowns, priestclokes," &c.

The English canon on the decent apparel of ministers was by his special approbation put in among those of Ireland.[26]

A quaint account survives of the above Commencements. We are told how the Lord President "delivered a proper speech in Latin to the doctors elect, while he also administered four academical consequences: (i) He set them in his chair; (ii) he gave them square caps; (iii) he delivered to them the Bible; (iv) he put rings on their fingers; after which he expounded to them the significance of each ceremony." On this occasion Ussher was selected to deliver the oration, which he did, choosing as his

25. Bernard's *Life of Ussher*, p. 46–7.
26. Bernard's *Clavi Trebales*, p. 64.

subject, after the controversial fashion of the day, the words, *Hoc est corpus meum.* He was then followed by the other doctors, who disputed on the same subject. A stately dinner was afterwards provided for the Lord-Deputy and Council in the College.[27] The total number of names in the books of that year was 109.

During the time when the buildings of the College were being erected, the weather, we are told, proved unusually propitious; "from the founding to the finishing of this College, the officious heavens, always smiling by day, though often weeping by night" till the work was completed.[28]

The foundation stone of the first building was laid by the Mayor, Thomas Smith, March 19th, 1592.[29]

---

27. See *Desid. Cur. Hib.,* p. 316–320.

28. Fuller's *Church History,* iii, 123. See also *Annals of Four Masters,* 1575, for a similar phenomenon. "The great interest and keen hopes of the city in the founding of the College are expressed in this legendary way." — J.P. Mahaffy, *Book of Trinity College, Dublin,* p. 8. We learn from a letter addressed by the Provost and Fellows to Burleigh, on August 15, 1594, that the original buildings cost £2000 — over £16,000 present currency. We also learn that the captains and soldiers of Ireland subscribed out of their reserved pay £623 "towards founding Trinity College, Dublin." Could this be the sum mentioned in the *MS. Book of Benefactions, T.C.D.,* as given towards founding the Library? We also learn from a letter addressed by Travers to Burleigh, that the new College was "built of brick, three stories high," thus authenticating Harris in his *History of Dublin,* that houses of brick began to be built in Dublin about this time, and refuting Petrie that there was not a brick house built in Dublin till the reign of Anne. — See *State Papers,* May 26 and August 15, 1594, and *Dublin Penny Journal,* I, p. 270; also Gilbert's *Cal. Anc. Records of Dublin,* ii, p. 7, where bricks are mentioned for the "citties use" in the year 1559.

29. Thomas Smith, who had the honour conferred on him of laying the foundation-stone of Trinity College, Dublin, was the son of Sir Thomas Smith, Secretary to Queen Elizabeth, and who had entertained his Sovereign at Audley End. Sir Thomas had obtained a grant of forfeited lands in the Ardes, county of Down, where his natural son was killed in 1572 "by such of his own household whom he trusted too much." Thomas Smith, the mayor, was the "city apothecary," and did business

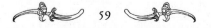

A king lies dying in agony, wracked with remorse for the devious murder of his own brother. . . . read about the blood "sign" he felt signaled God's judgment of his crime. Page 500, *The Annals of the World.*

Read more about
James Ussher's
The Annals of the World
www.nlpg.com/annals.asp

in Christ Church Lane, a narrow passage, about twelve feet wide, leading from Skinner's Row to Wine-tavern Street; he was thus a near neighbour of Ussher's. It was probably at his establishment the "bottell of poysoned drinke" was obtained by John Smith with a view to the nefarious purpose of "removing" Shane O'Neill, and at which the Queen was so greatly angered. Smith, who was Sir Henry Wallop's "only physician," used to complain greatly that his drugs were unsold owing to the Irish, who would use only the ministry of their own "leeches." He was therefore allowed a Government grant to enable him to supply "fresh and new drugs and other apothecary wares" for "the graver and civiller sort." Thomas Smith, who had also filled the office of City Treasurer, was a friend of Spenser while he resided in Dublin — See *Calendar of State Papers,* 1566; Shirley's *Farney,* p. 52; *Ulster Journal Arch.,* xi, p. 219; Morrin's *Calendar,* p. 231.

CHAPTER IV

STUDENT LIFE; THE YOUNG CONTROVERSIALIST; PURITANISM IN TRINITY COLLEGE

W hen Ussher entered Trinity College in 1593, he immediately directed his attention to Greek and Hebrew studies. He also devoted much attention to history and chronology. The words of Cicero — *Nescire quid antea quam natus sis acciderit id est semper esse puerum* — seemed to have had great weight with him. At the early age of fourteen he had begun his *Annales* and a year later he had drawn up a chronicle of the Bible, as far as Kings, the nucleus of the work he published later in life, and which still supplies the dates at the headings of the chapters in the Authorised Version of the Old Testament. By what authority Ussher's chronology obtained this position in our Bibles seems never to have been clearly ascertained.

In 1596, Ussher went up for the degree of B.A., having previously been elected to a scholarship. He performed the necessary exercises in the presence of the Earl of Essex, the Lord-Deputy and Chancellor of the University. On the death of his father, two years later, we are told that he resigned the whole of his estate

to his brothers and sisters, with the exception of a small portion which he retained for himself. He seems to have done so from a desire to be as free as possible from worldly cares, with a view to prosecuting his studies without interruption.[1]

Two circumstances now combined to give a marked bias to the theological opinions of Ussher. One was a natural reaction from the Roman Catholic leanings of some members of his family, the other the strong Puritanical element that prevailed in Trinity College. Stapleton, a polemical writer in the interests of the Church of Rome, had written a book called the *Fortress of the Faith*, in which he endeavoured to prove, by quotations from the Fathers, that the Roman Catholic Church was the old Church, and Protestantism altogether a new religion. To combat Stapleton, Ussher's attention was directed to the earliest Christian writers, and he commenced that study of the Fathers which only ended with his thirty-eighth year.

But Ussher found a still more formidable foe to his faith in the Jesuit Henry Fitzsymons. The career of this remarkable man deserves more than a passing notice. He was sprung of a good stock, who were all "of name and account in Dublin." His branch of the family was settled in Swords, and he himself was born in Dublin in 1566. His father was a senator or alderman of the city, and his grandfather was Sir Thomas Fitzsymons, Prime Serjeant-in-Law. By his mother, Anna Segrave, he was allied to the Stanihursts, and James Ussher was his cousin.[2] Fitzsymons seems to have been born a Roman Catholic, since he tells us that when ten years of age he was "inveigled into heresie," and at twenty-one he claimed that he was "able to convert into Protestancie any encounterer whatsoever." In 1583, he matriculated at Hart Hall, and subsequently returned to Ireland,

---

1. In this year the infant College was in a precarious condition. "For lack of maintenance it was ready to dissolve and break-up if it had not been relieved on this instant. The Queen's grant of £100 per annum was accordingly raised to £600." — *Calendar of State Papers,* 1596, p. 190.

2. See *Ussher Memoirs,* p. 29, 277; and *Dict. Nat. Biog.*

and gave "great disedification in Dublin by his error" — i.e., Protestantism. In 1587, we find Fitzsymons, in Paris, where, in controversy with Father Darbyshire, "an owld English Jesuit," nephew of Bishop Bonner, and formerly Archdeacon of Essex, his Protestantism was overthrown, and he was received into the Roman Catholic Church.

In 1596, Fitzsymons, who meanwhile had joined the Jesuit Order in Rome, was sent back to Ireland in response to a petition from O'Neill and others, to carry on a mission, and he opened a chapel in a nobleman's house in Dublin and celebrated the first high Mass that had been heard of in the city for forty years. As is always the way with converts, Fitzsymons, from being a warm supporter of Protestantism, had now become one of its most bitter assailants.

At length his aggressiveness became so great that the authorities were compelled to interfere, and Fitzsymons was seized and thrown into prison in the Castle of Dublin. His incarceration, however, could not have been very severe, as he was permitted to hold a religious controversy with Challoner, Hanmer, and Rider the Dean of St. Patrick's. Against the latter he maintained the thesis that "all antiquitie is repugnant to Protestancie." Fitzsymons himself, in the dedication of his "Britannomachia" to Aquaviva, the General of his Order, gives a graphic account of his controversial labours, and also of his interview with Ussher. "While I was in captivity in the Castle of Dublin for five years, I did everything in my power to provoke the parsons to a discussion. . . . Whenever I knew they were passing in the corridors or castle yard, I cried to see them, and by word or gesture to attract their attention. But they neither wished to look up at me in the tower, nor did they pretend to hear me when I challenged them in, a stentorian voice.[3] One indeed, a youth of eighteen,

---

3. The Castle was to Dublin what the Tower was to London. According to the *Carew MSS.*, it had some very loathsome "dungeons." — See also Hogan's *Celebrated Irishmen of the Sixteenth Century*, p. II, 12. Fitzsymons seems not to have been harshly treated, and to have enjoyed a considerable amount of liberty.

came forward in the greatest trepidation of face and voice. He was a precocious boy, but not of a bad disposition and talent as it seemed. Perhaps he was rather greedy of applause. Anyhow he was desirous of disputing about most abstruse points of divinity." Fitzsymons tells us he bid Ussher bring him some proof that he was considered a fit champion by the Protestants, and that then he would enter into a discussion with him. According to Fitzsymons, Ussher never appeared again.[4]

A letter from Ussher, however, is extant, which seems to throw doubt on this last statement that the combatants only met once. The letter is given by Fitzsymons himself, but an attempt has been made to question its genuineness. It runs as follows: "I was not prepared, Mr. Fitzsymons, to write unto you before you had first written unto me concerning some chief points of your religion, as at our last meeting you promised. But, seeing that you have deferred the same (for reasons best known to yourself), I thought it not amiss to inquire further of your mind concerning the continuance of the conference begun between us; and to this I am rather moved because I am credibly informed of certain reports, which I would hardly be persuaded should proceed from him who, in my presence, pretended so great love and affection to me. If I am a boy (as it hath pleased you very contemptuously to name me), I give thanks to the Lord that my carriage towards you hath been such as could minister no just occasion to despise my youth. Your spear, belike, is, in your own conceit, a weaver's beam; and your abilities such that you desire to encounter with the stoutest champion in the host of Israel, and, therefore, like the Philistine, you contemn me as being a boy. Yet this I would fain have you to know, that I neither came then, nor do come now, unto you in any confidence of any learning that is in me (in which respect notwithstanding, I thank God I am what I am), but I come in the name of the Lord of Hosts, whose companies you have reproached, being certainly persuaded that even

---

4. See preface to his *Britannomachia,* p. 14.

out of the mouths of babes and sucklings He was able to shew forth His own praises; for the further manifestation whereof, I do again earnestly request you that, setting aside all vain comparison of persons, we may go plainly forward in examining the matters that rest in controversy between us. Otherwise I hope you will not be displeased if, as for your part you have begun, so I also, for my own part, may be bold, for the clearing of myself, and the truths which I profess, freely to make known what hath already passed concerning this matter. Thus entreating you, in a few lines, to make known unto me your purpose in this behalf, I end. Praying the Lord that both this and all other enterprises that we take in hand may be so ordered as may most make for the advancement of His own glory, and the kingdom of His Son Jesus Christ. *"Tuas ad aras usque,"* JAMES USSHER.

The above letter, indeed, bears on its face evidence of being the effusion of a writer in his teens, and must therefore be excused for its overconfidence, especially when addressed by a youth to one considerably his senior. It is not the kind of letter Ussher would have written to an antagonist in later years, when time had matured his judgment and enabled him to realise the responsibilities of such controversies. Fitzsymons reply to the letter, if he ever wrote any, is not forthcoming.[5]

The future of this champion of the Roman Catholic Church in Ireland may be briefly told. In March 1604, after a declaration of his "loyalty and dutiful affection to his Majesty," Fitzsymons was released from prison by order of King James, and transferred to Bilboa in a ship. After various adventures in foreign parts he returned to Ireland, and having mixed himself up in treasonable plots, he was sentenced to be hanged. Flying from Dublin by way of the village of Rathfarnham, he sought a hiding-place at Glencree, among the bogs of the Dublin mountains, and when

---

5. According to Ware, the subject of the three first discussions between Ussher and Fitzsymons was "Antichrist," that fertile ground for controversy in the sixteenth and seventeenth centuries. They were to argue once a week, but only met two or three times — *Works*, ii, p. 327.

pursuit had ceased he made his way southwards, and probably died in Kilkenny about 1643. A list of his writings is given in the *Dictionary of National Biography*, and Ussher's copy of his *Catalogue of Irish Saints* may be seen in the Library of Trinity College, with marginal notes in the Archbishop's handwriting.[6]

Such was the career of a noted ecclesiastical plotter of his day, but the story of his life may be paralleled with that of many others of the same period, such as Archer, Holywood, and White (founder of the Irish College at Salamanca), and whose religious zeal was in many cases only a cloak to cover treasonable enterprises.[7]

There is a probability that it was not altogether in the interests of Protestantism that the young Ussher was thus put forward to challenge such a mature and experienced champion of the Roman faith. But if this be so, the efforts thus made by his Roman Catholic relatives to entrap him only recoiled on themselves and left Ussher more strongly confirmed in the Reformed faith. Richard Stanihurst, his uncle, seems to have abated no efforts with a view to converting him to the Roman Catholic religion. He left behind him for this purpose extensive notes, with the heading, *"Brevis premonitio pro futura concertatione cum Jacobo Ussuro."*[8] Ussher became strengthened in his Protestantism, and none of his writings is more valuable than

---

6. [*Class* Press A. 2, 8.] For the details of Fitzsymons' history the reader may consult his *Life* by the Rev. Edmund Hogan, S.J.; Articles in the *Month,* vol. lxxi, by the same author; Fitzsymons' *Britannomachia* and *Confutation;* Wood's *Ath. Oxon.;* and Article in the *Dictionary of National Biography.* We read that by Fitzsymons' death the Roman Catholics lost a pillar of their Church . . . he being esteemed the greatest defender of their religion in his time." — Wood's *Ath. Oxon.,* iii, p. 96. Fitzsymons' writings are full of violent and indecent attacks on the Reformers.

7. Ware says of Fitzsymons: "He was a great abettor and encourager of the rebellion of 1641." — *Writers of Ireland,* ii, p. 118.

8. See Ellington's *Life,* p. 35. "'Tis thought and verily believed by some that Ussher was too hard for his uncle in controversial points relating to divinity." — Wood's *Ath. Oxon.,* ii, p. 254.

his *Answer to a Jesuit*, to be noticed hereafter, in which he combats and overthrows with the strength of a giant the peculiar doctrines of the Roman Catholic Church.

But as this controversy gave a stronger bias to Ussher's Protestantism, so the atmosphere of Trinity College contributed to give that Protestantism a decidedly Puritan hue. Strange as the statement may appear, it is evident that while the Queen had a Catholic leaning in England, and encouraged the party which afterwards developed into the Laudian school, in Ireland she was either indifferent to the turn the Reformed religion might take or else encouraged the spread of Puritanism, believing that this phase of the Protestant movement best suited the requirements of the Irish Church.

Archbishop Loftus, though nominated first Provost of Trinity College,[9] only filled the office as a *locum tenens* until a regular and permanent Provost could be appointed. He was himself a strong Puritan, and, on leaving Armagh for Dublin, had suggested Hooker's opponent, Cartwright, who had been his chaplain at Armagh, as his successor in that archbishopric.[10]

The Presbyterian divine, Walter Travers, was ultimately selected. Travers had refused episcopal orders and had gone to Holland to receive ordination at the hands of the Dutch Presbytery at Antwerp, and on this account had been prohibited from preaching in London by Archbishop Whitgift. He had been for a period Lecturer at the Temple Church (where subscription to the Thirty-nine Articles was not required) when

---

9. Portraits of Loftus may be seen, one in the Provost's House, and the other (presented by Lord Iveagh) in the Fellows' Common Room. The Archbishop built himself a noble castle in the village of Rathfarnham, near Dublin, which is still standing and occupied. "The greatness of his mind and grandeur is sufficiently expressed in the stately edifice he built at Rathfarnham." — Borlase, *Reduction of Ireland*, p. 147–8. Loftus's high positions in Ireland are thus summarised": Primate, Chancellor, Provost, Lord Justice."

10. *Calendar of State Papers,* March 1577; Shirley's *Letters*, p. 321.

Hooker was Master, and as their views of Church doctrine and discipline were diametrically opposed, it used to be said, "The forenoon sermon spake Canterbury, and the afternoon Geneva."[11] Travers appealed against the Archbishop's inhibition to the Privy Council, but without success, although he had the powerful patronage of his friend the Earl of Leicester.

It was brought as a charge against him that he was in a conspiracy with Theodore Beza and others to set up a Presbyterian form of Church government. Hooker in his reply to a petition lodged by Travers, also charged against him that he had administered the communion, the recipients neither kneeling as was the custom of the realm, nor sitting as was the custom in the Temple Church, but standing and walking round the table.[12] According to Fuller, "Mr. Travers' utterance was graceful; gesture plausible; matter profitable, and his style carried in it *indolem pietatis,* 'a genius of grace' flowing from his sanctified heart. Some say that the congregation in the Temple ebbed and flowed in the afternoon, and that the auditory of Mr. Travers was far the most numerous. . . . The worst was, these two preachers . . . clashed

---

11. Fuller's *History,* vol. iii, p. 138–42, and *Appeal of Injured Innocence,* p. 518–9. See also Walton's *Life of Hooker,* S.P.C.K.Ed., p. 165–9. Travers' Letters of Orders by the Presbytery of Antwerp can be seen in *Fuller,* Vol. iii, p. 125. Walter Travers was of Irish extraction, and this may have had something to do with his appointment. He was the grandson of John Travers and Sarah Spenser, sister of the poet, a large portion of whose property in the county of Cork he inherited. Having no issue, he left his estates to his cousin John Travers. The family are now represented by the heir of Sir William St. Lawrence Clark-Travers, who married the only daughter and heiress of John Moore Travers of the county of Cork. The first of the family to settle in Ireland was the above-mentioned John Travers, who came over in 1580 in the retinue of Lord Grey de Wilton, Lord-Lieutenant of Ireland. — See Brady's *Records of Cork,* I, p. 351–2.

12. The counter-charges of Travers against Hooker were that he prayed before and not after the sermon; in his prayers he named bishops; he kneeled both when he prayed and when he received the sacrament. — Walton's *Life of Hooker,* p. 165–173.

one against another; so that what Hooker delivered in the fore-noon, Mr. Travers confuted in the afternoon. At the building of Solomon's Temple neither hammer nor axe nor tool of iron was heard therein; whereas alas! in this temple not only much knocking was heard but which was the worst — the nails and pins which one master builder drove in were driven out by the other."[13] Fuller quaintly goes on to describe the circumstances attending the inhibition of Travers: "All the congregation on a Sabbath in the afternoon were assembled together, their attention prepared, the cloth (as I may say) and napkins were laid, yea, the guests set, when suddenly as Mr. Travers was going up into the pulpit a sorry fellow served him with a letter forbidding him to preach any more. . . . Thus was our good Zaccheus struck dumb in the pulpit. Meanwhile his auditory (pained that their pregnant expectation to hear him preach should so publicly prove abortive and sent sermonless home) manifested in their variety of passions — some grieving, some groaning, some murmuring; and the wisest sort who held their tongues, shook their heads, as disliking the management of the matter."[14] Such was the man who was considered a suitable Provost under whose care the newly established college might start on its career.

When Tyrone's rebellion broke out, Travers resigned his provostship and returned to England,[15] when the same policy was pursued, and three years later another avowed Puritan was put by the Queen at the head of the college in the person of Henry

---

13. Fuller's *Church History,* iii, p. 128. The same kind of controversy was also proceeding elsewhere. At Cambridge; for example, "great clashing was now in the schools. Where one professor impugned — the other asserted the Church discipline in England." — Fuller's *Hist. Univ. of Cambridge,* p. 197.

14. Fuller's *Church Hist.,* Vol. iii, p. 129.

15. Where he died, according to Neal, "in silence, obscurity, and great poverty." We find in 1693 a John Travers, nephew of the Provost and grandnephew of Edmund Spenser, rector of St. Andrews, Dublin. — Gilbert's *Hist. of Dublin,* iii, p. 307.

Alvey, a Fellow of St. John's College, Cambridge, and an intimate friend of Hooker's opponent, Cartwright.[16] The influence exercised by these men over Ussher is plainly manifested in the Irish Articles of Religion he was mainly instrumental in drawing up some years later, and also in the *Eirenicon* he published in later years, wherein he sought a common standing ground between Episcopacy and Presbyterianism.

The effort to strengthen the Puritan element in Trinity College did not cease on the resignation of Alvey.[17]

His successor, William Temple, who had been Lord Essex's secretary, was a pronounced Puritan, and refused to obey the orders of Abbot, Archbishop of Canterbury and Chancellor of the University, who required him to wear a surplice in the College Chapel on Sundays and holy days. Ussher writes to Dr. Challoner, stating that this condition of things had annoyed the Archbishop, who had observed that no order was taken that the scholars should come into the chapel *clericaliter vestiti*. He objected also to the other things as "flat puritanical."[18] The king

---

16. Ussher's signature is first found in the college books on this occasion (October 1601), when he signs with the rest of the Fellows the certificate of Alvey's appointment. Henry Alvey is not to be confounded with Richard Alvey, also a Fellow of St. John's, Cambridge, who was Hooker's immediate predecessor as Master of the Temple, and who died in 1584. Elrington in one place (p. 15), by mistake, calls the new Provost "John Alvey."

17. Alvey fled from Dublin on the approach of the plague. He died at Cambridge, January 25, 1626. Dr. Ward, Master of Sidney, Sussex, visited him twice when he was sick, and found him "very patient and comfortable." Alvey desired to be "buried privately, and in a sheet only, without a coffin, for so, said he, was our Saviour. But it was thought fit that he should be put in a coffin, and so he was." Dr. Ward to Ussher. — Ussher's *Works,* xv, p. 369.

18. Ussher's *Works,* xv, p. 72. Temple was originally Master of the Free School of Lincoln. He was afterwards secretary to Sir Philip Sidney; and saw him fall at Zutphen. In 1609, he accepted the provostship "on the earnest solicitations of Dr. Ussher." — Wood's *Fasti Axon.* pt. I, p. 220; Borlase's Red of *Ireland,* p. 150.

(James I) was also "exceedingly offended thereat." "His Majesty sayeth that it is no reason to suffer those places to be the ground plotte of disorder and disobedience; neither is there any reason to be severe against the Papists if His Highness should be remiss against the Puritans."[19] The king apparently was bent on pursuing a different policy from that of his predecessor on the throne.

Ussher, we may observe, had been offered but refused the Provostship before it was given to Temple, for the reason that it might prove "a hindrance to his studies."[20] Temple refused to wear the surplice, on the ground that it was unreasonable to ask a layman to do so. He also intermitted the celebration of the Holy Communion till he was called to order through the intervention of Abbot. Still, Temple did some good work for the College. He obtained its first statutes, and he so improved in his churchmanship that he induced the students to wear surplices and attend Christ Church Cathedral. They also, we learn, used the Communion Book."[21]

That the Puritan element survived in Trinity College is shown by the fact that one of the divines who met in Westminster some thirty years later, and assisted in drawing up the Confession of Faith, was Dr. Hoyle, Professor of Divinity in the College.[22]

---

19. Archbishop Abbot to Archbishop Jones (Dublin), February 25th, 1613. Abbot was now Chancellor of the University of Dublin. — Elrington's *Life,* p. 32–3 (note).

20. Parr's *Life of Ussher,* p. ii. Ussher was then in his thirtieth year.

21. Stubbs' *History of Dublin University,* p. 35–8. It was considered noteworthy that Ussher always wore his episcopal robes in church, and required his chaplain to wear a surplice when celebrating the Holy Communion. It is also on record that the Archbishop never wore his hat in church, and always received the communion kneeling. — Bernard's *Clavi Trabales,* p. 60–1; Elrington's *Life,* p. 284.

22. Dr. Salmon, the present Provost of Trinity College, refers to this constant influence of Puritan divines on the Church of Ireland, bringing up the cases of Travers and Alvey. "Under these influences was trained the great boast of our University, James Ussher, who, more than anyone

else, imprinted his character on the Irish clergy of his day. — Report of the Dublin Church Congress, p. 126. Professor Mahaffy's view is that Travers, Alvey, and Temple were men who were "baulked in their English promotion by their acknowledged Puritanism." — *Book of Trinity College,* p. 17. In the MS. Room, Trinity College, Dublin, may be seen notes, made by Ussher when an undergraduate, of Travers' sermons preached in the chapel, Trinity College, Dublin, dated 1594 (Class C. 5, 13). Trinity College was not exceptional in its Puritanism. It had a rival in Emmanuel College, Cambridge, where the authorities discarded surplices and hoods at morning and evening prayer, as well as at the celebration of the Holy Communion. College suppers, as a rule, were given on Fridays. Bishop Hall writes to Wadsworth, afterwards tutor to the Infanta: "In Emmanuel College they receive the Holy Sacrament sitting upon forms about the communion-table, and doe pull the loafe one from the other after the minister hath begon. And so the cupp, one drinking, as it were to another, as good fellows, without any particular application of the saide words more than once for all." — Lewis's *Life of Hall,* p. 32–3. It was of this college that Dr. Preston became president. We also read that in the absence of Dr. Whitgift, on a certain Sunday, Mr. Cartwright and two of his adherents made three sermons so vehemently inveighing against all ceremonies of the Church that, at leaving prayer, all scholars save three cast off their surplices as an abominable relic of superstition. — See Fuller's *History of the University of Cambridge,* p. 197. Compare the surplice riots of our own day in St. George's-in-the-East, as described by Stanley, *Life and Correspondence,* ii, p. 25, &c.

CHAPTER V

USSHER AND THE ROMAN CATHOLICS

To return to our story, in the year 1600, Ussher went up for the degree of Master of Arts. It was a remarkable coincidence that on the same day the Earl of Essex, before whom he had performed the exercises for his B.A. Degree, was beheaded in London. Shortly afterwards, Ussher was elected a Fellow, and also Catechist, and at the same time made the first Proctor. As Catechist, it was his business to expound the principles of the Christian religion. Then as afterwards this took very much the form of controversial lectures against the errors of the Church of Rome. In fact, the Professorship of Divinity had this by statute for its principal business, and it is still the work of the Professor during the academical year to devote a certain portion of his lectures to the same subject. The Chair was originally called the "Professorship of Controversies."[1]

---

1. As Professor of Divinity, Ussher lectured chiefly on *Bellarmine's Controversies.* — Bernard's *Life,* p. 45; Smith's ditto, p. 63. Trinity College was recognised from the first as a great Protestant endowment. This is proved by the ferment into which the Jesuits were thrown by its erection. A petition was presented to the Pope against a "certain splendid college near Dublin

So successful was Ussher in his prelections, that he was soon pointed out as the proper person to address larger and more influential audiences, and so, though still a layman and not twenty years of age, he was selected with two others (also laymen) to deliver weekly lectures in divinity, and especially on the Roman controversy, before the Lord-Deputy and his household, in Christ Church Cathedral. This looks as if at the time of the Reformed Church of Ireland was but poorly provided with clerics of reputation, and that the authorities were glad to fall back on the services of educated laymen. Ussher was very reluctant to take upon himself the office, and it required much persuasion to overcome his youthful diffidence. His arguments and exhortations were so powerful that not a few Roman Catholics were led to conform to the Protestant faith. He had scruples, however, about discharging an office that was naturally clerical, and therefore determined to obtain orders.[2]

The difficulty arising from his not being of the canonical age was overcome by a dispensation from the Primate[3] and on the Fourth Sunday in Advent, 1601, he was ordained both deacon and priest by his uncle, the Archbishop of Armagh, being then but twenty-one years of age.[4] The first sermon after his ordination was preached on December 24th, being the day set apart for special prayer for success against the Spanish invasion. The

---

where the youths of Ireland were instructed in English heresy." In 1609, the College was officially called by its enemies "The Fanatics' College." See Hogan's *Hib. Ignatiana*, p. 35; Bagwell's *Ireland under the Tudors*, iii, p. 472. With a view to neutralising the influence of the College, Jesuit seminaries were founded by Irishmen at Seville, Salamanca, Lisbon, and other places.

2. Bernard's *Life*, p. 35.

3. Parr's *Life*, p. 8. Ussher's Letters of Orders, enclosed in a glass case, are to be seen in the Library of Trinity College.

4. This is the date given by all the biographers, but the Letters of Orders bear the date May 1602.

same day saw the battle of Kinsale fought and won. Immediately after this, Ussher was appointed afternoon preacher to the State in Christ Church Cathedral.[5]

The student life of Ussher may here be said to have ended; but it must be remembered that he was little more than a youth, whose precocious talents had forced him to the front.

He was still immersed in his books, and was carrying on in the midst of other labours those studies that were to bear fruit in his riper years, and hand down his name to after centuries as one of the most learned scholars of his day. He had yet a work to do in the founding of the noble Library of Trinity College, with which his collegiate career proper may be said to have closed.

We have already seen that the Government of Queen Elizabeth thought right to pursue a different religious policy in Ireland from that adopted in England. That that policy was one calculated to attract the Roman Catholics may well be questioned. There can be little doubt likewise that the unwise determination to have the Reformed Liturgy said in Latin in those parts of Ireland where the English language was not understood by the people was a most unhappy conclusion to arrive at. How different might the result have proved had there been then a Bedell at the head of affairs to encourage the use in public worship of their own tongue among the Irish-speaking population! The reformation of religion in Ireland would most probably have proved a success, and not the unhappy failure it has turned out to be.

The introduction of the penal laws had also a most deterrent effect, and Ussher was often called upon to preach before an audience who could hardly help being present, seeing they

---

5. A good deal of preaching went on at this time in Dublin, but apparently without much effect. Archbishop Loftus writes to Burleigh, December 1596, "I dare assure your lordship that there is not in any like place in England more often preaching of God's word (by godly and learned preachers) than in this city, where it little prevaileth." — *Calendar of State Papers,* A.D. 1596; p. 193.

would have been fined in their absence![6] In their zeal to propagate Protestantism, the Government required controversial sermons to be preached in different churches throughout the city, and Ussher was directed to preach in St. Catherine's Church, not far from the Castle. This custom of preaching controversial sermons, inaugurated in the sixteenth century, survived to a generation ago, and engaged the talents of some of the most eloquent preachers of the Irish Church, including O'Sullivan, McGhee, Fleury, and others. It was only the Protestants, however, who attended, and the Roman Catholics kept studiously away.[7]

The Statute of Recusants, as it was called, passed in the second year of Elizabeth, seems at this time to have been put in force more severely in Dublin than elsewhere. In virtue of this statute, Roman Catholics who did not attend the parish churches were liable to be fined one shilling for every offence of the kind, and the money thus received was spent in repairing Protestant churches and building bridges.[8] After a time it was felt that this statute was being pressed too severely, and orders came to the

6. When these unfortunate "Recusants" did go to church they made it extremely uncomfortable for the Protestant congregations. "If they come to church, they walk round about like mill horses, chopping, changing, making merchandise, so that they in the quire cannot hear a word, and those not small fools but the chief of the city." — John Shearman to Archbishop Long (Armagh), *Calendar of State Papers*, July 8, 1585; see Gardiner's *History*, i, ch. ix, for the position of the Recusants. It is to the credit of Laud that he could give no sanction to the stupid and wicked policy of taxing Roman Catholics into Protestantism. "This course," he wrote to Sir Edward Coke, "will never bring them to church, being rather an engine to draw money out of their pockets than to raise a right belief and faith in their hearts." See Hutton's *Laud*, p. 170–1; Hogan's *Dist. Irishmen*, p. 454.

7. The last great public disputation between champions of the rival Churches was the famous discussion between "Pope and Maguire," in the Rotunda, Dublin, in 1827.

8. See Bishop Rider's *Returns at the Royal Visitation of Killaloe* (1622), as given in Dwyer's *History of the Diocese*, p. 130, 146. In some instances, these fines were made very heavy, as much as £100 being levied from leading citizens — a sum approaching £1000 at the present day. See, for examples,

Lord-Deputy, Lord Mountjoy, to relax its requirements. In a letter dated February 26, 1603, Lord Mountjoy expresses the pleasure he felt at being permitted to adopt more moderate measures. Ussher, however, who was a strong Protestant, took umbrage at this interference with the Act of Uniformity, considering that it endangered religion and loyalty in the country; and when next called on to preach in Christ Church Cathedral, undeterred by any fear of the consequences, he boldly denounced what he considered to be the toleration of Popery.

He chose for his text the words: "And thou shalt bear the iniquity of the house of Judah forty days: I have appointed thee each day for a year" (Ezek. Iv, 6). When some forty years later the Rebellion broke out, people looked back on Ussher's discourse and regarded it as prophetic,[9] and the view taken of his sermon and some other later utterances gave rise to a small publication entitled *De Predictionibus Usserii*.

Ussher, indeed, had such a dread of the inroads of Popery that he thought it well that all Roman Catholic books should be withdrawn from the shelves of the College library. Thus, he writes to Dr. Challoner, from London, in 1612: "I would wish those English Popish books were kept more privately, as the books of discipline are, in a place by themselves, for it would be somewhat dangerous to have them remain in the public library."[10]

Calendar of State Papers, 1607–8, preface, 80–99; also *Desid. Cur. Hib.*, I, p. 274. The keeping up of the bridges was a *quasi* religious duty, formerly discharged by the monasteries, now dissolved. The old bridge of Dublin, the first of the six bridges of Ussher's time, had been built by the Friars Preachers, and had a chapel with a stoup for holy water to sprinkle passers-by on the centre. — Halliday's *Scan. Kingdom of Dublin*, p. 222–3 (note); Froude's *History of England*, x, p. 535.

9. Parr's *Life*, p. 39–40. Elrington argues that this sermon could not have been preached in 1601, amongst other reasons because Ussher was not ordained till the December of that year: but for some time he had preached as a layman.

10. Ussher's *Works*, xvi, p. 318–19.

And the fear still haunts him, for he writes again next year from the same place: "You may do well to have a care that the English Popish books be kept in a place by themselves, and not placed among the rest in the library, for they may prove dangerous."[11] He notes a few weeks later, in the course of his correspondence, apparently with a mild satisfaction, how "Latham, alias Molyneux, one of the learnedest and insolentest of the Popish priests here, was executed at Tyburn."[12]

To understand aright the position which Ussher took with regard to the Roman Catholic Church in Ireland, it would be necessary to take a retrospective glance at the history of the country. It is not too much to say that England has never understood the sister island, and though she has now held possession of the country for more than seven centuries, Ireland is still unreconciled, and her rule continues to be regarded by the majority of Irishmen as that of an alien and usurper. England has never succeeded in conciliating the race; she has failed in successfully implanting the Reformed religion on the soil; she has governed the country by alternately threatening and relaxing her hold of it. Annexed as it was to England by Henry II, Ireland has never been thoroughly conquered, or made an integral part of the United Empire, happy and contented by a wise and equable government.

The Irish difficulty exists today as it existed in Elizabeth's time, in that of Charles I, Oliver Cromwell, William III, and George III. Some evil must lie deep and undiscovered at the root, which has led to such untimely and undesirable results.

When we regard the ecclesiastical condition of the country at the time that Ussher was becoming a prominent figure in its history, we find the question of religion affecting to a greater or lesser degree its social and political condition. In the sixteenth and the opening of the seventeenth century, the Roman Catholics in Ireland were divided into two parties, the "Papists" and the

---

11. Ussher's *Works,* xv, p. 74.

12. *Ussher,* xvi, p. 320.

"Loyalists";[13] the distinction in itself is significant. When O'Neill rose in rebellion against Elizabeth, he proclaimed a religious war; he raised his standard "for the extirpation of heresy"; he got the Pope on his side, who sent him a consecrated plume, and styled him "Commander and Captain General of the Catholic Army in Ireland"; and the King of Spain, who supplied him with an armament. Thus Romanism and treason went hand-in-hand, and led to repressive measures.

The Queen, in an address issued in 1591, protested against the insinuation so eagerly made by her enemies that she was persecuting the faith: "We have saved our kingdoms by the efficacy of the laws enacted against rebels and those guilty of high treason, and not against religion, as has been falsely advanced by the favourers of these base views; which is the more flagrant from criminal suits, having been instituted in which none were condemned or put to death, except for treason, and for their avowal that they would aid and assist the Pope and his army if sent to invade our realms.

"It is a matter of notoriety also, that none of our subjects have been put to death for their religion; inasmuch as many possessed riches, and professing a contrary belief to ours are punished neither in their properties, their lives, nor their freedom, and are subject only to pay a certain fine for their refusal to frequent our churches, which is on our part, a clear refutation of the aspersions and calumnies which have been propagated in foreign countries by those who have fled from their own."[14]

There can be no doubt that the Queen was endeavouring to carry on the government of Ireland on the principle of giving freer and fuller liberty of worship to the Roman Catholics. The Roman Catholic historian Moore, and other authorities of that Church, acknowledge the fact.[15]

---

13. Cox, *History of Ireland,* p. 454.

14. Macgeoghegan's *History of Ireland,* p. 494.

15. See Moore's *History of Ireland;* iv, 108.

Lord Barry, a Roman Catholic peer, writing in 1600, in reply to Hugh O'Neill's letter, upbraiding him for his loyalty, gives expression to the feelings of the Loyalist Party: "Her Highness hath never restrained me for matters of religion. . . . I hold my lordship and lands immediately under God of her Majesty and her most noble progenitors, by corporal service and of none other by very ancient tenure, which service and tenure none may dispense withal but the true possessor of the Crown of England, being now our Sovereign Lady Queen Elizabeth."[16] But how was this toleration rewarded? When the Spanish General, Don Juan de Aquila, landed in Kinsale with the approbation of the Pope, he instantly issued a manifesto, coupling loyalty towards England with heresy: "Whoever shall remain in the obedience to the English we will persecute him as a heretic and a hateful enemy of the Church, even unto death."[17] The Irish Roman Catholics, with a few exceptions, were only too glad to rally to this cry, and found a leader in Eugene McEgan, the Vicar-Apostolic for Munster, an inhuman ecclesiastic who required all prisoners taken in battle to be murdered outright in his presence, and who died fighting against the Queen, "his sword drawne in one hand, and his portuis and beades in the other."

Nor was McEgan the only Roman Catholic priest of high standing who preached and practised sedition. Matthew de Oviedo, the titular Archbishop of Dublin, came over from Spain with men and arms to assist O'Neill in his revolt against the Queen's authority.[18] Can we wonder, if under those circumstances,

---

16. Carew's *Pacata Hibernia*, p. 21–22.

17. *Carew*, p. 202.

18. *Carew*, p. 366. McEgan is one of the "martyrs" of Elizabeth's reign, according to Roman Catholic authorities. He was not alone in his example of a desire to combine the temporal with the spiritual sword. Sir John Clotworthy, who was one of the Irish representatives at the Westminster Assembly, declared that Ireland was to be converted "with the Bible in one hand, and the sword in the other." — Nalson's *Impartial Collection,* Vol. ii, p. 536. Clotworthy was an advanced Puritan. He "dissembled not his

Elizabeth towards the close of her life felt compelled to adopt stricter measures, and required the oath of allegiance to be pressed on all indiscriminately, and proceedings to be taken against such persons as refused it, "peremptorily or obstinately"?[19]

On the death of the Queen, the Irish Roman Catholics looked forward with much expectation to the accession of James I. They remembered that he had Celtic blood in his veins, and that his mother, Mary Stuart, had been an unflinching member of the Catholic Church. Impressed with the notion that he would be favourably disposed towards them, they at once commenced to perform the rites of their Church with much outward pomp and ceremony. The service of the Mass was even celebrated in some of the parish churches from which the Protestant clergy were expelled. The Vicar-Apostolic of Waterford and Lismore had the hardihood, when announcing publicly the death of the Queen, to say, "Jezebel is dead."[20]

---

old animosity against the bishops, the cross and the surplice, and wished all might be abolished." — Clarendon's *Life,* Vol. ii, p. 380.

19. The national antipathy to the Queen ran very high. For example, on August 26th, 1600, the Lord-Deputy is in the Queen's County, and in one of the houses he finds "the Queen's picture behind the door, and the King of Spain's at the upper end of the table." — Carew, *Calendar of State Papers,* p. 432. The censures of that diabolical Church," writes Sir G. Carew, "is at the bottom of all the mischief, and were it not for this, ere May Day next, I would not doubt, by God's assistance . . . to settle Munster in as good quiet as Middlesex." — Ditto, p. 454. It is almost like a page of modern history to find, the Bishop of Cork writing a memorandum to Lord Runsdon, July 6th, 1596, to the following effect. Searching the books in a certain school in the diocese, he says, "I found to my great grief her Majesty's style and title torn out of all the grammars to the number of seventy-four in one school; the leaf in the grammar quite torn out which containeth it — 'Elizabeth, by the grace of God, Queen of England, France, and Ireland, Defender of the, Faith, &c., and in the end of the leaf — God save the Queen.' " — *Calendar of State papers,* 1596, p. 17.

20. "When Elizabeth's death became known, the citizens of Waterford, Kilkenny, and Cork burned the books of the heretics, ejected the ministers, and publicly had Mass said in the churches." Father Holywood to the General of the Jesuits, July 1603. — *The Month,* lxxxviii, p. 467.

Symptoms of revolt against the English authority began to show themselves once more, especially in the southern provinces. The result of this was that before long the Government of King James was forced to exchange the mild *regime* with which it had commenced for sterner measures. All Jesuits and even many priests were ordered by an edict of July 4, 1605, to leave the kingdom of Ireland, before a certain date. The people were required to attend the Protestant service in their respective parish churches at the risk of being fined for not doing so, and incurring the King's "high displeasure."[21] Where these orders and penalties were disregarded, a "mandate" was further issued under the broad seal, commanding attendance at church, with the alternative of being handed over to be dealt with by the Star Chamber and incur a heavier mulct, together with imprisonment. Here again it is evident that religion had to be punished, not because it was unreformed, but because it had united itself with treason and become dangerous to the State; and the Government from attempting toleration plunged under a panic into the opposite extreme of an excessive severity. The Pope as before took up the cause of his co-religionists, and issued a Bull declaring it the same as sacrificing to idols to be present at the reading of the English Liturgy.

When under the terror of the recent gunpowder plot the King proceeded to insist on an oath of allegiance which acknowledged him to be the rightful sovereign, and declared that the Pope had no power to depose him or release his subjects from their fidelity, Paul V replied on September 22, 1607, with another Bull declaring that the oath was one which could not be taken by Catholics as being dangerous to their salvation.[22] The loyal Roman Catholics had been prepared to take the oath

---

21. *Calendar of State Papers,* James I, 1606–08, p. 60–64, 80; *Hibernia Dominicana,* p. 611–12.

22. Hib. *Dom,* p. 613–15. See also King's *Church History,* supplement, p. 1318–20, where the Bull is given.

when the action of the Pope stumbled them. Such in brief was the condition of the country when Ussher found himself called upon to take a more prominent and responsible position in the affairs of Church and State. As might be supposed, his attention was largely occupied with the great question of the day — the rival claims of the two Churches which then as now, in the main divided Irish Christianity between them.

CHAPTER VI

USSHER'S FIRST ESSAYS IN LITERATURE

A n illustration of the extraordinary interest taken about this time (1602) in literary matters may here be noted. The army that had come over to suppress Tyrone's rebellion, and which for the time being had effectually crushed out the spirit of opposition by a victory over the Spanish contingent at Kinsale, was now on its way back to English shores. Before returning, the soldiers determined to show their interest in the advancement of learning in Ireland, and more particularly their interest in the young University of Dublin, by subscribing between themselves out of their arrears of pay, what was then the handsome sum of £1800, for the purchase of books for the use of the College library.[1]

---

1. Cox's *History of Ireland,* i, p. 446. The Lives of Ussher, including that by Elrington, give the above sum, but the MSS. *Book of Benefactions*, preserved in the Library of Trinity College, set down the sum as "about £700." In 1600 there seems to have been only forty books in the Library, ten of which were manuscripts. As the fruit of Ussher's and Challoner's labours they had reached 4,000 in 1610. — See Abbott's Article on the Library in *The Book of Trinity College,* p. 148; and for prices, Ussher's *Works,* xv, p. 74.

Towards the close of 1603, Dr. Challoner and James Ussher were selected to go to England with this sum and invest it to the best advantage. It is a remarkable coincidence that they met in London the famous Sir Thomas Bodley, founder of the Bodleian Library at Oxford, who was then in the City on a similar business for his own University.

Probably there never occurred before or since a like instance where an army of conquest and occupation exhibited a concern of this kind in the peaceful pursuits of literature. It shows how thoroughly the spirit of Shakespeare, Spenser, Ben Jonson, Hooker, Raleigh, and the other great writers who were then immortalising the English language by their works, had pervaded the entire nation.

On several subsequent occasions, Ussher visited England for the purpose of purchasing books for the University, and a list with prices annexed in his handwriting is preserved among the most cherished MSS. of Trinity College, Dublin.[2]

In the course of a visit in 1609, he preached before the London Court for the first time. On these occasions it was Ussher's practice to spend one month in Oxford, a second in

---

2. *Class* D, 3–20. On the occasion of Ussher's first visit to England, he halted at Chester to visit Christopher Goodman, a sturdy Nonconformist, mistakingly reputed by some, on account of his book against Mary, Queen of Scots, to have been the author of *The Monstrous Regimen of Women*, and who was then on his death-bed. In his time he had refused to subscribe to the Prayer-book and Articles. For his recusancy Archbishop Parker had him "beaten with three rods," and forbade him to preach. His Calvinism did not interfere with his cheerfulness, for in later days Ussher was in the habit of retailing many of his stories and wise sayings. — See Brook's *Lives of the Puritans*, ii, p. 125–6; Wood's *Ath. Oxon.* (Bliss's edition), I, p. 722–3; Fuller's *Church History*, bk. Ix, p. 77; and Ormerod's *Cheshire*. In 1566, Sir H. Sidney had recommended Goodman, who was then his chaplain in Ireland, for the archbishopric of Dublin, and he was afterwards recommended by Loftus for that of Armagh. — See Shirley's *Letters*, p. 284–5, and Wood's *Ath. Oxon.*, as above, p. 721.

Cambridge, and a third in London.[3] These visits brought him into communication with the most learned men of the day — Camden, Cotton, Selden, Ward, &c.

At the same time that Ussher was thus enriching the library of his University, he was also accumulating a large collection of books and rare coins on his own behalf. All these he bequeathed to his daughter before he died. In 1656, this property was notified for public sale, when, as we shall see, some of the English army then in Ireland came forward once more and purchased the books and coins for the Dublin University.

On his return from his second visit to London, in 1606, Ussher had been presented by Archbishop Loftus to the Chancellorship of St. Patrick's Cathedral, which carried with it the Vicarage of Finglas. Here he preached with great assiduity

---

3. Parr's *Life*, p. II. These frequent comings and goings of Ussher were remarkable considering the difficulties and delays of the passage across the Channel in those days, and speak much for his courage and perseverance. Thus we read in Lord Cork's Diary, an entry which shows how some members of his family along "with the onlie child of the good Lord Prymate embarqued at the Kingsend, neer Dublin, for England. They returned to Dublin that night, the wynde being east." We find Laud writing to Shafford many years later (July 30th, 1631): "What do you mean to do for your journey into Ireland? Will you stay till August be past and put yourself upon the flaws of September in that broken sea? You may find more danger in a ship to Ireland than over the Thames in a skuller." It was considered an occasion for a man making his will. Thus we find Ussher's brother-in-law, the Dean of Cashel, writing in 1609 to him, "I wish you a prosperous journey to England. Set all things in order and make your will." — *Rawlinson* MS., p. 369 B. The Irish Channel has always maintained its evil reputation of "sixty miles of stormy water." Nor was this the only danger and inconvenience; there was also the unpleasantness of being captured by pirates. In this way, in one of his passages Strafford lost his baggage. — Gardiner's *Hist. of Eng.*; viii, p. 38–9. Up to 1649 only one Government vessel carried the mails between Chester and Dublin. As the Irish mail subsidy question is now troubling the public, it may be interesting to know that in 1660 the grant was £500 a year — a sum approximating to £50,000 of our present currency. The delays were great. In 1605, the Government were three months without hearing from London.

every Sunday, and entertained his friends with much hospitality. In the same year, we find him Proctor of the College, and his accounts for the year 1606–7 are preserved in his own handwriting in the Library.[4] Before he vacated the benefice for the see of Meath, he endowed it with a glebe and tithes.

A year later, in 1607, Ussher proceeded to the Degree of Bachelor of Divinity, and was immediately afterwards appointed to the Professorship of Divinity in Trinity, College, then endowed with £8 a year, a position which he filled for the next fourteen years, lecturing chiefly on the Roman Controversy. These lectures are lost, with the exception of one volume.[5] His lectures seem to have been of benefit to the students, if we may judge from a letter to Dr. Challoner in September 1612, when he writes from London: "There goeth here current a very good opinion of the religious education of scholars in our College. God grant that we may answer that which is conceived of us."[6] Later on he is busy on a work on "The Original and First Institution of Corbes, Herenachs, and Termon lands," which was presented in MS. to James I by Archbishop Bancroft.[7] The Corbes were held by him to be Rural Deans, or Chorepiscopi; the Herenachs a class of inferior archdeacons, and the Termon lands property set aside for the endowment of churches. Ussher acknowledges the subject to be an obscure one.[8] At the same time he was engaged on the Canons of the Ancient Church.

In 1613, Ussher went to London to publish his first book, which was a historical exposition of the succession and character of the Churches of the West from the days of the Apostles, and was intended to be an answer to the oft-repeated gibe of the

4. *Class* D. 3. 18.

5. Ussher's collected *Works*, xiv.

6. Ditto, xvi, p. 316.

7. The treatise appears in Vol. xi of his *Works*. It was originally published by Vallancey from Ussher's MS. in T.C.D. Library.

8. The reader should consult King's *Early History of the Primacy*, p. 54–9, where Ussher's essay is examined; and Shirley's *Papers*, 1631–39, p. 27–8.

Romanists: Where was the religion of Protestants before Luther?[9] Ussher looked upon his work as a continuation of Jewel's "Apology" — *ille nunquam satis laudatus episcopus,* as he writes, and it was his design to bring the argument down to the time of the Council of Trent, but the third part was never published.

His purpose in this treatise, which was composed in Latin, was to prove that all along the line of Church history there were bodies of Christians who did not hold the errors and corruptions of the Roman Church. The abrupt reference to the "Roman beast" in the opening of the dedication gives the keynote to the entire essay. An attempted answer on the part of the Papal controversialists fell to the ground, and Ussher remained master of the field. The work was dedicated with a flattering preface to the King. In his dedication, Ussher acknowledges the good work that James I had done in endowing churches and schools in Ireland, and also granting a subsidy to Trinity College, which the King had lately endowed with £600 a year, raising the entire annual income of the College to about £1800. In presenting a copy to the King, Archbishop Abbot spoke of the work as "the eminent firstfruits of the University of Dublin."[10] The treatise at once established Ussher's reputation as one of the most learned theologians of his day, and was favourably received by the continental Reformers, on whose behalf it did good service. Towards the close of the volume he

---

9. The full title of the book is *Gravissimae Questionis de Christianarum Ecclesiarum in Occidentis presertim partibus ad Apostolicis temporibus ad nostram usque atatem continua successione* et *statu Historica Explicatio.* It bears beneath the following sentence from St. Ambrose: *Ecclesia videtur sicut luna deficere, sed non deficit, obumbrari potest, deficere non potest.* The work fixes the close of the millennium, the loosing of Satan, and the revelation of the Antichrist at the Pontificate of Gregory VII, A.D. 1073. Selden and Lightfoot took the same view.

10. See Ware's *Bishops,* I, p. 102, where a brief resume of the work is given. While Ussher was in London bringing out this book, we learn from one of his correspondents that he lodged in the Strand "right over against Salisbury House."

takes up the case of the Albigenses and Waldenses, whom he shelters from the indiscriminate charges of immorality and heresy brought against them by Roman Catholic writers.

In 1618, Ussher writes to Camden, informing him that "the Company of Stationers in London are now erecting a factory of books and a press among us here;[11] Mr. Felix Kingston and some others are sent over for that purpose. They begin with the printing of the statutes of the realm. Afterwards they purpose to fall in hand with my collections, *De Christianarum Succesione Continua et Statu,* and asks him to revise the edition for him.[12] Elrington informs us that there is in his library of Trinity College an imperfect interleaved copy of the first edition of this work, with MS. notes in Ussher's own handwriting.[13] In all his studies, Ussher seems to have proceeded with the utmost diligence on the principle of "verify your quotations." He tells us he "would trust no man's eyes but his own."[14] The footnotes throughout the work exhibit evidence of his enormous industry and wide reading.

Ussher had already qualified for the higher degree of Doctor of Divinity, which he took at the commencement of 1612, as already mentioned, selecting as the subject of his two Latin theses "The Seventy Weeks of Daniel" and "The Reign of the Saints with Christ for a thousand years," subjects which afford a clear indication of the current of theological thought in that day.[15]

11. Booksellers were then called "Stationers" (Stacyoneres), probably from the open stalls at which they did business, and of which our open-air cheap bookstalls are the survival. Dryden speaks of Tryphon the stationer when he means bookseller.

12. Ussher's *Works,* xv, p. 77, 135.

13. Elrington's *Life of Ussher* p. 37, *Class;* in the Library, D. 3. 14. The treatise is to be found in Vol. ii of Ussher's collected *Works.* The Jesuit Christopher Holywood ("Sacro Bosco") attempted a reply.

14. *Works,* xv, p. 78.

15. Smith is in error when he says, in his *Life of Ussher* (p. 34), that Hampton was Vice-Chancellor of the University, and as such conferred this degree on Ussher. Hampton simply acted on the occasion as Moderator of the Divinity Disputation (as Ussher himself did subsequently).

His friend and cousin, allied with him through intermarriage with the Ball family of Dublin, Dr. Luke Challoner, died at this time, leaving one daughter, Phoebe Challoner, to inherit his large fortune, much of which consisted of house property in the city. He had charged her to marry James Ussher, should an alliance open in that direction. The learned doctor proposed for her at the beginning of the year 1614, and they were married, with the result of forty years happy wedded life.

On the backs of some of Ussher's letters, preserved in the Rawlinson MSS. in the Bodleian Library, and written in his minute, neat hand, may be seen interesting items of Ussher's private expenses at this time, containing entries as to expenditure on food and drink, and servants, &c. "Phoebe's apparell" is set down, at £40; "Given to Phoebe 17s. for a hat"; 20s. for a petticoate; 10s. for shoes shee had."[16]

The fruit of the union was one daughter, born and baptized in London in 1620, who married Sir Timothy Tyrrell, of Shotover House, Stratford-on-Avon, and in his time the Royalist Governor of Cardiff Castle. If we are to judge from his letters, Ussher had entertained for some time tender feelings towards Phoebe Challoner, to whom, writing to her father from London in 1612, he desires his "most hearty commendations." A short time after their marriage, his future chaplain, Dr. Bernard, sends loving remembrances to Mrs. Ussher, "your little Phoebe and second self."

We find from the College accounts that incense was used at Dr. Challoner's funeral.[17] The remains of his statue in alabaster, which was destroyed by the weather, may still be seen behind the College chapel.

A Latin inscription was once to be read on the wall beside it, of which this rough rendering has been given: "Under this staircase lies Challoner's sad carcase, by whose prayers and entreaties,

---

16. See Ball Wright's *Memoirs*, p, 89–90.

17. Stubbs *History of the University of Dublin,* p. 24.

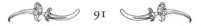

this house now so great is."[18] In 1614, we find Ussher elected Vice-Chancellor of the University by the Provost and Fellows. He also held the office of Vice-Provost during the temporary absence of its head.

Visit www.nlpg.com/annals.asp for excerpts from *The Annals of the World*

18. Stubb's *Hist.,* p.321. For another, and more refined rendering, see Fuller's *Church History,* Vol. iii, p. 136. The monument was erected by his daughter Phoebe. Dr. Luke Challoner is commemorated as "the first mover and the earnest solicitour for the buildinge and founding of Trinitie Colledge, by Dublin." — *Funl. Entries, Ulster Office,* cited in Ball Wright's *Memoirs,* p. 108. Dr. Challoner left several MSS. which are preserved in the Library of Trinity College, Dublin, including a catalogue of his books, an account of his lands at Finglas held from the Archbishop of Dublin, and a Common-Place Book (*Class* D, I. 9).

CHAPTER VII

THE IRISH ARTICLES OF 1615; CORRESPONDENCE

U ssher was now to play a prominent part in moulding the theology of the Reformed Church of Ireland as far as compiling Articles of Religion could do it. Up to this time it is difficult to say what were the doctrinal standards of that Church. In the matter of reformation, it naturally lagged behind the Church of England, which had in a large measure reformed itself before it introduced the principles of the Reformation into Ireland. It is not certain whether the Elizabethan Articles possessed at this time the authority of law in Ireland. There is no evidence to show that they had been accepted in any way by the Irish Church or had received the sanction of the Irish Parliament. In the year 1566, as we have seen, a book of *Twelve Articles of Religion* had been published by authority of the Lord-Deputy Sidney and the archbishops and bishops, and directions given that they should be read by the clergy at their possession-taking, and thrice every year afterwards.

These Articles were of the same nature with a similar set of nine Articles (the Lambeth Articles) published in England, and which were afterwards superseded by the Thirty-nine Articles.

In the year 1615, a Convocation of the Church of Ireland was summoned in conjunction with a new Parliament,[1] Dr. Jones, Archbishop of Dublin and Lord Chancellor of Ireland, was President of the Upper House, and the Rev. Randolph Barlow, chaplain to the Lord-Deputy Chichester and afterwards Archbishop of Tuam, was Prolocutor of the Lower House.

This Convocation of the clergy, which was strictly modelled after that of Canterbury, sat in St. Patrick's Cathedral, Dublin, from May 24th, 1613, to April 25th, 1615, when the subsidies were granted. It is regarded as the first Convocation held in Ireland.[2]

Dr. Hampton, Archbishop of Armagh, who had been consecrated only sixteen days previously, has in a letter to the Archbishop of Canterbury given us an account of the opening proceedings: "When the day of the Convocation came, my Lord Chancellor would have the sermon after dinner, but yielded to me therein that it should be at nine o'clock of the morning, after the manner of England, and I did requite his Lordship's kindness therein with relenting in the matter of our habits, albeit I and most of my suffragans were provided of scarlet robes. Yet, finding my Lord Chancellor unfurnished thereof for Convocation, I persuaded my suffragans to leave their scarlets at home, and to go to Convocation in our rochets to cover my Lord Chancellor and his omission. After sermon his Lordship, taking the first place, caused the bishops to be called, and first himself by the name of Thomas, Archbishop of Dublin, then by three suffragans; afterwards Christopher, Archbishop of Armagh, Primate of all Ireland. Before I would answer to my name I excepted against the injury that I held it a wrong done to the Primate to be called in a national Council after the Archbishop of Dublin and all his suffragans. His Lordship answered, 'It was God's

---

1. For an account of the proceedings of this Parliament, see Cox, vol. ii, p. 21-31.

2. Ball's *History of the Reformed Church of Ireland*, pp. 108-9; Elrington's *Life of Usher*, p. 38.

business.' I replied He was the God of order, and His business might be done in order."[3]

The principal business of the Convocation was to draw up Articles of Religion for the Church of Ireland, a task in which Ussher, as the Professor of Divinity, had a chief share.[4] These Articles are 104 in number, and are an additional proof of the strong hold Puritanism had got on the Church of Ireland. The Lambeth Articles, which, under the advice of Andrewes and Overall, Queen Elizabeth had refused to sanction for use in the Church of England, are here reproduced almost word for word.[5]

The Westminster Confession of Faith is largely modeled on these Irish Articles.[6] There is a marked similarity between the

---

3. See Dr. Reeve's *Convocation, &c.,* paper read at the Dublin Church Congress — *Report,* p. 752: also Whitelaw and Walsh, *History of Dublin,* ii, p. 1027–8. The last Convocation of the Irish Church was held in the tenth year of Queen Anne, 1711. An informal Convocation was held in St. Patrick's Cathedral immediately after the passing of the Irish Church Act in 1869.

4. See Carte's *Ormonde,* I, p. 147; Leland's *History of Ireland,* Vol. ii, p. 458–9. Ussher, at the time of the adoption of these Articles, had "not yet got over the tincture he received in his first studies from the modern authority of foreign divines." — *Carte's Ormonde,* i, p. 77.

5. The Lambeth Articles are reproduced "almost verbatim." — Cox's *History,* ii, p. 31. Marginal references to the Lambeth Articles are to be found in the original editions of the Articles of 1615 — Maskell's *Second Letter on Articles of* 1615, p. 21–2. "It is true that almost every word of the nine Lambeth propositions is to be found in the Articles agreed upon by the archbishops and bishops and the rest of the clergy of Ireland in 1615, and through these Articles probably much of the phraseology passed into the Westminster Confession of Faith." — Tulloch's *Rational Theology,* Vol. I, p. 44. "The Irish Articles of 1615 remain the abiding memorial of the hardy predestinarianism of the Irish Protestant Church. Ussher, their reputed author, was Provost of Trinity College" — Ditto, p. 82. Of course this last statement is a slip on the part of Tulloch. Gardiner makes the same mistake in *Diet. Nat. Biog.,* ix, p 246.

6. See Professor Mitchell's *Introduction to the Minutes of the Sessions of the Westminster Assembly,* p. xlvii,; and Stanley's *Essays on Church and State,* p. 390.

two documents in the order and titles of many of the chapters, as well as in the language of entire sections.

We may see in the drawing up of these Irish Articles the same desire to be independent of the Church of England that was manifested two centuries later, when the Book of Common Prayer was revised. Had the Church of Ireland in Ussher's time been possessed with a desire to conform to that of England, there was no reason why the Irish Convocation should not have met at this time *pro forma,* and adopted the English Articles. The Puritan element was at work then as it was in our own day, and on both occasions that strange feeling was uppermost that always had been antagonistic to English influences. "Whether they wearied of their dependence," says Mant, "or abated of their reverence for the Church of England, there were at this time some of the clergy of the Church of Ireland who were ambitious of establishing an independent character, of framing Articles of Religion of their own, and by their own authority, and so of distinguishing themselves by their own peculiar character as a free independent Church.

But the more powerful and real actuating motive was that innovating spirit which, having failed some years before in the attempt to engraft the doctrines of Calvin on the profession of faith of the Anglican Church by means of the notorious Lambeth Articles, was now to be employed in attempting to substitute in the Irish Church a new profession with which those Articles should be incorporated.[7]

These Irish Articles certainly betray no desire to lessen the differences which existed between the Established Church and the Roman Catholic community. On the contrary, they were all calculated to widen the gulf. On the other hand, there is a clear approximation towards Presbyterianism. There is no mention, for example, of the three orders of Bishop, Priest, and Deacon. A Sabbatarianism as severe as the most rigid Scottish divines could have desired may be found in them. The Bishop of Rome is the "Man of Sin" and

---

7. Mant's *History of the Church of Ireland,* Vol. ii, p. 383. See also, for a similar view, Ball's *Reformed Church of Ireland,* p. 110–111.

the "Anti-Christ,"[8] foretold in the Apocalypse and by the Apostles; the chief errors of the Church of Rome are condemned, the endless torments of the wicked are unequivocally declared.

The doctrine of sacramental grace corresponds with that afterwards laid down in the Westminster Confession. Baptism deals unto us our new birth, and consequently our justification, adoption, and sanctification by the communion which we have with Jesus Christ; in the sacrament of the Lord's Supper, the Body and Blood of Christ are really and substantially presented unto all those that have grace given unto them to receive the Son of God, but they are not otherwise present with the visible elements than symbolically and relatively.

The Articles were of such a nature as to permit their acceptance by several Presbyterian ministers, who crossed from Scotland and were ordained and licensed to benefices in the north of Ireland. These Articles of Religion "agreed upon by the archbishops and bishops, and the rest of the clergy of Ireland, in the convocation holden at Dublin in the year of our Lord God 1615, for the avoiding of diversities of opinion and the establishing of consent touching true religion" — so ran their official title — were, as Ussher testified,[9] duly signed by the President and the Prolocutor, and then ratified by the Lord-Deputy as representing the King; but they never received the authority of Parliament.

As might be supposed, many "hard questions" were submitted from time to time to one who had now gained a reputation in theological knowledge. Thus a Mr. Edward Warren,[10] writes from Kilkenny, in 1617, asking for Ussher's views on the extent of Christ's knowledge as a man, and whether habitual knowledge grew by degrees in Him as in other men, a subject which has

---

8. This was at the time as much an Article of Faith with the Puritans as any clause in the Apostles Creed.

9. Bernard's *Life of Ussher,* p. 49–50. See also Parr's *Life,* p. 14.

10. Warren was a Fellow of Trinity College, Dublin, and became Dean of Ossory in 1626 — *Dublin University Calendar* for 1877, pt. ii, p. 194.

not ceased to interest Christian thinkers and the discussion of which has been revived in our own day.[11] He also inquires about the knowledge Adam possessed, whether it was as great "as the nature of man was capable of." Unfortunately, Ussher's answers are not always forthcoming. Thanking him for his reply on June 11th, 1617, Warren goes aside to notice the fact that "Mass was said in Kilkenny very lately by one, to an assembly of women (and one boy that by chance fell in among them, by whom also the matter was discovered) that when it was ended the priest transformed himself into a he-goat with some other unmannerly pranks which I had rather that he should do than I relate."[12]

Another question with which the same correspondent plies Ussher is that of God tempting man to evil. A further voluminous and gossiping correspondent was Sir Henry Bourgchier, afterwards Lord Bath, who keeps him well posted in London news.[13] If he wanted a book, Sir Henry was the man to get it. Ussher was not only a bookworm, but an inveterate borrower and purchaser of books. *"Peto primo, secundo, et tertio, instanter, instantius, et instantissime"* (he writes to Lydiat, in 1617), "that you will let me have the use of your Geminius and Albategnius."[14]

---

11. See, e.g., Mr. Gore's essay in *Lux Mundi*. Ussher discusses this difficult question of the nature and extent of Christ's knowledge in his *Tract. de Controv. Pont.*, under the head *De Scientia Anima: Christi — Works*, Vol. xiv, p. 187. The reader will find there a suggestive and helpful contribution to the study of the subject.

12. Ussher's *Works*, Vol. xvi, p. 342–3.

13. Henry Bourgchier was a Fellow of Trinity College, Dublin, in 1601, and came to his title in 1636. Lady Bath in 1671, bequeathed £200 to the Library "as a signall memoriall of the kindness her Lord had for the College." — *Dublin University Calendar* for 1877, pt. ii, p. 164. Dunton, in 1698, speaks of the Countess of Bath's library filled with many handsome folios and other books in Dutch binding, gilt with the Earl's arms."

14. *Works*, Vol. xv, p. 128. Thomas Lydiat was brought to Ireland by Ussher in 1609, where he became a Fellow of Trinity College in the following

Sometimes correspondents complain that he is keeping their books a long time or has not returned them, and Ussher himself has to make the same complaint of others. Sir Henry, writing under date 1618, says: "Here are few books lately published; if there be any old or new which you desire you may command my purse and credit as your own." In the same letter he tells Ussher of "one Thrasco, a minister," who had been imprisoned for diverse fanatical opinions. . . . The particulars would stuff a letter too much." But he tells him how he was compelled to "stand on the pillory with his ears nailed and branded in the forehead, that so he that was *schismaticus* might likewise be *stigmaticus.*" A brutal jest! But then "it was," says the writer, as a kind of apology, "the Lord Chancellor's phrase."[15] In a former letter he had let Ussher know that the Reformed Church had held a synod at Rochelle, and that Sir Walter Raleigh was then at Southampton.

A third correspondent was Heartwell, who, writing in 1618 of the Papal Church, says "the beast rages now, "and mentions that a massacre was nearly taking place in Venice, but was by a wonderful providence discovered."[16] He excuses the thinness

---

year. Ussher got him rooms in College, and a Readership worth £3 6s. 8d. a quarter. An entry in the College account-book has the following: "Mr. Lydiat, partly for reading, partly by way of benevolence, '£5, December 23rd, 1609." Subsequently, Lydiat returned to England, where he was thrown into prison for a debt incurred for others, and was only liberated by the kind offices of Ussher, seconded by Laud. In gratitude to the latter he dedicated to him a treatise "On the Setting up of altars in Christian Churches, and bowing in reverence to them." Kippis, in his *Biog. Brit.,* vi, p. 4067, is in error when he represents Lydiat as Ussher's brother-in-law, and that he signed himself as such. The signature is really "your most assured loving friend and brother." — See Ussher's *Works,* xv, p. 112, 150; Todd's *Graduates,* p. 357; *Ath., Oxon.* iii, p. 185–9.

15. Ussher's *Works,* xvi, p. 359. Thrasco was considered to be a broaker of Judaism." — Fuller, *Church History,* Vol. iii, p. 274. His sect was identified with. "Sensualists" and "Antinomians."

16. This was the conspiracy aimed against Paolo Sarpi and the Protestants in Venice.

of his communication by saying in the quaint language of the day, "whilst you fill your sides with ambrosia and nectar, raining down heavenly manna therein, I am glad for barrenness to patch up anything in post to you again." He desires further — "out of your belly may flow rivers of the water of life to water the Lord's garden, and long may you flourish as a palm-tree and a cedar in the courts of our God, until filled with your reward, He gives you to drink out of the river of His pleasures,"[17] a mixture of figures of speech which may well have puzzled the recipient. About the same time, Ussher is exercised about "our great St. Patrick and his miracles," and asks Camden to search for a MS. in Sir Robert Cotton's library; written before the time of Bede, "bound in blue leather," and which was found among Jocelin's remains.[18]

---

17. Ussher's *Works,* xvi, p. 356–7.

18. In addition to the above, Ussher enjoyed a learned correspondent in William Brouncker, afterwards second Viscount Castlelyons. He was the first President of the Royal Society. His grandfather, Sir Henry, had been President of Munster, and died and was buried in Cork in 1607. Brouncker made two important mathematical discoveries. "He was the first to introduce continued fractions, and to give a series for the quadrature of the equilateral hyperbola." — *Dict. Nat. Biog.,* vi, p. 470.

CHAPTER VIII

USSHER, A COURT PREACHER; BISHOP OF MEATH

At this time the ever-vacillating King, who at one moment would send representatives to the Synod of Dort, and the next rail at the Puritans, was in the latter mood, and hearing of Dr. Ussher and his proceedings in the Irish Convocation, had conceived a strong dislike to him which he did not care to conceal. The acute Sabbatarianism of the Irish Articles in particular had vexed him. Ussher, being about to visit London, and knowing the sentiments of the King, who was listening to Ussher's enemies, determined to go armed with a letter of commendation from the Irish Government to the Privy Council in England.[1]

"We are desirous," say the Irish Lord-Deputy and Council (September 30th, 1619), "to set him [Dr. Ussher] right in his Majesties opinion, who it seemeth has been informed that he is somewhat transported with singularities, and unaptness to be conformable to the rules and orders of the Church. We are so far from suspecting him in that kind, that we may boldly recommend

---

1. According to the *Montgomery MSS.*, p. 104–5, Ussher did not ask for this letter of commendation.

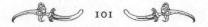

him to your Lordships as a man orthodox and worthy to govern in the Church, when occasion shall be presented, and his Majesty may be pleased to advance him, he being one that had preached before the State here for eighteen years, and has been his Majesties Professor of Divinity in the University for thirteen years; and a man who has given himself over to his profession; an excellent and painful preacher, a modest man, abounding in goodness, and his life and doctrine so agreeable, and those who argue not with him are yet constrained to love and admire him. And for such a one we beseech your Lordships to understand him, and accordingly speak to his Majesty."[2]

The Puritan faction being at this time in strong disfavour, there is reason to believe that some leading Irish Roman Catholics were only to glad to affix the name of Puritan to persons who had made themselves obnoxious to their Church by their zeal in propagating Protestant principles; and as Ussher was now well known for his devotion to the Reformed faith, they had fastened the unpopular designation on him.

The letter of the Irish Government had, however, a good effect upon the King, whose interest was further excited when he met Ussher, and listened to his learned discourse. His Majesty declared with his wonted sententiousness, after one or two interviews, that "the knave Puritan was a bad, but the knave's Puritan, an honest man."[3] Elrington, in his *Life*,[4] observes that no record

---

2. Parr's *Life of Ussher*, p. 15, 16. This was not the first letter of commendation carried by Ussher to London. In 1612, his former tutor, James Hamilton, thus writes to Sir James Semphill on his behalf: "Clear them to his Majestie that they are not Puritants, for they (Ussher and Challoner) have dignitariships and prebends in the cathedral churches here." — *MS. Archiv. Eccl. ,Scot.*, xxviii, No. 18; see *McCries' Life of Melville*, p. 380 (note).

3. Parr's *Life*, p. 17. "Spalato . . . was the first who, professing himself a Protestant, used the word 'Puritan' to signify the defenders of matters doctrinal in the English Church. Formerly, the word was only taken to denote such as dissented from the hierarchy in discipline and Church government." — Fuller's *Church History*, Vol. iii, p. 305.

4. *Life of Ussher*, p. 52.

of the particulars of these interviews between Ussher and the King has been preserved. Fortunately, the writer was here in error, for the Montgomery MSS., since published, contain a full and interesting account of what took place. Montgomery, then the Bishop of Meath and his great friend, happened to be in London when Ussher arrived, and, we learn, sent for him at once to come to his lodgings.

Ussher had only just alighted from his horse at the inn, and was preparing to stay there incognito for a day or two after his long journey. He also wanted to get new habits according to the use of the English clergy. When Ussher got the Bishop's message, he forthwith had his clothes brushed, and "went (Nicodemus-like) when it was night" to the Bishop's lodgings. After "caressings, salutation, and a glass of wine, they sat down together," though Ussher hesitated to do so, from his native modesty, and the great deference he entertained for the Bishop. Montgomery told him to let him know when he got his new clothes that he might introduce him to kiss the King's hand. On the following day, Montgomery brought Ussher to the Court, where everyone was anxious to see one of whom so much had been spoken, especially the clergy, "who observed the countenance and deference with which he was treated by the King's favourite bishop." When James saw Ussher, he informed him that he had long "grieved to see him of whom he had heard a great deal of praise." His Majesty then called for Ussher's letters of recommendation, and having read the names subscribed thereto, he said he should love them all his life the better for their love to Ussher.

The King now made Ussher his chaplain-in-ordinary until better provision might be forthcoming, and the new chaplain thereupon fell on his knees and thanked his Majesty, who bade him rise and discoursed with him on divers abstruse points of religion, to which he received "learned, pertinent, answers." A little later, Ussher was again called into the royal presence, and told he must preach before the King's Highness within a week; and, opening a little Bible, King James chose a text in the Book of Chronicles, "which was very hard bones to pick," but which Ussher handled with such warmth that he extracted "abundance of good oyl from it," to the great admiration of all that heard him.[5] Shortly afterwards, the Bishopric of Meath became vacant by the death of Bishop Montgomery, when the King nominated Ussher, and living long enough to hear of his success, and of his many and earnest labours, he boasted with considerable pride that he "was a bishop of his own making." In Ireland, the appointment was received with much satisfaction by the authorities. The Lord-Deputy Grandison wrote at once from Dublin (February 20th, 1620) to congratulate the bishopelect. "I thank God for your preferment to the Bishoprick of Meath; his Majesty therein has done a gracious favour to his poor Church here. There is none here but are exceeding glad that you are called thereunto, even some Papists themselves have largely testified their gladness of it. Your grant is, and other necessary things shall be, sealed this day or tomorrow. I pray God bless you and whatever you undertake."[6]

The King was now in trouble with his people. His Protestantism was suspected. A reaction had set in after the conclusion of the Synod of Dort, and his enemies regarded this as a conversion of the King to Popery. The proposed alliance of the King's son with the Infanta of Spain was not acceptable. "The new chapel for the Infanta goes on in building," writes Sir Henry Bourgchier to Ussher, "and our London Papists report that the angels descend every night and build part of it." To do away with such prejudices the King determined to call a new Parliament, and as the Protestantism of many of the members of the House of Commons was suspected, he arranged that they should take the test of the Communion and hear a sermon from one who's Protestantism was beyond question. Dr. Ussher, bishop-elect for Meath, accordingly received the royal orders to preach before Parliament at St. Margaret's Church, Westminster.

---

5. *Montgomery* MSS., edited by Hill, p. 104–6.

6. Ussher's *Works,* Vol. xvi, p. 374, and Elrington's *Life,* p. 52.

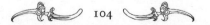

Some notes of the occasion are preserved among the Bishop's memoranda:[7] "February 14 being Shrove Tuesday, I dined at Court, and betwixt four and five I kissed the King's hand and had conference with him touching my sermon. He said, "I had charge of an unruly flock to look to next Sunday. . . . He bade me tell them I hoped they were all prepared (for Communion), but wished they might be better; to exhort them to unity and concord; to love God first and then their prince and country; to look to the urgent necessities of the times and the miserable state of Christendom with *bis dat qui cito dat.*" This last a timely suggestion with reference to the supplies to be voted in favour of the Elector Palatine and the support of Protestantism in the Low Countries.

The sermon, which was preached February 18, 1620, pleased the house much, and the King forthwith sent two of its members, Sir James Perrot and Mr. Drake, to request its publication.[8] The discourse was accordingly printed in the following year, and is to be found in the second volume of Ussher's collected works.

It is one of the only two sermons published with his permission. In the course of the sermon, Ussher enters largely into the differences which separated the Churches of England and Rome, and especially on the subject of the sacraments. We need scarcely say it is very unlike a sermon that would be preached in the present day before the House of Commons; indeed, the delivery of such a discourse under the circumstances would now be an impossibility.

Then as now, controversy ranged chiefly round the nature and efficacy of the sacraments, and to this question Dr. Ussher largely devoted himself. The danger to the realm from Jesuitical sophistries, especially in the matter of the oath of allegiance to the Sovereign, also came under notice. The text of the preacher on the occasion was the words of St. Paul, as recorded in

---

7. Parr's *Life*, p. 17, 18.

8. It would appear that the House of Commons at this time desired to offer Ussher the appointment of Precentor in St. Margaret's Church. — See Stanley's *Mem. West. Abbey*, p. 358 (note).

I Corinthians x, 17. On them he founded the doctrine of the Unity of the Church — all partaking of the one Bread. "The enemy desires dissension, *Hoc Ithacus velit et magno mercentur Atrida. . . . Divide et impera. . . .* The face of Christendom, so miserably rent and torn as it is this day, cannot but present itself as a rueful spectacle unto all our eyes. . . . Out of Christ there is nothing but confusion; without Him we are nothing but disordered heaps of rubbish, but in Him all the building fitly framed together, groweth unto an holy temple in the Lord.

Of ourselves we are but lost sheep, scattered and wandering in every direction. From Him it is that there is one fold and one Shepherd."[9] The Lord's Supper is itself too often a cause of separation instead of union. "It is a lamentable thing to behold how this holy Sacrament, which was ordained by Christ to be a bond whereby we should be knit together in unity, is by Satan's malice, and the corruption of man's disposition so strangely perverted the contrary way that it is made the principal occasion of that woeful distraction which we see amongst Christians, at this day, and the very fuel of endless strifes and implacable contentions."[10]

Ussher goes on to develop the Protestant view of the Sacrament as against the Roman doctrine of Transubstantiation. "The bread and wine are not changed in substance from being the same with that which is served at ordinary tables. But in respect of the sacred use whereunto they are consecrated, such a change is made that now they differ as much from common bread and wine as heaven from earth. Neither are they to be accounted barely significative, but truly exhibitive also, of those heavenly things whereunto they have relation as being appointed by God to be a means of conveying the same unto us, and putting us in actual possession thereof. So that in the use of this holy ordinance, as verily as a man with his bodily hand and mouth receiveth the earthly creatures, so verily doeth he with his spiritual hand and

9. Ussher's *Works,* ii, p. 423–4.

10. Ditto, p. 426.

mouth, if any such we have, receive the body and blood of Christ, and this is that real and substantial presence which we affirmed to be in the inward part of this sacred action. . . . We do not receive here only the benefits that flow from Christ, but the very Body and Blood of Christ, that is Christ crucified."[11]

To the question how is it possible that there could be union between us and Christ, seeing the body of Christ is in heaven and we are upon earth, he answers: "If the manner of this conjunction were carnal and corporal, it would be indeed necessary that the things conjoined should be in the same place; but it being altogether spiritual and supernatural, no local presence, no physical or mathematical continuity, or contiguity is any way requisite thereto. It is sufficient for the making of a real union of this kind, that Christ and we, though never so far distant in place from each other, be knit together by those spiritual ligatures which are intimated unto us in the words alleged out of the sixth of John, to wit, the quickening Spirit descending down from the Head to be in us a fountain of supernatural life and a lively faith wrought by the same Spirit ascending from us upward to lay hold upon Him."[12]

On being appointed to the Bishopric of Meath, Ussher resigned the Professorship of Divinity in the University of Dublin. There was some difficulty in finding a successor. The Chair was first offered to Mr. Preston, the "patriarch of the Presbyterian party," who refused it in favour of the Presidency of Emmanuel College, Cambridge.[13]

---

11. Ussher's *Works,* ii, p. 429.

12. Ussher's *Works,* ii, p. 431–2.

13. John Preston, as Fellow of Queen's College, was suspected of inclination to Nonconformity. He was prosecuted by the Commissary, and recanted, preaching a sermon "warily expressing his allowance of the Liturgy and set forms of prayer, and so escaped." — Fuller's *Hist. Univ. Cambridge,* p. 308. "After long controversies with the Puritan chief," says Fuller, "Ussher would say, 'Come, Doctor, and let us say something about Christ before we part.'" They kept up the friendships to the last. Preston concludes one of his letters with a postscript, "I suppose you remember me, as I do you,

After a delay of four years it was given to Mr. Hoyle, one of the Senior Fellows, whose sympathies were entirely with the Puritans. Hoyle subsequently was a witness against Laud on his trial, and sat, as we have seen, among the Westminster divines who drew up the Confession of Faith.

It would seem, from a correspondence shortly after Ussher's appointment, that Dr. Hampton, Archbishop of Armagh, was inclined to think that the bishop-elect was a little too hasty in exercising his episcopal rights, not yet having been conse-crated. Ussher writes that, in consequence, he has directed his Commissary to surcease immediately from dealing any way with the jurisdiction, in order that he might not seem to stand by any right of his own to the derogation of any point of the Archbishop's authority. As Dr. Hampton had also a similar case against the Bishop of Clogher, Ussher, urges him not to bring it into Court.

At the same time, he is not prepared to yield to the legal view of the matter propounded by the Archbishop.[14]

---

daily." (In a Latin dedication of the above *History,* Fuller acknowledges his gratitude and obligations to Ussher.) It is stated that Dr. Preston always preached "as if he knew God's will." "He was," adds Fuller, "the greatest pupil-monger in England in man's memory, having sixteen fellow-commoners joint heirs to fair estates admitted in one year at Queen's College." "He was a perfect politician, and used (lapwing-like) to flutter most in that place which was furthest from his eggs." — Fuller's *Worthies,* iii, p. 116–17. It is remarkable as an evidence of the tendency of Puritanism in the direction of free thought that Emmanuel College, erected by Sir Walter Mildmay as a Puritan foundation, shortly begat some of the most prominent leaders in Anglican rational theology — e.g., Whichcote, Smith, Cudworth, &c. A strain of the same kind may be seen in the Church of Ireland, where theology has been Puritan, with a decided leaning towards a tone of thought unhampered by dog-matism.

14. *Works,* xx, p. 155, &c. The correspondence is interesting as touching on the rights of the Dean and Chapter of Armagh during a vacancy in that see. As we shall find, Ussher afterwards, as Archbishop of Armagh, occupied a somewhat similar position towards Bishop Bedell.

It is evident that Ussher's elevation to the episcopate had been anticipated by his friends for some time. As early as 1617, Mr. Warren, writing from Kilkenny, had addressed him as "Bishop of Meath";[15] and two years previously, Mr. William Eyre, writing from Colchester, *"gratulor tibi purpuram si verus sit rumor."* There had also reached him a report of Ussher's state of health, and he adds, *"Nobis etiam ipsis vitam et valetudinem tuam gratulari debeo propter tristem rumorem de morte tua apud nos sparsam. Cura, quaeso valetudinem.* "[16]

During Ussher's visit at this time to England, his daughter and only child was born. The parish register of St. Dunstan, London, contains the following entry: "1620. Sep. 19. Elizabeth dau. of Doctor Ussher and Phoebe, was baptized."[17]

Visit www.nlpg.com/annals.asp for an
in-depth look at *The Annals of the World*

15. *Works,* xvi, p. 343. This is certainly puzzling, but it may be explained perhaps on the principle that "coming events cast their shadows before"; and great secrets will sometimes ooze out. We now learn that Montgomery had got a promise from the King of the bishopric of Meath in reversion for Ussher some time before his death. The vicarage of Trim was probably the "good fat benefice" *in commendam* to which the Bishop refers. — See *Mont. MSS.,* p. 106–8. Bishop Reeves in the MS. marginal notes to his copy of Ware, now in the Library of Trinity College, refers to the interesting notices of Ussher in these *Mont. MSS.*

16. *Works,* xv, p. 87.

17. Ball Wright's *Ussher Memoirs,* p. 110.

CHAPTER IX

USSHER'S ADVICE TO PREACHERS; A PROVINCIAL VISITATION; THEOLOGICAL OPINIONS

Ussher was consecrated Bishop of Meath in St. Peter's, Drogheda, December 2nd, 1621.[1] The consecrating prelates were Archbishop Hampton, Primate; Robert [Echlin], Bishop of Down and Connor; Thomas [Moygne], Bishop of Kilmore; and Theophilus [Buckworth], Bishop of Dromore.[2] Forthwith he entered on the high duties of his office. He started with the purpose of being a preaching Bishop of the type of Latimer; and he bound himself by the legend on his episcopal seal — *Va mihi si non Evangelizavero*.[3] The pulpit through his life was a favourite place with Ussher.

---

1. On his consecration, his friends presented Ussher with an anagram on his new signature, "James Meath" — Bernard's *Life* p. 52.

2. Ware's *Bishops,* p. 52.

3. We are told by Bernard, who was his chaplain, that at the first confirmation held by Ussher after his consecration, when a great number received the rite, the Bishop delivered a powerful address on the antiquity and good use of Confirmation. — Clavi, *Trabales,* p. 63.

Years afterwards, when an exile from Ireland and visiting Oxford, he desired no greater pleasure than to preach to the students. Several of his sermons on these occasions were taken down and published after his death. That he had great admirers of his style, etc., is evident from the many references of contemporaries to his sermons. Amongst others, the learned Hebraist, Ralph Skynner, writes, October 31, 1625: "My lord, I would gladly be your scholar to learn your method and facile way, of preaching. O that I might be beholden unto you for some of your directions in that kind, and that I might see but a sermon or two of your Grace's in writing, according to those directions: for therefore did I enter in the last hour of the day of my life into God's house"; and he concludes with the Hebrew text of Psalm xcii, 13.[4]

We learn that as a preacher Ussher preferred the extempore method. "As he was," says one of his biographers, "all excellent textuary, so it was his custom to run through all the parallel places that concerned the subject on, which he treated, and paraphrase and illustrate them as they, referred to each other and their particular contexts: he himself, as he passed on, turning his Bible from place to place, and giving his auditory time to do the like: whereby, as he rendered his preaching extremely easy to himself, so it became beneficial to his auditors, acquainting them with the Holy Scripture, and enabling them to recur to the proofs he cited by which the memory was very much helpful to recover the series of what was discoursed upon for them. He never cared to tire his auditory with the length of his sermon, knowing well that as the satisfaction in hearing decreases, so does attention also, and the people instead of minding what is said, only listen when there is like to be an end."[5]

No doubt, Mr. Skynner's desire to know the secret of Ussher's art as a preacher was gratified if he came across the admirable instructions on the subject the Bishop was in the habit

---

4. Ussher's *Works,* xv, 314–15.

5. Parr's *Life,* p. 86. He "constantly used a set form of prayer before his sermon, and that with a decent brevity." — *Clavi Trabales,* p. 61.

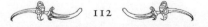

of addressing to the candidates for ordination. As they are not as well known as they deserve to be, they are set down here:

I. Read and study the Scriptures carefully; wherein is the best learning and only infallible truth; they can furnish you with the best materials for your sermons, the only rules of faith and practice, the most powerful motives to persuade and convince the conscience, and the strongest arguments to confute all errors, heresies, and schisms. Therefore, be sure let all your sermons be congruous to them; and to this end it is expedient that you understand them, as well in the originals as in the translations.

II. Take not hastily up other men's opinions without due trial, nor vent your own conceits, but compare them first with the analogy of faith and rules of holiness recorded in the Scriptures, which are the proper tests of all opinions and doctrines.

III. Meddle with controversies and doubtful points as little as may be in your popular preaching, lest you puzzle your hearers, or engage them in wrangling disputations, and so hinder their conversion, which is the main design of preaching.

IV. Insist most on those points that tend to affect sound belief, sincere love to God, repentance for sin, and that may persuade to holiness of life; press these things home to the conscience of your hearers, as of absolute necessity, leaving no gap for evasion, but bind them as close as may be to their duty; and as you ought to preach sound and orthodox doctrine, so ought you to deliver God's message as near as may be in God's words; that is, in such as are plain and intelligible, that the meanest of your auditors may understand; to which end it is necessary to back all practical precepts and doctrines

with apt proofs from the Holy Scripture; avoiding all exotic phrases, scholastic terms, unnecessary quotations of authors and forced rhetorical figures, since it is not difficult to make easy things appear hard, but to render hard things easy is the hardest part of a good orator as well as preacher.

V. Get your hearts sincerely affected with the things you persuade others to embrace, that so you may preach experimentally, and your hearers perceive that you are in good earnest, and press nothing upon them but what may tend to their advantage, and which yourself would venture your own salvation on.

VI. Study and consider well the subjects you intend to preach on, before you come into the pulpit, and then words will readily appear themselves; yet think what you are about to say before you speak, avoiding all uncouth phantastical words or phrases; or nauseous, indecent or ridiculous expressions, which will quickly bring preaching into contempt and make your sermons and persons the subject of sport and merriment.

VII. Dissemble not the truth of God in any case, nor comply with the lusts of men, or give any countenance to sin by word or deed.

VIII. But above all you must never forget to order your own conversation as becometh the Gospel, that so you may teach by example as well as precept, and that you may appear a good divine everywhere as well as in the pulpit; for a minister's life and conversation is more heeded than his doctrine.

IX. Yet after all this, take heed you be not puffed up with spiritual pride of your own virtues, nor with a vain conceit of your parts or abilities, nor yet be transported with the

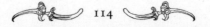

applause of men, nor dejected or discouraged with the scoffs or frowns of the wicked and profane."[6]

Shortly after Ussher's appointment to the Bishopric of Meath, a Royal Commission was issued for the Visitation of the Province of Armagh, and it was one of the first duties of the new Bishop to see that his diocese was duly reported. The return from Meath, dated May 28, 1622, and which is still extant,[7] shows the lamentably impoverished condition of the Church of Ireland at this period. The Bishop's diocese being largely within the Pale, was comparatively prosperous; and yet the story of ruined churches, no glebes, no incomes, is painfully monotonous.[8]

The fact is, the lay impropriators had been allowed to fatten on the ecclesiastical revenues, and enrich themselves at the expense of the Church. When the Lord-Deputy Grandison with

6. Parr's *Life,* p. 87–8.

7. See Elrington's *Life of Ussher,* appendix V, where the return is printed in full as "a certificate of the state and revennewes of the Bishoppricke of Meath and Clonemackenosh." A MS. copy is to be seen in the Library T.C.D. *(Class* E 5.6). Among the returns mention is made of "a Mr. John Gregge, a Mr of Artes, a good preacher, of good life and honest conversacion, and very paynfull in his ministry." He was the first Vicar of Trim, and died Dean of Lismore. For a notice of him, see Butler's *History of Trim,* p. 159, also the *Journal* of the Royal Hist. and Archaeol. Society, April 1873. John Gregg's tomb was discovered some years ago in a shattered condition in the churchyard of Trim. It records his death as the first Vicar, January 21, 1629. It is a coincidence that there should have been a second John Gregg, a minister of the Church of Ireland, to whom the above testimony may also be truly applied, and who died Bishop of Cork, May 26, 1879. The church and chancel of Trim were then "in reasonable good repair," and for a rectory there was "a fayre castle and a hall." It is noteworthy that at this time bishops' residences were also called castles, and not palaces.

8. The fabrics of the Irish Church seem to have been in a state of chronic ruin. About 1440, the Archbishop of Armagh writes to his suffragans to put their churches in repair. The snow and rain came through the roofs, while the windows were unglazed and unframed. — See Prene's *Register,* Vol. ii (unpaged).

laudable zeal attempted to force the spoliators to disgorge their plunder, he was attacked on all sides, and the Roman Catholics joining in the outcry for their own ends, the Deputy was recalled by order of the King, and Lucius Cary, second Lord Falkland, was sent as Deputy in his place. The new Viceroy apparently had like good intentions towards the Church. "My Lord of Falkland," writes Dr. Ryves to Ussher, "It is wonderfully inquisitive of the defects of that Church. . . . He intends to get particular warrants from his Majesty for the benefit of that Church."[9]

The success of the Roman Catholics in driving out Lord Grandison awakened a feeling of strong resentment in the breast of Ussher, who was loth to lose his friend. Accordingly, on the occasion of his first sermon in Christ Church Cathedral before the new Deputy, he made use of the opportunity to warn the Government of the necessity that existed for restraining the liberties of the Roman Catholic population. He selected for his text the words "He beareth not the sword in vain," and delivered thereon an address so vigarous as to excite general alarm. Ussher subsequently wrote an account of the sermon to Lord Grandison, and justified

---

9. Ussher's *Works*, xvi, p. 392. That the standard of education in Trinity College under the fostering care of Ussher was then high, may be judged from the progress made in his studies by the young Lucius Cary, who accompanied his father to Ireland in 1622, and began his studies at Dublin, being then about twelve years old. "He made," says Clarendon, "better progress in academic exercises and languages than most men do in more celebrated places; insomuch, as when he came into England, which was when he was about the age of eighteen years, he was not only master of the Latin tongue and had read all the poets and other of the best authors with notable judgment for that age, but he understood and spake and writ French as if he had spent many years in France." — Clarendon's *Life*, p. 42–3. Quoted by Tulloch (in his *Rational Theology*, i, p. 81), who holds it likely, that it was while in Trinity College; Dublin, Cary received his "first impulse towards those latitudinarian views of Church government for which he was afterwards distinguished. For the University authorities in Dublin, and Ussher conspicuously — strange as this may seem were no less remarkable for their liberal ecclesiasticism than for their rigid doctrinal orthodoxy." — Ditto, p. 82.

himself for the language he had used. He quotes a Mr. Ankers, a preacher of Athlone, who told him "that going to read prayers at Kilkenny in West Meath, he found an old priest, and about forty with him in the church, who was as bold as to require him (the said Ankers) to depart until he had done his business!"

Ussher also refers to the case of some friars, "who were going about to re-edify an abbey near Mullingar for the entertainment of another swarm of locusts."[10] So great was the excitement, that even the Primate, Dr. Hampton, felt himself called on to rebuke the preacher for his strong language, which he did in a letter at once firm and gentle. He says he cannot play the part of a Gallio and care for none of these things. "If my wishes may take place," he writes (October 17th, 1622), "seeing so many men of quality have something against you, tarry not till they complain, but prevent it by a voluntary retraction and milder interpretation of the points offensive, and especially of drawing the sword, of which spirit we are not, nor ought to be; for our weapons are not carnal, but spiritual. Withal it will not be amiss, in my opinion, for your lordship to withdraw yourself from those parts and spend more time in your diocese, that such as will not hear your doctrine may be drawn to love your lordship for your hospitality and conversation. Bear with the plainness of an old man's pen, and leave nothing undone to recruit the intercourse of amity between you and the people of your charge. Were it but one that is alienated you would put on the bowels of the evangelical shepherd; you would seek him and support his infirmities with your own shoulders; how much more is it to be done when so many are in danger to be lost! But they are generous and noble,

---

10. Ussher's *Works*, xv, p. 180–1. Ussher was charged with having said, "the sword had rusted too long in, the sheath;" "whereas in my whole sermon," he writes, "I never made mention of either rust or sheath." He had never intended the practice of "violence or cruelty towards the peasants." Killen, in his *Eccles. Hist. of Ireland*, ii, p. 508, considers Ussher's text to have been singularly ill advised; but the memory of the "sword" is still kept up in the "Prayer for the Chief Governor," in the Irish Prayer-book.

and many of them near unto you in blood and alliance [alluding to Ussher's Roman Catholic relatives], which will plead effectually and conclude the matter fully whensoever you show yourself ready to give them satisfaction."[11] A year later, the Archbishop has to write to Ussher, "If your lordship light upon petulant and seditious libels too frequent nowadays, as report goeth, I beseech you to repress them and advise our brethren to the like care."[12]

The mild hint that the Bishop was too fond of Dublin, and might with advantage to himself and his episcopal charge spend more time in his diocese, was perhaps not altogether unnecessary. Ussher enjoyed preaching, study, and the society of learned people, for all of which things he found larger opportunity in the capital than in the backward and thinly populated regions of Meath.

Besides, was not that noble library within the walls of the College growing apace? And what comparison could there be between the fat kine that roamed lazily over the rich pasture lands of Meath and the wealth of learning gradually accumulating under the shelter of his alma mater!

But however much he might have been inclined to obey the injunctions of his Metropolitan, circumstances were against it. Ussher was now a Privy Councillor and in daily communion with the heads of the Government. A man of his ability and ready speech was a necessity, and his services could not easily be dispensed with. An occasion was now at hand when those services would have a fresh demand made upon them.

Strong as the language of the Bishop had been, it did not bear the harsh interpretation put upon it by the Roman Catholics. As several "Papists" of leading position in the country were refusing to take the oaths of supremacy and allegiance pressed upon them in consequence of the alarm created by the action of the Pope in flooding the island with his new bishops and clergy, Ussher was requisitioned to address the offenders. This he did in a speech so

---

11. Ussher's *Works*, xv, p. 184.

12. Ditto, p. 199.

well reasoned and eloquent as to carry conviction to the minds of several who accordingly took the oath. The rest were censured.

A copy of the speech was sent to the King, who acknowledged the receipt in a letter to the Bishop, in which he expressed his "gracious and princely thanks for Ussher's zeal to the maintenance of our just and lawful power."[13] The service done to the King had at the same time its practical reward in a royal mandate to the authorities in Ireland, to suffer Ussher to absent himself from his see and prosecute in England his studies on the antiquities of the ancient British Churches.[14]

Among the questions submitted to Ussher by his various correspondents at this time was one touching the orientation of churches in ancient times, on which the learned Selden had asked his opinion. Ussher replies in an interesting letter, dated "Dublin, April 16, 1622."[15] He quotes Strabo as saying they did not much care how they turned their churches, yet for the most part they turned to the east at prayer, and most of their churches were built in that fashion. It was so also in Ireland, according to Joceline's *Life of St. Patrick.* About this time, we find Ussher displaying much interest in the discovery of copies of the Samaritan and Chaldaean Pentateuchs.

His letters give the impression of hard mental work in the midst of all his episcopal duties, while he ever and anon discusses with such correspondents as Dr. Ward vexed questions concerning predestination, free grace, and the liberty of the human will.[16]

---

13. The speech is given in full in Ussher's *Works,* Vol. ii, p. 461–7. Leland characterises it as "vehement, artful, and pathetic." *History,* ii, p. 482 (note).

14. *Calendar of State Papers,* 1622, p. 353, where the mandate is given.

15. Ussher's *Works,* xv, p. 170–5.

16. "Now also began some opinions about predestination, free-will, perseverance, &c., much to trouble both the schools and pulpit." — Fuller's *Church History,* Vol. iii, p. 146. Ward, who became Master of Sidney Sussex, was a distinguished Orientalist, and one of the translators of the

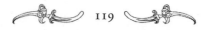

On June 20th, 1624, we find Ussher preaching before the King at Wanstead. The subject of his discourse is the universality of Christ's Church. According to the pronounced opinion of Ussher, from which he never wavered, the Church of Rome was the Babylon of the Apocalypse, and the Pope, Antichrist. The sermon pleased King James, and he commanded its publication. Ussher's text on this occasion was Eph. Iv. 13.

The sermon, which is furnished with elaborate notes, is published in Vol. ii of the Archbishop's collected writings. He defines the Catholic Church as of one entire body "made up by the collection and aggregation of the faithful unto the unity thereof." The Bishops of the ancient Church, though they had the government of particular congregations only committed unto them, yet in regard to this communion which they held with the Universal did usually take to themselves the title of Bishops of the Catholic Church. Ussher then points out the false claim of the Church of Rome to be alone the Catholic Church. He asks, "What then must become of the poor Muscovites and Grecians, to say nothing of the Reformed Churches in Europe? What of the Egyptian and Ethiopian Churches in Africa? What of the great company of Christians scattered over all Asia, even from Constantinople to the East Indies? . . . Must these, because they are not the Pope's subjects, be therefore deemed not to be Christ's subjects? Because they are not under the obedience of the Roman Church, do they therefore forfeit the estate which

---

Authorised Version. — Todd's *Life of Walton,* i, p. 120. Ward had filled (ad interim) the Chair of Divinity in Trinity College, Dublin, during the vacancy preceding the appointment of Hoyle. Urwick in his *Early History of Trinity College, Dublin* (p. 26), confounds the above with Samuel Ward of Ipswich, who was imprisoned by Laud as a contemner of the Book of Common Prayer. Ward, the Master of Sidney Sussex, was a Royalist, and was imprisoned as such by the Cromwellians in his own College. He died at Cambridge, September 7th, 1643, and was buried in the College Chapel. See a notice of him in the *Life and Death of Bedell,* by T. Wharton Jones, p. 93.

they claim in the Catholic Church out of which there is no sal-vation?"[17]

To the taunt, "Where was your Church before Luther?" Ussher replies, "Our Church was ever where now it is: In all plac-es of the world where the ancient foundations were retained arid these common principles of faith upon the profession whereof men have ever been wont to be admitted by baptism into the Church of Christ: there we doubt not but that our Lord had His subjects and we our fellow-servants. That which in the time of the ancient Fathers was accounted to be truly and properly Catholic — namely, that which was believed *everywhere, always, and by all,* that in the succeeding ages hath been preserved and is at this day entirely professed by our Church."[18]

17. Ussher's *Works,* vol. ii, p. 479–80.

18. Ussher's *Works,* ii, 493–4. Another reply of Ussher has the retort: "Where was the Popish religion before Luther? Most of those poisonous errors were down, and up and down, before then, but not collected fully into a body, and so owned and headed by the Papacy till then." — Bernard's *Judgment of the Archbishop,* &c., p. 84. Bramhall uses the illustration of the difference between "a garden weeded, and a garden unweeded." — *Works,* Vol. i, p. 199. At the request of Ussher, Bedell also wrote an answer to the question, "Where was your religion before Luther?" but the MS. was lost in 1641. Hooker and Field address themselves to the same question. See also Simpkinson's *Laud,* p. 49–50.

CHAPTER X

THE ANSWER TO A JESUIT

At this time, Ussher took advantage of his visit to England to publish his famous polemical work,[1] *The Answer to a Challenge Made by a Jesuit in Ireland.* Writing from Finglas on March 18th, 1622, Ussher had confided to Dr. Ward, Master of Sidney Sussex College, that he was preparing such a work for the press, "being drawn thereto by a challenge made by a Jesuit in this country." At the same time, he forwards to Ward a copy of his essay, "Concerning the Religion Professed by the Ancient Irish."[2] Dr. Morton, Bishop of Coventry, also received a copy, and in his acknowledgment he writes to Ussher, "At the sight of the inscription I was compelled to usurp that saying, *Num boni quid ex Galilea.*"[3] So much for the esteem in which an English bishop of the time could hold Irish Church history and antiquities.

The Jesuit answered by Ussher in the above work was Father Malone, who was born in Dublin about 1586, and was educated at Rome, where he joined the Order and was for a time the Rector

---

1. Vol. iii of Ussher's collected *Works.*

2. Ussher's *Works,* Vol. iv.

3. Ditto, xv, p. 195.

of the Irish College. The challenge is thus epitomised by Ussher: "What Bishop of Rome did first alter that religion which we commend in them of the first four hundred years? In what Pope's days was the true religion overthrown in Rome?" To which he thus briefly and generally answers in the opening chapter: First, we do not hold that Rome was built in a day; or that the great dunghill of errors, which now we see in it, was raised in an age; and therefore it is a vain demand to require from us the name of any one bishop of Rome by whom and under whom this Babylonish confusion was brought in. Secondly, that a great difference is to be put betwixt heresies which openly oppose the foundations of our faith, and that apostasy which the spirit hath evidently foretold should be brought in by such as speak lies in hypocrisy. . . . Thirdly, that the original of errors is oftentimes so obscure and their breed so base, that howsoever it might be easily observed by such as lived in the same age, yet no wise man will marvel if in tract of time the beginnings of many of them should be forgotten, and no register of the time of their birth found extant."[4]

Ussher then goes on to discuss the following points in which the Church of Rome has wandered from the primitive faith, and lapsed into heresy and superstition: Traditions; The Real Presence; Confession; The Priest's Power to Forgive Sin; Purgatory; Prayers for the Dead; *Limbus Patrum* and Christ's Descent into Hell; Prayers to the Saints; Images; Free Will; Merits.

On the first of these subjects he thus speaks: "That the traditions of men should be obtruded unto us for articles of religion, and admitted for parts of God's worship, or that any traditions should be accepted for parcels of God's word, besides the Holy Scriptures and such doctrines as are either expressly contained therein, or by sound inference may be deduced from thence, I think we have reason to gainsay;"[5] and he goes on to establish his position from Scripture. The ancient Fathers are next taken up

---

4. Ussher's *Works*, iii, p. 9, 10.

5. Ditto, p. 41–2.

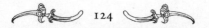

one by one, beginning with Tertullian, and from their writings Ussher collects a catena of passages all averse to a traditional theology outside of Holy Scripture.

Thus from Origen: "But if any thing do remain which the Holy Scripture doth not determine, no other third Scripture ought to be received for to authorise any knowledge"; from St. Athanasius: "The Holy Scriptures given by inspiration of God are by themselves sufficient to the discovery of truth"; from St. Ambrose: "The things which we find not in the Scriptures, how can we use them?"; from St. Hilary: "It is well that thou art content with those things which be written"; from St. Basil: "Believe those things which are written, the things which are not written seek not"; from St. Augustine: "In those things which are laid down plainly in the Scripture all these things are found which appertain to faith and direction of life," and so forth.[6]

On the next question of the "Real Presence," Ussher repeats his views, as already given in his sermon before Parliament: "In the receiving of the Blessed Sacrament we are to distinguish between the outward and the inward action of the communicant. In the outward, with our bodily mouth we receive really the visible elements of bread and wine; in the inward, we do by faith really receive the Body and Blood of our Lord, that is to say, we are truly and indeed made partakers of Christ crucified to the spiritual strengthening of our inward man."[7]

He contests the position that after the act of consecration there remaineth no longer any bread or wine to be received, but that the Body and Blood of Christ are in such a manner present under the outward show of bread and wine, that whosoever receiveth the one, be he good or bad, believer or unbeliever, he doth therewith really receive the other. Here, too, Ussher fortifies his position with numerous quotations from the Fathers and early English writer's, Aelfric, Wulfstane, &c.

---

6. Ussher's *Works*, iii,pp, 43–4.

7. Ussher's *Works*, iii, p. 52.

On the subject of confession, Ussher thus delivers himself: "Be it, therefore, known . . . that no kind of confession, either public or private, is disallowed by us that is in any way requisite for the due execution of that ancient power of the keys which Christ bestowed upon the Church; the thing which we reject is that new picklock of Sacramental confession obtruded upon men's consciences as a matter necessary to salvation by the canons of the late Conventicle of Trent, where those good Fathers put their curse upon anyone that either shall deny that sacramental confession was ordained by divine right, and is by the same necessary to salvation, or shall affirm that in the sacrament of penance it is not by the ordinance of God necessary for the obtaining of the remission of sins to confess all and every one of those mortal sins, the memory whereof by due and diligent premeditation may be had.

This doctrine, I say, we cannot but reject as being repugnant to that which we have learned both from the Scriptures and from the Fathers."[8] The quotations made throughout this chapter from the early writers are very effective and to the point.

The next chapter, "of the Priest's power to forgive sins," is a continuation of the subject. "We must, in the first place," says Ussher, "lay this down for a sure ground, that to forgive sins properly, directly and absolutely, is a privilege only appertaining unto the Most High."[9] Having supported this statement by many references to the teaching of the early Church, he goes on: "Having thus, therefore, reserved unto God His prerogative royal in cleansing of the soul, we give unto His under-officers their due when we account them as of the ministers of Christ and stewards of the mysteries of God; not as lords, that have power to dispose of spiritual graces as they please; but as servants that are bid to follow their master's prescriptions therein; and in the following thereof, do but bring their external ministry (for which itself also they are beholding to God's mercy

8. Ussher's *Works*, iii, p. 90–1.

9. Ditto, p. 119–20.

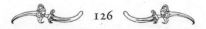

and goodness); God conferring the inward blessing of His spirit thereupon when and where He will."[10]

The chapter on Purgatory opens in this quaint style: "For extinguishing the imaginary flames of Popish Purgatory, we need not go far to fetch water. Seeing the whole current of God's word runneth mainly upon this — that 'the Blood of Jesus Christ cleanseth us from all sin'; that all God's children die in Christ, and that such as die in Him rest from their labours, that as they be absent from the Lord while they are in the body, so when they be absent from the body they are present with the Lord, and in a word that they come not into judgment, but pass from death unto life. And if we need, the assistance of the ancient Fathers, behold, they be here, ready with full buckets in their hands." Then follow copious extracts from Tertullian, St. Gregory, of Neo Caesarea, St. Basil, St. Augustine, St. Cyril, &c. "The first whom we find to have held that for certain light faults there is a purgatory fire provided before the day of judgment, was Gregory the First, about the end of the sixth age, after the birth of our Saviour Christ." Ussher goes on to show that even this "Gregorian fire," founded on the misapprehension on the part of Gregory "that the end of the world was at hand, and that revelations were being made of the condition of departed souls, did not suit the Romanists, who, from this small beginning, went on to elaborate a purgatory of their own unknown to the Greek Church, and so unto this day the Romish purgatory is rejected as well by the Grecians as by the Muscovites, and Russians, the Cophites and Abassines, the Georgians and Armenians, together with the Syrians and Chaldeans, that are subject to the Patriarch of Antioch and Babylon, from Cyprus and Palestina unto the East Indies, and this may suffice (concludes the Bishop) for the discovery of this new-found creek of purgatory."[11]

---

10. *Works,* iii, p. 126–7.

11. Ussher's *Works,* iii, p. 196–7. Ussher was writing at a time when English sailors were everywhere awakening interest by the discovery of new creeks, islands, &c.

In the following chapter on "Prayers for the Dead," Ussher shows with much learning the distinction between the commemoration of the faithful departed, as observed by the primitive Church, and the prayers founded on the Popish doctrine of Purgatory. The important point laid stress on by Ussher is this, that these early prayers and commemorations are on behalf of the dead in Christ who are in bliss, and always take the form of thanksgivings for their happiness; in no case do they take the form of a prayer for deliverance from purgatorial fires.

The chapter on the "*Limbus Patrum,* and the Descent of Christ into Hell," is an exhaustive treatise in itself of some 140 pages, and bristles with authorities from Origen to Suarez. Ussher's own view seems to amount to this: that hell is but a synonym for the grave. "To lay down all the places of the Fathers wherein our Lord's 'rising again from the dead' is termed His rising again from Hades, inferi, or hell, would be a needless labour; for this, we need go no further than the canon of the Mass itself, wherein the prayer that follows next after the consecration, there being a commemoration made of Christ's passion, resurrection, and ascension; the second is set out by the title *ab inferis resurrectionis* of the 'resurrection from hell.' . . . If, then, 'the resurrection from the dead' be the same with the resurrection from 'Hades, inferi, or hell,' why may not 'the going unto Hades, inferi, or hell,' be interpreted to be the 'going unto the dead'?" Ussher shows how the passage in I Peter iii, 19, 20, was interpreted by St. Jerome, St. Augustine, and others, as meaning that Christ by His spirit acting on Noah, a preacher of righteousness, wrought among those ancients.

He quotes the Venerable Bede to the effect, "He who in our time coming in the flesh preached the way of life unto the world, even He Himself also before the flood coming in the Spirit preached unto them which then were unbelievers and lived carnally."[12] As we have said, the entire chapter is a study

---

12. Ussher's *Works*, iii, p. 307–8.

in itself and an exhaustive examination of the question. Ussher ends this portion of his "Answer" by protesting that in the discussion he has aimed at peace. "In the Articles of our faith, common agreement must be required, which we are sure is more likely to be found in the general than in the particular. And this is the only reason that moved me to enlarge myself so much in the declaration of the general acceptions of the word Hades and the application of them to our Saviour's descent spoken of in the Creed."[13]

In the chapter dealing with "Prayers to Saints," Ussher contrasts *in abundantiam* the teaching of the early Church with that of Rome. In one passage, he briefly sums up a number of authorities, SS. Basil, Gregory Nyssen, John Chrysostom, John Damascen, and others, all laying down the same principle, that prayer is essentially a converse or conference with God, "and, therefore, where the names of the martyrs were solemnly rehearsed in the public Liturgy of the Church, St. Augustine interpreteth it to be done for our honourable remembrance of them, but utterly denieth that the Church therein had any intention to invoke them." *(De Civ. Dei,* 22, cap. 10.) In contrast to this teaching of the early Church, Ussher quotes among other Roman documents, Bonaventure's *Lady's Psalter:* "Lady, how are they multiplied that trouble me. . . . My Lady, in thee have I put my trust; deliver me from mine enemies, O Lady. O come let us sing unto our Lady; let us make a joyful noise to Mary our Queen that brings salvation. O sing unto our Lady a new song, for she hath done marvellous things,"[14] &c.

In the chapter on Images, Ussher clearly shows that the teaching of the acknowledged Fathers of the Roman Catholic Church involved the highest kind of worship to images; thus, "It is the constant judgment of divines that the image is to be honoured and worshipped with the same honour and worship wherewith

---

13. Ditto, p. 419.

14. *Works,* iii, p. 490–1.

that is worshipped whereof it is an image."[15] "We impart *latria* or divine worship to the image of God, or of Christ, or to the sign of the cross also; *hyperdulia* at the image of thy holy Virgin, but *dulia* at the image of other saints."[16]

In the eleventh chapter, Ussher grants man the possession of a free will as essentially belonging to him as reason itself. Even in doing works of grace, our free will is not suspended, but being moved and guided by grace does that which is fit. The Manichees, who bring in the necessity of sinning, are condemned. At the same time, since the fall of man, the ability which the will once had for spiritual duties is "quite lost and extinguished." Ussher completely endorses the teaching of Art. X on the subject of "Free Will."[17] In carrying on this part of the controversy, St. Augustine is Ussher's great authority. Pelagius and Celestius were the first two who taught a doctrine of free will contrary to that anciently received in the Church, to the effect that supernatural assistance was not needed for the conversion of man and the right direction of his will. In the closing chapter, on "Merits," Ussher clearly shows how late "in this main and most substantial point which is the foundation of all our comfort, the Church of Rome departed from the faith of its forefathers," contrasting the teaching of Roman authorities as recent as the thirteenth century with those that followed in the fifteenth and sixteenth.

As an instance of the manner in which the Roman authorities had perverted the grace of the Gospel, Ussher refers to the form for preparing men for their death which was commonly to be found in all libraries, and particularly was found inserted among the *Epistles of Anselm*, Archbishop of Canterbury, who was commonly accounted to be the author of it. The substance of this treatise was to be found in a tractate, written by a

---

15. Azarius the Jesuit cited, ditto, p. 501.

16. Jacobius de qraffiis, ditto, p. 502.

17. Ussher's *Works*, iii, p. 518–19.

Cistercian monk, entitled "Of the Art of Dying Well" (which, says Ussher, "I have in written hand, and have also seen printed in the year MCCCCLXXXVIII; and MDIV"), and in a book called *Hortulus Anima.* From treatises of the kind the Spanish Inquisition command, such interrogatories as these to be blotted out: "Dost thou believe to come to glory not by thine own merits, but by the virtues and merit of the passion of our Lord Jesus Christ?" "Dost thou believe that our Lord Jesus Christ did die for our salvation, and that none can be saved by his own merits or by any other means but by the merit of His passion?" In some copies of this same instruction the last question propounded to the sick man was this: "Dost thou believe that thou canst not be saved but by the death of Christ?" and he was instructed to say: "Lord, I oppose the death of our Lord Jesus Christ betwixt me and Thy judgment; nor otherwise do I contend with Thee. . . . Lord, I put the death of the Lord Jesus betwixt Thee and my sins. Lord, I set the death of our Lord Jesus Christ betwixt me and my bad merits, and offer His merit instead of the merit which I ought to have, but have not. . . . Lord, I interpose the death of our Lord Jesus Christ betwixt me and Thine anger."[18]

This laborious treatise of Dr. Ussher has been a mine of wealth for later controversialists. Those who have since crossed swords with the champions of Rome have been indebted to it for many of their arguments. Its learning is unquestioned, as well as the accuracy and relevance of its references. Nearly four hundred authorities in all are quoted, including ancient liturgies and conciliar edicts, and ranging from the spurious Gospel of Nicodemus to Johannes de Selva, A.D. 1500. Nothing richer or fuller in the way of a general answer to the particular tenets of the Roman Catholic Church has since been presented to the world. The work, which forms Volume iii of Ussher's collected writings, is dedicated to James I. It professes to base itself entirely

18. Ussher's *Works*, iii, p. 567–8.

upon "the judgment of antiquity," and bears upon its title-page the significant saying of our Lord: "From the beginning it was not so."[19]

The publication of this important work synchronised with a time when the Jesuits were making unusual efforts, fair or foul, to extend the influence of their Church. We find Dr. James writing from Oxford, on January 28th, 1623, to draw Ussher's attention to the enormous corruption by shameless forgeries and otherwise in the Roman Catholic editions of the Fathers: "The notedest cozenage which is rife and most beguiling in these days is a secret *Index Expurgatorious,* and therefore the more danger-ous; that is, the reprinting of books, not making mention of any castigation or purgation of them, and yet both leaving and adding, and otherwise infinitely depraving them. . . . There are about five hundred bastard treatises and about a thousand places in the true authors which are corrupted." Dr. James adds that he has got together "the flower of their young divines, who will examine into and collate such corruptions."[20]

Another correspondent, writing in September of the same year, observes, "Never were the Popish priests and Jesuits more busy than at this day, seeking by all means to seduce and pervert unstable souls and such as are not firmly grounded in the knowl-edge of the true religion."[21] It will be thus seen that Ussher's work appeared at a most seasonable moment in the religious history of the country. The approaching marriage of the King's son

---

19. Malone attempted a reply in 1629, but it was so stuffed with inaccura-cies and falsities that Ussher took no notice of it. — See Parr's *Life,* p. 25. The reply was published without the name of printer or place of publication, but it is supposed to have been printed at Douai. All cop-ies were seized and detained at the London Custom House, and few got abroad. — Ussher's *Works,* xv, p. 434. The book was answered by Hoyle, Singe, and others. For lists of forbidden and intercepted Popish books, see Arber's *Stat. Reg.,* I, p. 393–4, 492.

20. Ussher's *Works,* xv, p. 206–7.

21. Ussher's *Works,* xvi, p. 407.

with the Spanish Infanta was also exercising public opinion, and many were dubious as to the consequences. Dr. Ryves, however, writes to the Bishop, October 8th, 1623, that the Prince had returned from Spain a better Protestant, and that it was the same with the Duke of Buckingham: "They all return more resolved Protestants than ever, being thoroughly persuaded, *ex evidentia facti,* that Popery is idolatry if ever any were."[22] Among other correspondents was the Bishop of Elphin, who writes to Ussher from Elphin, 1623, to say that he (Ussher) is "with him every day in Latin and English." The Bishop, like all his contemporaries, is in hourly dread of Popery. "The devil beginneth to act his part more busily. . . . It is time that the Lion of the tribe of Judah doth destroy the roaring lion with all his works, both in his sheep's and lion's skin."

He goes on to witness to Ussher's increasing literary labours: "I know your lordship's indeffesible studies and intolerable toils do not permit you to answer every one"; but he pleads that he may be among Ussher's "unfeigned friends, whom he makes choice to answer for."

During Ussher's absence in England, his mother, who had joined the Roman Catholic Church, to the great grief of her son, died in Drogheda; Ussher was much afflicted by the event and the fact of his absence. He would have desired to have been with her when she passed away, that he might have helped the departing soul by his counsels and commended her to God in his prayers.[23]

---

22. Ditto, xv, p. 201–2.

23. Smith's *Life,* p. 8–9.

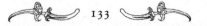

CHAPTER XI

BOOKS AND MANUSCRIPTS; ARCHBISHOP OF ARMAGH; THE QUESTION OF TOLERATION

At the close of the year of 1623, Ussher lost his earliest and one of his most learned correspondents by the death of Camden the historian. Sir Henry Bourgchier thus communicates the event: "The latest [news] which I must send you is very sad and dolorous, being of the death of our late worthy friend, Mr. Camden, whose funeral was solemnised at Westminster on Wednesday last in the afternoon, with all due solemnity, at which was present a great assembly of all conditions and degrees."[1]

The Bishop's correspondence at this time illustrates the conditions under which literary work was in a large measure carried on in the seventeenth century. As libraries were not as numerous and accessible as they are now nor books as plentiful, a considerable business went on in lending and borrowing. Ussher was also always alert to the possibility of enriching his collection by purchase.

---

1. Ussher's *Works,* xv, p. 203.

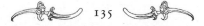

The above correspondent informs him, in November 1624, that there are come to London "two dry-fats of mart books, and they expect but one more; you may perceive by the catalogue what they are. Here will be very shortly some good libraries to be had."[2] Dr. Ward writes that he has sent Sir Robert Cottons manuscripts of Bede's *Ecclesiastical History* to Ussher, and expects the book back when he has done with it, for that he would keep it till Sir Robert restores a book of his which he had borrowed from Mr. Patrick Young.[3] The Bishop in his turn writes to Ward, entreating him to borrow for him a history of the Church of Durham. Later on, Dr. Ward writes to Ussher to say he has borrowed for him the two books he mentioned, and Dr. Maw entreats him to set down some limited time for which he would borrow them, and asks for a receipt of them in some note under his hand.[4] The learned Mr. Selden is also a borrower on a large scale, and Ussher notes at the foot of one of his letters, under date September 19, 1625, the books lent, among which were *The Book of Hoath* and *Fragments of the Annals of St. Mary's Abbey, Dublin.*

Sometimes, as might be supposed, these borrowed books never came back to their owners, and there is a strange story of one of his books having been discovered by Ussher, exposed for sale on a bookstall in the streets of London.[5] Ussher went further afield than England in search of rare MSS. and precious tomes. He had an agent in the East in the person of the Rev. Thomas Davies, chaplain to the British Factory at Aleppo and a predecessor of

2. Ussher's *Works* ,xv, p.227. "For books," says Parr, "he (Ussher) had a kind of laudable covetousness, and he never thought a good book, either manuscript or print, too dear."

3. Ditto, xv, p. 229.

4. Ditto, xv, p. 293.

5. Ussher's *Works,* xv, p. 116. See also xvi, p. 570–3. Ussher was exceedingly anxious to get hold of the original MSS. of the *Book of Howth* and the other Carew MSS. for the Library of Trinity College, and asked the refusal of them before any other; but they went eventually to the Lambeth Library, on the death of Sir Thomas Stafford. — Ussher's *Works,* xv, 433–4.

Edward Pococke. It was through his instrumentality that in the year 1624 the rare "find" was made of the "five books of Moses in the Samaritan character," which he discovered "by a mere accident with the rest of the Old Testament joined with them." "But the mischief," adds Mr. Davies in his letter to Ussher, "is, there wants two or three leaves of the beginning of Genesis and as many in the Psalms." A search for the Old Testament in the Syriac tongue was made about the same time at Mount Lebanon and also at Tripoli in vain. Mr. Davies was an enthusiastic henchman. "I should think myself happy," he writes to Ussher, "that I were able to bring a little goat's hair or a few badger skins to the building of God's tabernacle."[6] Elsewhere in his letter the Bishop acknowledges his deep indebtedness to Davies.

But Ussher had other cares besides literary ones. His advice was sought on many subjects, great and small. Thus we find a Mr. Randolph Holland requesting him to write to the Bishop of Cork to interfere with one Stuke, of Bandon, on account of errors in "faith and piety." Doing so, the Bishop will be "like to the prophet Elisha with his cruse of salt seasoning the bitter waters of Jericho," and making the new corporation of Bandon Bridge, now leavened with errors, "a commodious seat for honest and faithful Christians."[7] Sir Henry Bourgchier as usual lightens his correspondence with the gossip of the day. "Out of Ireland," he writes to the Bishop, January 5th, 1624, "there is no late news that I hear of." He tells him of the burning of Donnybrook[8] and that Sir Edward Herbert, late Ambassador in France, is made Lord Herbert of Castleisland, in the county of Kerry.

---

6. Ussher's *Works*, xv, p. 222. Dr. Hall, Bishop of Norwich, uses an identical figure of speech in a letter to Ussher, *Works*, xvi, p. 598. A successor to Pococke, in the same chaplaincy in 1670 was Huntingdon, who in 1683 became Provost of Trinity College, Dublin, and afterward Bishop of Raphoe.

7. Ussher's *Works*, xvi, p. 405.

8. "Donnybrook (Domnach-broc, the Church of of Broc) at that time was a small hamlet, situated at a considerable distance from the city. It was destroyed by a great fire in the above year. That the Usshers had some

At this time, Ussher is found residing at Much Hadham in Hertfordshire. He is invited thither by Mr. Theophilus Ailmer, who writes, "Mine earnest desire is that it would please your lordship and the virtuous gentlewoman your wife to take one whole week's repast with me at my poor house in Hadham, that your mind may have some relaxation from daily studies by taking view of my poor library. . . . How will the great Bishop Nazianzus, with that prince of eloquence, the Caesarian Archbishop; how will his Nicene brother, that treasure of learning; how will that golden-mouthed Constantinopolitan Archbishop rejoice to see that bishop in whom themselves shall see all their particular prayers jointly concurring? Your lordship cannot conceive with what desire Epiphanius, Eusebius, and immortal praise-deserving Athanasius, do expect you, since I named the expectation of your coming. Some of them have decked themselves in new and fresh apparel, as desirous to be somewhat answerable in outward hue to the view of their fellow bishop; others of them have covered themselves with old and dusty garments, as lamenting your so long absence." The writer sends a coach to meet them, and horses for the men to ride on, and to attend them. In a postscript he humbly entreats the Bishop and "the virtuous Mrs. Ussher" to take up into the coach, which he shall send, his daughter, Elizabeth Cole, in case they should meet with her.[9]

But to return to the Bishop's public life, Ussher was now to ascend to the highest position he could occupy in the Irish Church.

---

interest in Donnybrook is plain from the fact that Sir William Ussher, Constable of Wicklow Castle, lived there in 1605." Henry Ussher, as Arch-deacon of Dublin (afterwards Archbishop of Armagh), was Rector of Donnybrook in 1580. Arthur Ussher, son of the above Sir William, was "drowned in Donybrook River" (the Dodder) on March 2, 1628. — See Beaver Blacker's *Sketches of Donnybrook,* pt. I, p. 66; *Notes and Queries,* second series, Vol. viii, p. 438.

9. Ussher's *Works,* xvi, p. 412–13. At this time, Ussher was looking for a house at Godstow or Water Eaton, near Oxford, "for facilitating his studies." — *Works,* xv, p. 211.

In January 1624, Primate Hampton had died, and the King forthwith nominated the Bishop of Meath to succeed him.[10]

One of the first to hear of Ussher's likely preferment was the Bishop's old friend Dr. Ward, who wrote to him from Cambridge, March 21st, 1624: "I did hear at London of the decease of the late Primate of Armagh, and of your lordship's designment by his Majesty to succeed in that place."[11] The Bishop of Kilmore, Dr. Moygne, also congratulates him, "out of an assured and most firm persuasion that God hath ordained him as a special instrument for the good of the Irish Church," and, adds the Bishop, "my good lord, now remember that you are at the stern not only to guide us in a right way, but to be continually in action and standing on the watch-tower to see that the Church receive no hurt."[12] Ussher had only held the bishopric of Meath for four years; he was to be acting Primate for the next sixteen.

As Archbishop of Armagh, Ussher became at once one of the most important functionaries in the country; he stood next to the Lord-Deputy himself. The King not only conferred this mark of his favor and approval on Ussher, but he also wrote to the custodian of the temporalities, directing him to hand them over, free of all deductions, to the new Archbishop.

This was the last official act of James in connection with the affairs of Ireland, as he died shortly afterwards. Perhaps nothing is more to the credit of the King than the steady friendship he maintained toward Ussher, and the appreciation which he evinced of his devotion to the Protestant religion. The patronage of the

---

10. According to Mr. Justice Philpot, it was on Hampton's earnest representation that Ussher was selected to succeed him in the Primacy. — Ussher's *Works*, xvi, p. 419–20. He was appointed by letters under the Privy Seal, dated at Westminster 29th January, and had restitution of the temporalities the next day (*Rolls*, 22, Jac. 1.). Ware says he was made Archbishop of Armagh "to the universal satisfaction of all the Protestants of Ireland." — *Works*, i, p. 105.

11. Ussher's *Works*, xv, p. 268.

12. Ditto p. 272–3.

Sovereign was not, however, to tease with the death of James, as his son and successor warmly took up the Irish prelate, and wrote to the Lord-Deputy and Treasurer to bestow upon the Archbishop the sum of £400 out of the funds of the kingdom.[13] Ussher was in England at the time of his translation, and was suffering from a severe attack of ague. Writing to Sir Robert Cotton, from Much Hadam, May 1625, he says, "My weakness is such that I am thereby disabled as to write any letter myself, so to dictate very few."

Before he returned to Ireland, however, Ussher was to prove once more how able and convincing a controversialist he could be when it was a question between the claims of the rival Churches of England and Rome.

John, Lord Mordaunt, afterwards the first Earl of Peterborough, was a zealous Roman Catholic. His wife, a daughter of Lord Howard of Effingham, was a decided Protestant, and as each was most anxious for the conversion of the other to what they believed to be the true faith, they decided that the points of difference between the two Churches should be argued before them. Lord Mordaunt chose as his champion an English Jesuit, who went under the feigned name of Beaumont, but whose real name was Rookwood. Lady Mordaunt selected Archbishop Ussher. The scene of the combat, which took place towards the close of 1625, was his lordship's seat of Drayton, Northamptonshire. Ussher left a memorandum of the proceedings among his papers. The first three days of the disputation were in the hands of the Archbishop, who chose the subjects of Transubstantiation, Invocation of Saints, Worship of Images, and the Visibility of the Church, as points where the Church of Rome had gone astray from the true faith. On the fourth day, Rookwood was to reply; but when it arrived the Jesuit was nowhere to be found! Ussher

---

13. "English money, out of any casualty or casualties that should first happen in Ireland." — *Calendar of* (English) *State Papers,* Oct. 19, 1626; Reeves' *Ware,* i, p. 106, MS. note. It was said that the King had committed the jewel of his royal prerogative over all persons and causes ecclesiastical into Ussher's hands. — See Clogy's *Memoirs of Bedell,* p. 117.

had proved altogether too formidable an antagonist, and Rome's champion sent a message to the effect that all his arguments, which he thought he knew as perfectly as his Paternoster, had been forgotten, and that he believed it was the last judgment of God upon him for daring to dispute with a man of Ussher's eminence and learning without the permission of his superiors.

Lord Mordaunt, disgusted with the result, adopted the Reformed faith, and became a sincere Protestant, while his wife lived to show herself Ussher's staunchest friend and be his stay and comfort in the dark days that were before him in the future. It was at her house in Reigate that he breathed his last, thirty years later. As for Rookwood, he was admonished to "beware of Drayton House, lest he should there chance to light upon another Ussher, and be again put to flight, to the great disgrace both of himself and his profession."[14] The Primate, after this encounter, returned to Ireland via Liverpool and was duly installed in the Chair of St. Patrick. On his arrival in Dublin he was welcomed by a large gathering of the nobility, bishops, and clergy.

Ussher did not enter on his high office without trouble from Dr. Ryves, Judge of Faculties and Prerogatives in Ireland, who claimed by virtue of his patent to exercise authority independent of the Primate. The matter was the subject of more than one communication between Ussher and Dr. Williams, Bishop of Lincoln, the Lord Keeper, and Lord Treasurer of England. He claims that his powers as Archbishop of Armagh should at least be equal to those exercised by the Archbishop of Canterbury, and asks, "Did ever any reasonable man hold it to be a thing

14. See Bernard's *Life*, p. 54–6, for an account of this controversy. Such theological duels were common enough in those days. Thus we find that two years previously Bramhall, then in his twenty-ninth year, took part in one at Northallerton with a Jesuit named Hungate. According to some authorities, Ussher had a similar controversy with another learned Jesuit with whom he crossed swords under the guise of being only a simple country parson. The Jesuit declared that the country vicar had more learning than all the English bishops. — See the *Biographia Britannica*, vi, p. 4,070.

unreasonable that a substitute should be ordered by him that hath, appointed him to be his substitute?"[15]

As might be supposed, the Archbishop had many applications for patronage; one, John Parker, writes to him from St. Patrick's Close, April 26th, 1625: "I could wish to live under your command and jurisdiction, and to enjoy the comfort of my ministry there. The height of my ambition is to be once able before I die to preach on these words of St. Paul, 'Owe nothing to any man.' For next unto the pardon of my sins, I desire that blessing, and therefore if your Grace will be pleased to be mindful of me when you have remembered those that have nearer relation unto you for some addition that may help me out of that Egyptian bondage of debt which I have fallen into . . . I shall be found a thankful receiver."[16]

On July 12th, 1625, Ussher writes to Sir Robert Cotton warning him that if Arabic, Syriac, Hebrew, and Persian books were to be sought from the East, it must be done very speedily, because "the Jesuits of Antwerpe are already dealing for the Oriental press." The same month, the Archbishop's agent at Aleppo advises him that he has forwarded the first five books of Moses with parcels of the New Testament in the Chaldean tongue. He also sends him some of the works of Ephrem, but has not been able to come on the New Testament in the Ethiopic language. In August, Dr. Ward, writing from Cambridge, mentions that the plague is raging there; but he is careful that his letter is conveyed "by persons safe from all infection." It is to be observed that in his later years Ussher came to the conclusion that the study of these Eastern languages was a mistake and a bootless labour.[17]

---

15. See the correspondence, Ussher's *Works*, xv, 278–9, 296, &c.

16. Ussher's *Works*, xvi, p. 425.

17. "In discourse with him [Ussher], he told me how greate the loss of time was to study much the Eastern languages; that excepting Hebrew, there was little fruite to be gathered of exceeding labour." — Evelyn's *Diary*, i, p. 294.

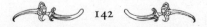

England at this time was going through one of those "scares" about Irish matters with which she is periodically affected and under which she has always shown a tendency towards panic legislation. Both France and Spain were hostile, and the Pope, Urban VIII, had issued a fresh Bull against the oath of supremacy as interfering with his rights in claiming supreme Vicar of God. The result was an agitation throughout the country antagonistic to the English interests, and Charles determined to increase his Irish army. At the same time, with a strange inconsistency, the penal laws were to be relaxed in favour of those Roman Catholics who willingly subscribed towards the cost of the new levies. Nothing could be worse in the way of policy. It was one of those crooked enterprises of Charles I which brought so much trouble on himself and misery on his people. The Protestant party were outraged, at the same time that the "recusants" came forward cheerfully to buy religious liberty with their offerings. A toleration of this kind, and under the circumstances, was what the heads of the Established Church in Ireland could not endure, and eleven of the bishops assembled in the house of Archbishop Ussher in Drogheda to draw up a protest, which was published on April 23rd, 1627. As seven or eight of the bishops, however, remain to be accounted for, this action of theirs cannot be regarded as having been unanimous.[18]

The "judgment" of the bishops "concerning toleration of religion," did not mince matters. The religion of the Papists was denounced as superstitious and idolatrous; their faith and doctrine, erroneous and heretical; their Church, in respect of both, apostatical. To give them, therefore, toleration, or to consent to allow them freely to exercise their religion and profess their faith and doctrine, was, "a grievous sin."

Fairly enough, indeed, the bishops contended that to grant the Roman Catholics toleration "in respect of any money to be given, or contribution to be made by them, was to set religion to sale, and with it the souls of the people whom Christ our Saviour hath

---

18. See the judgment in Parr's *Life*, p. 28–9.

redeemed with His most precious blood." In a letter to Archbishop Abbot, Ussher writes: "Some of the adverse party have asked me the question, where I have heard or read before that religion and men's souls should be set to sale after this manner? Unto whom I could reply nothing but that I had read in Mantuan that there is another place in the world where *calum est venale, deoque.*"[19]

One thing is certain, very few Protestants, if any, would put their hand to such a document in the present day, and the fact that Christian bishops could draw up a denunciatory judgment of the kind only shows how little the principles of Christian toleration were generally understood even so late as the seventeenth century.

"A religious establishment," in the words of Bishop Butler, "without a toleration of such as in conscience think they cannot conform to it, is itself a general tyranny." Strange to say, Milton, the great apostle of religious liberty, put the Church of Rome beyond the borders of toleration on the ground of her "idolatry."[20] It was reserved at this period for Jeremy Taylor, alone of all the great divines, to conceive a constitution broad and tolerant enough to throw the shield of its protection even over Roman errors.[21] The episcopal declaration was followed up by violent sermons preached before the Court in Christ Church Cathedral. The Bishop of Derry, Dr. Downham, occupied the pulpit the first Sunday, and read out the judgment. He ordered the congregation to say "Amen" after it, when the church shook with the response, to the great annoyance of Lord Falkland.[22]

On the following Sunday, Archbishop Ussher preached. He charged the authorities with endeavouring, like Judas, to sell their Lord for thirty pieces of silver.

---

19. Ussher's *Works,* xv, p. 366.

20. See Milton's *Treatise of True Religion, Heresy, Schism, and Toleration.* — *Works,* 2nd ed. 1753.

21. See *Liberty of Prophesying,* sect. xx.

22. Fuller's *Worthies,* p. 189; *Ware,* I, p. 292.

The excitement of the protestant party, led on by the Bishops, was now intense and it was felt that if peace was to be preserved, an entire change of tactics was necessary. Archbishop Ussher, at the request of the Lord-Deputy, had unequivocally condemned this sale of indulgences to the Roman Catholics; the money, however, was required for the King's purposes, and should be raised in some other way.

Ussher was quite ready to back up the King's demands, provided that they did not endanger the interests of the Protestant religion and encourage the Roman Catholics in the public exercises of their faith. Accordingly, at a meeting of the Council in the Castle of Dublin, the Primate set forth in very powerful language the reasons why the country should come to the aid of the King. The dangers of a foreign invasion and of a domestic rebellion were imminent. The Duke of Medina Sidonia had declared in '88 that his sword knew no difference between a Catholic and a heretic, but that he had come to make way for his master; the translating of the throne of the English to the power of a foreigner is the thing that mainly intended, and the re-establishing of the Irish in their ancient possessions which were gained from them by the valour of our ancestors.

As a divine, he told them plainly that to supply the King with means for the necessary defence of the country was not a thing left to their own discretion either to do or not to do, but a matter of duty, which in conscience they stood bound to perform, on the principle of rendering unto Caesar the things which are Caesar's.[23] The eloquence of Ussher, however, was thrown away. The Irish Roman Catholics who professed their willingness to contribute to the royal necessities, in return for a removal or moderation of their religious disabilities, refused to do so as a matter of duty to the King, and the supplies were not granted. It has been said that if the army in Ireland had been brought to its

---

23. The speech is given in full in Parr's *Life*, p. 29–35.

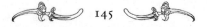

full strength at this time, the dreadful outbreak of 1641 would never have taken place.[24]

That may be as it may, but the method taken to raise the supplies was indefensible. The Roman Catholics had either a natural right to the free exercise of their religion, or it was a right that could not be purchased with money. It was a measure fruitful in future evils.

In the lull that followed this excitement, Ussher had time to return to his studies. He laid himself out once more to collect rare books and manuscripts, and his agent at Aleppo was busy. We have already seen how he furnished his patron with one of the first, if not the first copy of the Samaritan Pentateuch known to the Western world,[25] a volume which with other books was placed at the disposal of Walton when compiling his Polyglot,

---

24. Ussher, as we have already seen, was regarded in his day as a prophet, because he was believed to have foretold this and several other leading events. "He was wonderfully endowed with a spirit of prophecy whereby he gave out several true predictions and prophecies of things a great while before they came to pass." In 1678, there was published in Dublin a small quarto, entitled *Strange and Remarkable Prophecies and Predictions of the Holy, Learned, and Excellent James Ussher, late Lord Archbishop of Armagh, and Lord Primate of Ireland.* The book, which sets forth Ussher's predictions regarding the rebellion of 1641; the confusion and miseries of England in Church and State; the death of the King; his own poverty and want; the divisions in England in matters of religion; and "lastly, a great and terrible persecution which shall fall on the Reformed Churches by the Papists," was "published, earnestly to persuade us to that repentance and reformation which can only prevent our ruin and destruction." The title-page is garnished with the text: "Shall I hide from Abraham the thing that I do?" (Gen. xviii, 17). Ussher is also credited with having foretold the burning of London — that it would be "burnt to a cinder." See *Biog. Brit.* vi, p. 4,079.

25. Selden's *Mar. Arundel,* and Walton's *Preface* to the Polyglot Bible. See also *Ware,* i, p. 207: *"Vix aliud exemplar, si forte illud,"* Smith, in *Life of Ussher,* p. 59. According to Bernard, *Life of Ussher,* p. 85, the Archbishop received four Samaritan Pentateuchs, of which he gave one

and which now rests in the Bodleian Library, with an inscription from the pen of the Archbishop who had presented to Laud, and with these words written underneath in Laud's handwriting: *Qui librum hunc mihi dono dedit, W Cant.* Ussher was now contemplating an edition of the Syriac version of the Old Testament, and had literary agents to assist him.[26]

The loan moneys required at this time by the new King were not being levied off the Irish clergy without much discontent and grumbling; and on January 27th, 1626, we find the Primate writing from Drogheda to Lord Faulkland, promising to do what he can towards getting in the money, and he will give a particular certificate of those who will not pay in order that the Deputy may deal with them as he thinks fit.

From the Latin Diary of a Dr. Arthur, a Roman Catholic physician, in Limerick, we learn that at this time Ussher was in ill-health. Dr. Arthur seems to have been very successful in treating a disorder that had baffled the English physicians. On April 14th, he took him over to Lambay Island, off Malahide, where amid the salubrious air of the place he gradually regained

---

to the Library at Oxford, a second to Leyden, a third to Sir Robert Cotton's Library, and the fourth he kept himself. A previous copy had been received in Paris from the famous traveller Pietro dele Avale, from which Morinus published a copy in the Polyglot of Le Jay. — Todd's *Life of Walton,* i, p. 185 (note). Walton places Ussher at the head of his literary benefactors in his Polyglot; the Archbishop collated no less than sixteen MSS. for him, the various readings of which are admitted into the Polyglot. — Ditto, p. 79, 182–3.

26. "It is impossible even to imagine the pains, labour, and expense which Ussher bestowed upon Oriental studies till we take up his correspondence, and not the numerous agents he maintained at Constantinople, Smyrna, and throughout the East, seeking for and purchasing ancient MSS. I would venture to say that there is not at the present time a single scholar in the British islands who takes one quarter the trouble in this respect that Primate Ussher took more than 200 years ago." — G.T. Stokes, in *F.R.S.A Ireland,* fifth series, i, p. 17, 18. See also Dunton's *Life and Errors,* p. 497–8.

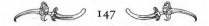

his strength. They returned to Dublin on June 9th, and were received in state by the Viceroy and his Court. Lord Falkland was so pleased that he appointed Arthur physician to himself and his family. Ussher gave him a fee of £61 5s. 4d.[27]

The killers of famed Roman Emperor Julius Caesar are destroyed with the same swords used to murder him, and reports of one, Brutus, seeing "some-one" on the nigh before his final battle. Page 649, *The Annals of the World.*

Order your copy of
James Ussher's
The Annals of the World
www.nlpg.com/annals.asp

27. The *Journal* of the Kilkenny Archaeological Society for 1867, where Dr. Arthur's fee-book is printed, and Ball Wright's *Memoirs,* p. 92–3. Lambay Island was part of the Ussher property at this time, subject to £6 rent per annum to the See of Dublin. — Ditto, p. 106 (note). The house where he lived on the island is still to be seen. There must have been in idea at one time that the island was rich in ore, for we find John Challoner writing to Cecil on May 28, 1563, asking permission "to work the silver and copper veins in the island of Lambay." — *Calendar of State Papers,* Elizabeth, of above date.

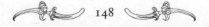

CHAPTER XII

THE PROVOSTSHIP OF BEDELL; USE OF THE IRISH LANGUAGE IN PUBLIC WORSHIP; RELIGIOUS DISSENSIONS; GOTTESCALCUS

The question of a new appointment to the Provostship of Trinity College was now occupying much of the Archbishop's time and attention. On January 10th, 1627, he writes from Drogheda to the Archbishop of Canterbury, to say the time had come when he had succeeded in prevailing on Sir William Temple, who had been provost for seventeen years, to resign the office. On the same day, Ussher writes to the same effect to the Society of Lincoln's Inn, and in both letters he suggests Mr. Sibbes, the Preacher of Gray's Inn, as his successor. Failing Mr. Sibbes, he suggests Mr. Bedell, or Dr. Featley; and if the Archbishop can persuade the Fellows of the College to elect Bedell, "that poor house shall ever have the cause to bless his memory."

Writing back from London on March 19th, Archbishop Abbot says: "I send unto you Mr. Sibbes. . . . I hope that College shall in him have a very good Master which hitherto it hath not had."[1] The Fellows were now divided into two parties, and neither of them would elect Mr. Sibbes. Archbishop Ussher next recommended Mede, "a single man, very eminent in learning, and one that will wholly apply himself to the government of the house without seeking any further preferment."[2] The Senior Fellows, who claimed the sole right of appointment, nominated Mede, and the Juniors, Robert Ussher, a cousin of the Archbishop's. Mede, on being pressed, refused the office. He was not willing "to adventure into a strange country upon a litigious title." He was, moreover, "slow and difficult of speech," and knew not how far that would disqualify him for the duties of the place.[3]

The King now interfered, and Mr. Parry, one of the Senior Fellows, afterwards Bishop of Killaloe, writes to Ussher that his Majesty has granted a letter for the appointment of Mr. Bedell to the Provost's place, and so will put an end to all tumults, and effect the long desired settlement of the College.[4] Archbishop Abbot, who was Chancellor of the University, writes to the Senior and other Fellows to the same effect: "It hath pleased his Majesty to give a remedy thereunto [the distractions of these frequent elections] by appointing unto you for that place Mr. Bedell *(sic)*, a man of great worthe, and one who hath spent some time in the parts beyond the seas, and so cometh unto you better experienced than an ordinary person."[5] Dr. Ward also writes from Cambridge of Bedell in the

---

1. Ussher's *Works,* xv, p. 375.

2. *Ditto,* xvi, 453–4. Sibbes was a pious and eloquent Puritan theologian. Among other treatises, he wrote, *The Saints' Cordial, The Soul's Conflict with Itself,* and *The Bruised Reed,* books which still command some attention.

3. Ussher's *Works,* xvi, p. 455. See also Stubbs' *Hist. Univ. Dublin,* p. 390–1. Mede was afflicted with a bad stutter. It was a hopeless matter with him to pronounce the letter "r." "R was a shibboleth to him," says Fuller, *Worthies,* i, p. 520.

4. Ussher's *Works,* xvi, p. 457.

5. Elrington's *Life,* p. 87 (note).

highest terms as a "sincere honest man, not tainted with avarice or ambition, pious, discreet, wise, and stout enough, *si res exigat.*"[6]

William Bedell, thus appointed to the Provostship, was born in Essex in 1570, and was therefore eleven years older than Ussher. He was elected a Fellow of Emmanuel College, Cambridge, in 1593, and received his orders from Dr. John Sterne, the Suffragan Bishop of Colchester. Inconsequence of the promiscuous way in which these Suffragans dispensed holy orders, the institution was allowed to fall into disuse, only to be revived in our own day.

This particular Suffragan being called to account for his carelessness, replied that he had ordained one man (meaning Bedell) better than anyone ever ordained by any Bishop. When Sir Henry Wotton was sent by King James as Ambassador to Venice, Bedell went with him as chaplain; there he fell in with Father Paul (Sarpi), the learned friar and historian of the Council of Trent, who took Bedell "to his very soul." He taught him Italian, and in return Bedell taught Father Paul English.[7] So great was the intimacy between the ambassador and his chaplain and the leading citizens of the Republic, that it was at length given out that Venice was about to turn Protestant, and an attempt was made to assassinate Father Paul. After eight years thus spent, Bedell returned to his living of Bury St. Edmunds. In 1615, he was presented to the parish of Horninger, in the diocese of Norfolk.

He refused to pay the exorbitant fees for institution and induction on the ground that it was simony, and the Bishop then instituted him without them.[8] Here Bedell remained for twelve years,

---

6. Ussher's *Works,* xv, p. 402.

7. Walton's *Life of Sir Henry Cotton* (S.P.C.K. edition), p. 107–8. Monck Mason's *Life of Bedell,* p. 62–6.

8. The Bishop was Dr. John Jegon, according to *Dict. Nat. Biography;* Dr. Samuel Horsnet, according to Clogy's *Memoirs of the Life and Episcopate of Bedell,* p. 25 (note). These memoirs were first printed in 1862, with notes from the original MS. in the Harleian Collection, British Museum. Clogy was a native of Scotland, admitted to holy orders by Bedell and promoted to the vicarage of Cavan. Bedell seems on principle to have objected to

until 1627, when he was invited to become Provost. According to Sir James Ware, he only accepted the office on the strong representation of the King, who promised that it would lead to something better. As a matter of fact, two years later he was made Bishop of Kilmore. Bedell himself tells us what his feelings were as to his acceptance of the Provostship. "Thus I stand," he writes to a friend from Bury, March 6, 1627, "I am married. I have three children; therefore if the place require a single man the business is at an end. I have no want, I thank my God, of anything necessary for this life. I have a competent living of above one hundred pounds a year in a good air, and seat, with a very convenient house near to my farm, a little parish not exceeding the compass of my weak voice."

"I have often heard it said [he adds] that changing seldom brings the better, especially to those who are well; and I see well that my wife (although resolving, as she ought, to be content with whatsoever God shall appoint) had rather continue with her friends in her native country than put herself into the hazard of the seas and a foreign land with many casualties in travel. All these reasons I have if I consult with flesh and blood, which move me rather to reject this offer, yet with all humble and dutiful thanks to my Lord Primate for his mind and good opinion of me. . . . If I may be of any better use to my country, to God's Church, or of any better service to our common Master, I must close thine eyes against all private respects; and if God call me I must answer, 'Here I am.' " He is ready to obey if it were not only to go into Ireland, but into Virginia,[9] and even though "death itself" should meet him

---

fees of every kind, and would take none afterwards from his clergy, when Bishop of Kilmore. He would see them to the door lest anyone else might exact them after they left his presence. See Bedell's *Life of the Bishop*, p. 72; Clogy's *Memoirs*, p. 55. *The Life of Bishop Bedell*, by his son, was published by John E.B. Mayor, Fellow of St. John's, Cambridge, from the Tanner MS., British Museum (Class 278, f. 15 sq.) in 1871. Bedell, we learn, always addressed his clergy as *"fratres et compresbyteri."* — Clogy's *Memoirs*, p. 47.

9. Sir Walter Raleigh had a short time before he planted the English flag on the shores of Virginia.

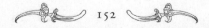

in the performance.[10] The Senior Fellows on their part write to Bedell, tendering him all hearty entertainment and due respect.[11]

Immediately on being sworn in, a meeting of the Board was held, at which it was agreed that all former quarrels should be forgotten. Bedell never showed himself quite confident of his ability to fill the place; he evidently accepted it with misgivings.[12] Writing to Ussher from Ringes (qy. Ringsend), September 10th, 1627, he says: "I have taken upon me the government of that society, though with privity to myself of very much insufficiency thereto. I have endeavoured hitherto to set order first in the worship of God (much neglected, as appeared by the very ill array of the chapel itself, and omitting of communions these many years)."[13] He finds the statutes which he is revising to consist of a few papers tacked together, part English, part Latin, and all out of order.[14] He arranges for the keeping of two "common places" weekly instead of one. The finances of the college are in a bad way. He finds no money in the chest to pay for commons and stipends as they are due. From the first, things did not run smoothly.

On April 1, 1628, he complains "of a new broil, that old grudges and factions are revived," and hints at his possible resignation. On April 15th he writes to Ussher that he had informed the

---

10. Ussher's *Works*, .xvi, p. 442–3. See also Stubbs' *History of the University,* who prints a copy of the appointment from the College Register. It was evidently considered a serious business in those days to cross over into Ireland; it was a "foreign land."

11. Stubbs' *History,* p. 393. Bedell's salary as Provost was £100 a year, and he received £20 a year additional as Lecturer in Christ's Church Cathedral. — Bedell's *Life,* p. 41.

12. On the day of his arrival in Dublin, Bedell took lodgings at the house of Dr. Siler in Copper Alley, and in the afternoon paid his respects to the Lord-Deputy at the Castle. — Bedell's *Diary,* August 16, 1627.

13. Ussher's *Works*, xvi, p. 458. There was no communion table in the College chapel in 1627 when Bedell entered on his duties, as we learn from his diary.

14. Ussher's *Works,* xvi, 458; Stubbs' *History,* p. 395.

Archbishop of Canterbury that he feared he would be "a bad pilot in such rough seas," and that he was deaf.[15] Still later he writes again to Ussher from his old parish in Suffolk, whither he had gone to bring over his family to Dublin, that he considers it has been an error all this while to neglect the faculties of law and physic, and "attend only to the ordering of one poor college of divines." Archbishop Abbot had approved of the new statutes,[16] as Bedell informs Ussher, but while it was insisted upon that the students should always wear their gowns in college, Abbot did not approve of their being excused when they went into the town — a point which, he says, of all others should have been provided for. Bedell replied that "the streets in Dublin were very foul," and the Archbishop's rejoinder was that they might "if the streets were never so foul take their gowns under their arms."[17]

In another letter to the Archbishop of Armagh, Bedell complains of the "new-fangleness in apparel, and long hair and ruffles, wherein this city (Dublin) and the very greatest of the clergy are, methinks, very exorbitant."[18]

---

15. Ussher's *Works*, xv, p. 396. These constant quarrels and emeutes arose very much from the enmity that existed between the British and Irish students, who divided the College between them. — See Bedell's *Life of Bedell*, p 44.

16. Bedell's statutes were subsequently revised by Jeremy Taylor, and were in consequence called Taylor's statutes, but their foundation was Temple's statutes. — Todd's *Catalogue of Graduates*, p. vii.

17. Ussher's *Works*, xv, p. 396.

18. Ditto, xvi, p. 458. Bedell was an enemy to all kinds of clerical dandy-ism, and set an example of simplicity of dress as a Bishop. Among his synodical instructions to his clergy was the following — "*ut clerici comam ne nutriant, et habitu clericale . . . incedant.*" — Clogy's *Memoirs*, p. 63. We are told that he would not wear silk, but dressed in plain stuff. In Dublin, he would not ride up and down the streets with his three or four men attending, as was the common usage of the bishops there, but always walked with one man. He very seldom used to ride with the State to church on Sundays, and when he did so it was with as little show as possible. — Ditto, p. 48–9. Clerical vanity was as rife in the English

The College continued to be an unruly place, as we can easily see from Bedell's Register. Thus he notices how two students, Dean and Wilson, are mulcted a month's commons for their insolent behaviour, assaulting and striking the butler. Sir Springham is said to keep a hawk. Rawley, for drunkenness and knocking Strank's head against the seat of the chapel, is to have no further maintenance from the house. Booth, for taking a pig of Sir Samuel Smith's, and that openly in the daytime before many, and causing it to be dressed in town, is condemned to be whipped openly in the hall, and to pay for the pig.[19] Writing to Ussher, he tells him how on St. Matthews day, the scholars at night pulled down, between supper and prayer-time, a wooden enclosure, "every stick, and brought it away into the college to several chambers; upon warning, at prayer

---

Church. Bishop Hall writes to his brother, about to become a clergyman. His attire should not be "youthfully wanton, nor affectedly ancient, but grave and comely like the mind, like the behavior of the wearer." Archbishop Bancroft likewise, in his letter on Pluralities (1610), speaks of clerical pride in dress as never so great as it was then, from the dean to the curate. Nothing was left to distinguish a bishop from any of them. Deans, and even archdeacons and inferior clergy, were to be found in their velvet or satin cassocks with silk stockings. Their wives were likewise given similar failings, and this caused a great outcry against "double beneficed men," and much envy and heart-burning. — See Lewis's *Life of Bishop Hall,* p. 117–121. The clergy had also begun to smoke at this time, and Hall condemns the new habit before Convocation in 1623. Even of the mouths that were sacred to God, "there were some which out of a wanton custom savoured of nothing by Indian soot, and took more pleasure to put forth a cloud of smoke than the thunderings and lightnings of the Law." — Ditto, p. 66. See Simpkinson's *Laud,* p. 13.

19. See Monck Mason's *Life of Bedell,* p. 163–4; Stubbs' *History of the University,* p. 58–9, where these extracts from Bedell's Register are given. Bedell's insistence on religious instruction during meal times does not seem to have profited the students much; we are told that he required "a chapter to be read in the Latin Bible, and after meat was brought in, and a little space of time allowed, the reader was to go up to the Fellows' table (where seldom but the Provost himself was present), and there recite some verse of the chapter that was read to give occasion of savoury and profitable discourse." — Bedell's *Life of Bedell,* p. 43.

time, they brought it all back, and there was a great pile reared up in the night. This "insolency grieved" Bedell "much."[20]

One of the first enterprises of the new Provost was to set himself to learn the Irish language, with the praiseworthy purpose of being able to give religious instruction in it.[21] He writes to Ussher, asking for a loan of an Irish Psalter.[22] He quickly turned his attention to the great work of giving the Irish people the Bible and Book of Common Prayer in their own tongue. He also established in the college an "Irish lecture," which gave the King great pleasure.[23] The instruction of the Irish people by clergymen of the Church of Ireland who could speak their language was a matter on which the previous King (James I) had set great importance. He had written to the Earl of Cork, complaining that Trinity College, which had been founded by Elizabeth with the object of thus instructing the Irish-speaking people, had failed in this respect.[24]

The ordinance of Queen Elizabeth, already referred to, that where the natives did not understand the English language the Liturgy should be said in Latin, had been, as might be supposed, a most effectual check of the progress of the Reformation. A natural result was that the clergy of the Established Church did not care to master a language that could be of no practical value to them in the discharge of their public duties. On the other hand, the Roman Catholic clergy kept the language alive among the people by ministering to them, if not in public, at least privately, in a tongue they loved to hear.[25] An Act passed in the twenty-eighth year of Henry VIII (cap. xv.) had provided that spiritual promotions should be

20. Ussher's *Works*, xvi, p. 427.

21. While in Venice, Bedell had learned Italian, and had translated the English Prayer-book into that tongue.

22. Ussher's *Works*, xvi, p. 476.

23. Ditto, xv, p. 443.

24. Stubbs' *History*, p. 58 (note).

25. Bedell complained to Laud of the clergy in his diocese that they had not "the tongue of the people," and could not perform any divine offices

given only to such persons as could speak the English tongue, and *none other*, and promise to maintain a school *to learn English.*

By the statute of Queen Elizabeth, (2nd Eliz. cap. xiii), it was enacted that where the parish minister had not the use of the English tongue, "it shall be lawful to say or use all their common and open prayer in the Latin tongue." The eighty-sixth (Irish Canon) sought to get rid of the difficulty by permitting the parish clerk to read the most important portions of the service after the clergyman in the Irish tongue. We shall see what further efforts Bedell made in this direction, and how they were thwarted.

All this time, affairs were in a very unsatisfactory state in Ireland. The discontent of the Recusants was slumbering; Laud, then Bishop of London, was commencing to turn his attention to Irish matters, and was in correspondence with Ussher.[26] The Roman Catholics had refused the bounty, but they had made overtures to the King, and sent representatives to London with an offer of a large sum of money.

---

nor confer with them, which was no small cause of the continuance of the people in Popery. — Letter to Laud, April 1st, 1630. — See Clogy's *Memoirs,* p. 36–8. Bedell drew up an Irish Catechism for the people, which he called *ABC, or the Institution of a Christian.* It was printed in Dublin by the Company of Stationers in 1631; on the reverse of the title-page is a coarse woodcut representing children picking up fruit from a tree. The whole, which contains among other things the Creed and the Lord's Prayer, consists of eight leaves. This Catechism is extremely rare, only one copy of it being known to exist, in the Library of the British Museum. — See Cotton's *Fasti* Hib., iii, p. 162, and T. Wharton Jones' *Bedell,* p. 172–4.

26. It is curious to see how far back the opposition to the use of the Irish tongue in religious instruction goes. We find that it required a special act of Parliament in 1485, to allow of the Archbishop of Dublin sending an Irish-speaking of his flock who only understood that language. — See Hardiman's *Patent Rolls, temp.* Richard II. It was regarded in the light of treason to back up the Irish. Thus in 1421, the Bishop of Cashel was accused by the Bishop of Lismore "that he made very much of the Irish, and that he loved none of the English nation, and that he bestowed no benefice upon any Englishman, and that he counselled other bishops not to give the least benefice to any of them." — Marleburrough's *Chronicle,* p. *222;* Ware, i, p. 480–1.

The favours they asked for in return were not altogether of a religious nature, but embraced also domestic and political advantages for the entire country. A free and general pardon was promised in return, and that all landholders should be confirmed in their estates. The Roman Catholics were elated, and considered, in accordance with the instructions issued from London, that they had again full licence to celebrate, without let or hindrance, the observances of their religion. The consequence was, they seized upon some of the parish churches for the purpose, and established a Popish seminary in the city of Dublin. It was now the turn of the Protestant party to be irritated, and they called on the Lord-Deputy to interfere and put the laws in force against the Recusants. In response to this demand, Lord Falkland was compelled to issue a proclamation to the effect that "the late intermission of legal proceedings against Popish pretended titular archbishops, bishops, abbots, deans, vicars-general, jesuits, friars, and others, deriving their pretended authority from the See of Rome, in contempt of his Majesty's royal power and authority, had bred such an extravagant insolence and presumption in them; that he was necessitated to charge and command them in his Majesty's name to forbear the exercise of their Popish rites and ceremonies."[27]

This proclamation was very badly received, and in Drogheda (the residence of the Archbishop) was treated with the utmost contempt, so much so as to draw forth a strong remonstrance addressed to Ussher by the Lord-Deputy, April 14th, 1629. "It was done," writes Lord Falkland, "in scornful and contemptuous sort, a drunken soldier being the first set up to read it, and then a drunken sergeant of the town, both being made by so much drink incapable of that task." It was more like a "May-game" than anything else. He had expected that Ussher, from the eminent place he held in the Church, and being a Privy Councillor, would have communicated with him on the subject.[28] The Primate was

---

27. Leland's *History* iii, p. 4–5.

28. Ussher's *Works,* xv, p. 438.

deeply hurt by the tenor of his letter, and the Lord-Deputy subsequently apologised.

Representations adverse to the government of the Lord-Deputy followed, and the English Government recalled him. Lord Falkland, on his departure from Ireland, took an affectionate leave of Ussher, and, kneeling down, begged his Grace's blessing."[29]

The Roman Catholic party, looking on his recall as a great triumph, suddenly burst out into the wildest licence, and paraded the streets of Dublin with public ceremonies, monks and friars walking in procession in full ecclesiastical habiliments, a thing that had been unheard of for many years. The consequence of these proceedings was a serious riot in the city, on the occasion of the Archbishop of Dublin (Bulkeley) and the Lord Mayor attempting by force to put down a religious service in Cook Street. The Archbishop was attacked, and was compelled to fly for his life, and take refuge in a neighbouring house.[30] How far it was becoming for a minister of religion, and especially one of his high rank, to appear at the head of a body of men armed with muskets and pole-axes, it is not for us to pronounce. The English Government, however, took his side.

The house where the service was celebrated was demolished, as "a mark of terror to the resisters of authority," and the building, which had been set apart as a Roman Catholic seminary, was confiscated and handed over to the University of Dublin.[31] Protestant lectures were delivered there, which were attended occasionally by

---

29. *Illius benedictionem plexis genibus rogavit.* — Smith's *Life,* p. 65.

30. The religious order was that of the Capuchins, who established themselves in Ireland in 1623, under the rule of one Father Ling, an Irishman. For a notice of the riot, see Leland's *Hist. of Ireland,* iii, p. 7. Butler, in his *History of the Roman Catholic Church*, represents the Archbishop to have been Ussher, but the Primate was not present. It was Dr. Bulkeley, Archbishop of Dublin. — See Elrington's *Life,* p. 280, Wall and Leland (and after them Elrington) seem to have been mistaken in representing the order as that of the Carmelites. — See *Todd,* as below.

31. It was called St. Stephen's Hall, and was known for some time as "the College in Bridge Street." — See Todd's *List of the Graduates of the University of Dublin*, introduction, p. lxiv–lxv.

the Lords Justices. It was subsequently brought as a charge against Lord Strafford on his trial, that he had restored the building to the Roman Catholics. His answer was that he had done so in consequence of a successful suit before the Privy Council.[32]

The Protestants were still excited, and representations were made to the King on the state of affairs. In return, Charles addressed a letter to the four Archbishops, in which he called on them to exercise greater vigilance in their work, to exhort their clergy to do their duty by preaching and catechising in the parishes committed to their charge, and to live answerably to the doctrine which they preached to the people. The Bishops were not to hold any benefice or ecclesiastical dignity whatsoever along with their bishoprics; and when livings fell vacant they were to fill them up at once, and not keep the revenues in their own hands.[33]

This severe letter, almost amounting to a reprimand, in return for the complaint of the Protestant party, was written, no doubt, at the suggestion of Laud, who was at this time busying himself about Irish matters, and in particular with the abuses of the Established Church. The entire letter suggests that the Church was itself responsible for much of the growing strength of the Roman Catholics.

And in truth the abuses at this time were manifold and glaring. How could a Church be a successful missionary institution which owned Bishops like Dr. Boyle, Bishop of Waterford and Lismore? A Fellow of St. John's, Oxford, by the interest of his relative, the Earl of Cork, he had got possession of the See of Waterford and Lismore, with a patent to hold in addition any amount of dignities and promotions. His nephew, the Bishop of Cork, afterwards Lord Primate and Lord Chancellor, perpetuated this shameful abuse, seizing on the livings in his diocese under the excuse that he could not find clergymen to occupy them. Things were not better in the northern dioceses. Bishop Moygne, the immediate predecessor of Bedell in the See of Kilmore, "had set

32. See Rushworth's *Tryal of the Earl of Strafford*, p. 27.
33. See the letter in Parr's *Life*, p. 38–9.

up such a shop of mundination and merchandise as if all things spiritual and temporal belonging to episcopacy had been ordinary vendible commodities, as in the "Church of Rome . . . orders and livings sold to those who could pay the greatest fines."[34]

Of a far different character in his life and work was the Archbishop of Armagh, and if other prelates before and after him had been men of the same zeal and determination of purpose, the Reformed Church of Ireland would have flourished and made converts through the diligence of its pastors, bishops, and parochial clergy alike. Ussher, we are told, devoted himself to missionary work among those who had been "bred up in the Roman Catholic religion from their infancy; for which end he began to converse more frequently and more familiarly with the gentry and nobility of that persuasion,[35] as also with divers of the inferior sort that dwelt near him, inviting them often to his house and discoursing with them with great mildness of the chief tenets of their religion, by which gentle usage he was strangely successful, convincing many of their errors, and bringing them to the knowledge of the truth."[36]

---

34. Clogy's *Memoirs*, p. 34–5.

35. The proselytizing of the sons of the nobility has been carried on with consistent impartiality by both Churches. Ussher took into his house two young scions of noble houses, James Dillon, afterwards Earl of Roscommon, and the young Viscount Iveagh (Arthur Mac Ongusa or McGuinness), who both became Protestants. Mac Ongusa afterwards married the daughter of Hugh O'Neill, Earl of Tyrone. — See Elrington's *Life*, p. 109; O'Hart's *Irish Pedigrees*, p. 157.

36. Parr's *Life of Ussher*, p. 39. The general want of missionary enterprise, on behalf of the Roman Catholic population of Ireland, arrested at a later date the attention of the famous Puritan, John Owen. "How is it," he asks, "that Jesus Christ is in Ireland only as a Lion staining all His garments with the blood of His enemies, and none to hold Him up as a Lamb sprinkled with His own blood, to His friends. . . . For my part, I see no further into the mystery of these things, but that I could heartily rejoice that innocent blood being expiated, the Irish might enjoy Ireland so long as the moon endureth, so that Jesus Christ might possess the Irish — *Sermon before Parliament on the Day of Humiliation*, Feb. 28, 1650.

The Archbishop also laid himself out to reform the secular abuses of the Church, restraining impropriations, as far as he could do so, and endeavouring to protect the property of the Church from falling into the hands of the great landed proprietors, in which good work he was ably seconded by Laud.[37] But none of these troublesome questions were allowed to interfere with Ussher's studies. He received a letter from his agent at Aleppo, informing him, that he had shipped off a parcel of books for him — an imperfect copy of the Old Testament in the Chaldean; a Syriac tract of St. Ephrem's, &c.

Later, he writes again (July 29th, 1628), "The books in the Ethiopian tongue I have not been so happy as to be able to procure. Jerusalem yields none of them."[38]

In March 1629, we find Ussher writing from Drogheda to Dr. Ward, informing him that he is about to edit the history of Gottescalcus with two of his confessions never before published.

In 1631, Archbishop Ussher issued from the press this work, and thereby gratified the strong Calvinistic opinions he held at the time. It was one of the first books printed in Ireland in the Latin tongue.[39] Gottescalcus was a Benedictine monk in the diocese of Soissons who flourished about the ninth century. He devoted himself to the Pelagian controversy, and maintained the doctrines of predestination and irresistible grace, against Maurus, the Archbishop of Mentz, Johannes Scotus, and others. On his side appeared Ratramnus of Corbey, Prudentius of Troyes, and

---

37. Irish Churchmen, at least, have every reason to regard the memory of Laud with gratitude. He laboured hard to regain its possessions for the Church. Even a strong Protestant like Fuller writes: "He was a worthy instrument in moving the King to so pious a work." — Ch. *Hist.* iii, p. 426.

38. Ussher's *Works,* xvi, p. 472.

39. Ussher says he supposes it was the first Latin book ever published in Ireland (*Works,* xv, p. 583), but, as Elrington points out (*Life,* p. 123), Ware had already published two Latin treatises in Dublin, and Professor Killen mentions a Latin book printed in Dublin in 1619 — a medical treatise on hereditary diseases. — See Reid's *Hist. of Presbyterianism,* i, p. 29 (note).

Remigius, Archbishop of Lyons. His opinions were ultimately condemned, he was sentenced to be degraded and whipped, his book, in which he appealed to Scripture, thrown into the flames, and himself imprisoned in the monastery of Hautvilliers. Refusing to retract, he lingered in prison for twenty years, and after his death was denied Christian burial.[40]

It casts a strange light on the theological controversies of the seventeenth century that Ussher thought it worth his while to produce this history.[41] He leans strongly to the side of Gottescalcus, and defends him as an Augustinian. It is also remarkable that the English Court should have thought the subject worthy of its notice, and that the King should have issued an order against reviving the Predestinarian controversy. Although the Archbishop's book escaped notice, a publication by Downham, Bishop of Derry, *A Book against the Arminians and the totall and finall Apostacie of the Saints from Grace,* as Prynne calls it, was not so fortunate, having been suppressed by royal authority.[42]

At the same time that this was done, three Puritans were expelled from Oxford — Ford, of Magdalen Hall, Thorn, of

---

40. See, for an account of this controversy, Kurtz' *Church History,* i, p. 546–548; Hagenbach's *Hist. Of Doctrines,* ii, p. 293–297.

41. *Gotteschalchi Praedestinatianae controversiae ab eo motae Historia: uma cum duplice ejusdem confessione nunc primum* in *lucem edita Dublinii,* 1631. The work, which is dedicated to Vossius, is a treatise of 233 pages, and forms the first part of Vol. iv of the Archbishop's collected writings. — Ussher's *Works,* Vol. iv.

42. The King, through Laud, ordered Ussher to call in Downham's book. The Archbishop's reply was found in Laud's study at Lambeth, endorsed with his own hand. In the course of it, Ussher says he had caused all the copies unsent into England to be seized. He adds that he had no eye to the Dublin press, because it was out of his province, and the case, he supposed, more properly belonged to his brother of Dublin. Bedell was then ordered to overlook the press in Ireland. Ussher's book escaped because it was written in Latin, and because of the eminence of the writer. — Collier, *Eccl. Hist.* ii, p. 750; *Doom of Canterbury,* p. 172. See also for a note on Downham's treatise, Reid's *Hist. Pres.,* i, p. 164.

Balliol, and Hodges, of Exeter; and Prideaux, Rector of Exeter, College, was publicly censured for defending them.

If we are to believe some, Gottescalcus taught an extreme antinomianism. One of his opponents — Archbishop Rabanus — wrote that he had seduced many, who had become less careful of their salvation, since they had learned from him to say: "Why should I labour for my salvation? If I am predestinated to damnation I cannot avoid it; and on the contrary, if I am predestinated to salvation, whatever sins I may be guilty of, I shall certainly be saved." However this may have been, his opinions sufficiently interested Archbishop Ussher to induce him to write a book on the subject.

The Archbishop seems afterwards to have considerably modified his theological opinions. Having begun as an extreme Calvinist, under the training of men like Travers and Alvey, he ended as a man of more reasonable views on such subjects as the extent of Christ's atonement, election, reprobation, &c.

"Another very eminent contemporary," says Bishop Christopher Wordsworth, "whose sentiments concerning the Calvinistic points appear to have undergone at a much later period of his life a change very similar to that which took place in those of his friend, Dr. Sanderson, was the truly pious and primitive Archbishop Ussher, who had often exerted himself as an earnest and public advocate and propagator of those notions which he latterly disclaimed." Dr. Hammond gives similar testimony.[43]

---

43. Wordsworth's *Eccl. Biography*, iv, p. 437 (note). It is worth dwelling upon this point, as there are those who believe Ussher remained all his life an extreme Puritan and Calvinist. Collier says "Ussher was a strict Calvinian, and held the Predestinarian controversy in the sense of the Lambeth Articles; but some time before his death he changed his opinions touching the five points, and came over to the other side." — *Eccl. Hist.*, p. 868. See ante, p. 107; "In later years the effects of this *prava disciplina* were almost obliterated." — Elrington's *Life*, p. 17. See also the subject fully entered into in Todd's *Life of Walton*, i, p. 203–9.

CHAPTER XIII

ARCHBISHOP USSHER AND BISHOP BEDELL; THE STORY OF THE IRISH BIBLE

I n March 1629, Ussher met with a severe domestic affliction in the death of his only brother, the learned Ambrose Ussher.[1] Like the Archbishop, he was deeply read in Eastern languages, especially Arabic and Syriac. He had been a scholar and Fellow of Trinity College. Ambrose Ussher only published one book, a short Catechism, but there is an extensive collection of his MSS. in the library of the college. Ware gives a full list of them.[2] The Primate does not allude to his loss in any of his published letters.

About this time, the Archbishop received a communication from the Lord-Deputy and Council thanking him for some trouble he had taken in examining into certain acts of the titular Bishop of Raphoe and the affairs of Popish conventual houses in that town. The Bishop had been accused of making a priest at a public Mass in an orchard.[3]

---

1. "A very learned young man, who died too early." — Dr. Parr to Archbishop Bancroft, Jan. 5, 1682.

2. Ware's *Works,* ii, p. 128–9.

3. Ussher's *Works,* xv, p. 440.

On May 12th, 1629, Bedell writes to Ussher informing him that he had that day received letters from the King touching the bishopric of Kilmore and Ardagh. The King expresses in them his desire that the college should not proceed to elect another Provost until they further knew the royal pleasure in the matter, and he recognises the good work that had been done on behalf of the college by Bedell.[4]

Immediately before he resigned the Provostship, Bedell had considerable trouble with two of the students, and he informs Ussher of the matter in a letter dated August 20th, 1629. Great efforts had been made to win these students over to the Roman Church. The story is significant, as showing the way in which the Roman Catholic Church was working at this time. The two youths had been met by a Mr. Bodkin in a house in Castle Street, who introduced them to one Plunket, a Carmelite friar, "who laboured to encourage them in their intended resolution of being Roman Catholics," but was a poor controversialist.

Then a friar by the name of Dominick Nugent tried his hand on them, and argued very subtilely. Friar Barnwell, a Capuchin, also discoursed them "very learnedly of the non-errability of the Church, producing arguments against the Lord Primate very solidly," and promising them "pardon and reconcilement." The following day, Father Plunket and Father Browne, Provincial of the Carmelites, met them in a house in Bridge Street, where for privacy sake they retired to an arbour in the garden and discussed "controverted points between the Protestants and the Papists," such as the sacrament of the altar, the supremacy of the Pope, the marriage of priests, &c. They were offered a safe course for a journey into Spain, or to "Galloway" (Galway). Bedell gives Ussher an account anything but flattering of these youths. One had been irregular in his attendance at hall, absented himself from prayers, lodged out of his chambers in Trinity Hall, and had disorderly meetings "at a very suspected house." The other was

4. Ibid., xvi, p. 487.

equally incorrigible; he lodged and slept at an ale-house. What to do with them is doubtful, and he writes to Ussher for advice. At the close of the letter he says that September 13th will stand for his consecration.[5]

Bedell was accordingly consecrated Bishop of Kilmore and Ardagh on September 13th, 1629, in St. Peter's Church, Drogheda, by the Primate, and the Bishops of Down and Connor, Dromore, and Clogher.[6] He was scarcely installed when he got into difficulties with Dr. Allen Cook, his lay chancellor. He complains of him in a letter to Ussher, dated Kilmore, December 28th, 1629, and maintains that his patent is insufficient. He appeals to the Primate to try the case by himself, and adds, "I have resolved to see the end of this matter."[7] Affairs did not go smoothly with the new Bishop. It appears from a letter written from Farnham early in the following year, that charges were made against him that he was "a Papist, an Arminian, an equivocator, politician, and traveller into Italy"; that he bowed his knee at the name of Jesus,[8] pulled down the late bishop's seat because it was too near the altar, preached in

---

5. Ussher's *Works,* xvi, p. 494–501.

6. Bedell gives a lamentable account of his diocese shortly after he entered on his episcopal duties. The Cathedral Church of Ardagh and the bishop's house were "down to the ground." The Cathedral Church of Kilmore had no "bell or steeple, font or chalice." The parish churches were "ruined, unroofed, and unrepaired." The people, with the exception of a "few British planters," were all "obstinate recusants. " — *Rushworth,* ii, p. 47.

7. Ussher's *Works,* xv, p. 458.

8. This was one of the most serious charges that could be brought against the orthodoxy of Protestants at this time. Carte goes so far as to say that Ussher was "horribly afraid of bowing at the Name of Jesus," but gives no authority. — *Ormonde,* i, p. 78. The Puritan, Sir Edward Deering, on the other hand, had the courage to say that to refuse to bow at the Name of Jesus was "going up the back stairs to Socinianism." — Speech before Parliament, 1642 — See H. Monck Mason's *Life of Bedell,* p. 245.

his surplice, &c.[9] Bedell defended himself from these random charges in the Cathedral in the presence of his clergy.[10] Ussher was not well at the time, and Bedell writes expressing his sorrow. In a long letter addressed to the Primate, February 15th, 1630, he defends his action against his lay chancellor; and refers to the shameful charges raked up against himself. He has been "blazed a Papist," "a neuter," "a niggardly housekeeper," "an usurer"; he prays "towards the east"; "would pull down the seat of his predecessor to set up an altar"; denied burial in the chancel to one of Cook's daughters. He is also charged with having compared Ussher's preaching "to one Mr. Whiskins, Mr. Creighton, Mr. Baxter, and preferred them." Ussher had been deceived in him.

"Omitting all the rest," writes Bedell, "I cannot but touch on the last, touching the preferring others to your Grace's preaching." This he felt was a serious charge. He protests to the Primate that he never heard Mr. Whiskins preach. Mr. Price, a candidate for holy orders, declared "he would be quartered" if the charge were true. As for Dr. Cook, his patent was bad, and couched in "false Latin." In one sentence "there were above 500 words hanging in the air, without one principal verb." The seal hanging to it was not the Bishop's seal. His fees had been exorbitant. On these grounds Bedell had inhibited Dr. Cook. Very injudiciously, Bedell now falls foul of the Primate, and tells him he has heard it said among great personages that "my Lord Primate is a good man, but his court is as corrupt as others; some say worse."[11] What most offended the

---

9. A letter addressed by Bramhall to Laud, Dec. 20, 1634, gives an insight into the state of the Church in the north of Ireland about this time. "It would trouble a man to find twelve Common Prayer-books in all their churches, and those only not caste behind the altar, because they have none, but in place of it a table ten yards long, where they sit, and receive the sacrament together like good fellows." — Shirley's *Papers*, 1631–9, p. 41.

10. Ussher's, *Works*, xv, p. 459. See also Clogy's *Memoirs*, p. 139–140.

11. Ussher's *Works*, xv, p. 463–72.

Primate was the Bishop's statement that in Ussher's triennial visitation the clergy saw no profit but the taking of money.[12]

To this long letter, Ussher replies with some heat. He says most of the slanders wherewith Bedell was troubled, he had never heard of till Bedell had mentioned them himself. Of Mr. Whiskins', Mr. Creightan's, and Mr. Baxter's preaching, Ussher had never heard, till now; "would God" write the Archbishop, "that all the Lord's people might prophesy and there might be thousands of His faithful servants that might go beyond me in doing the Lord's work; the spirit that is in me I trust shall never lust after such envy."[13] He goes on to warn the Bishop against judicially declaring Dr. Cook's patent to be void. If he interferes with the civil magistrate he runs the risk of a *premunire*. The next paragraph in the Primate's letter is noteworthy as proving that there were plenty of bad landlords in Ireland at the time. "Complaints I know will be made against my court and your court and every court wherein vice should be punished, and that not by delinquents alone, but also by their landlords, be they Protestants or others, who in this county care not how their tenants live so as they pay them their rents. Bishops, he continues, should be careful about taking the jurisdiction out of the hands of their chancellors and keeping it entirely in their own hands.

"I know a bishop in this land who exerciseth the jurisdiction himself; and I dare boldly say that there is more injustice and oppression to be found in him alone than in all the chancellors in the whole kingdom put together." Ussher himself is thankful to have a lay chancellor. The law is a ticklish matter. "My chancellor is better skilled in the law than I am, and far better able to manage matters of that kind. . . . How easy a matter it is for a

---

12. Bedell did not at all relish the Primate's "bull of prohibition," as Clogy calls it, giving notice of his triennial visitation, and the suspension for the time of the Bishop's episcopal jurisdiction. He threw it away, we are told, as a man throws away an unclean thing, and stamped on it with his foot. — Clogy's *Memoirs*, p. 72–3.

13. Ussher's *Works*, xv, p. 474.

bishop that is ignorant in the law to do wrong unto others and run himself into a *premunire;* and where wrong is done, I know right may more easily be had against a chancellor than against a bishop." If his chancellor does wrong, Ussher will be the first man to throw stone at him. As for the Archbishop's visitation of the Bishop's diocese, had there been presentations made and reformation neglected there would have been cause for complaint. In a bantering tone he notices the complaints about fees. "If your clergy can get but half so much for their money from you as they did from me, they may say you were the best bishop that ever came among them." The Primate ends his reply by excusing himself from further notice of some other matters adding: "I am quite tired, and what I have written I fear will not be so pleasing to you"; and he ends, "your most assured loving friend and brother (notwithstanding any unkind passages which may have slipped from me in this letter)."[14]

To this communication, Bedell briefly replies, March 29, 1630, excusing himself for the way he had dealt, "with the papists," and on some of the other subjects referred to in their correspondence. He will not enter further into the controversy between them, but "will lay his hand upon his mouth."[15] The case of Dr. Cook, the lay chancellor, was eventually decided in the Court of Chancery, against the Bishop, with £100 costs, and the chancellor was confirmed in his appointment.[16]

---

14. Ussher's *Works,* xv, p. 475–6.

15. Ditto, p. 486. Dr. Parr, in his preface to the Archbishop's letters, says the correspondence between Ussher and Bedell "was more especially published for the doing right to the Archbishop's character, which might otherwise have suffered by some injurious reflection upon him in the Life of that Bishop lately written" (probably Burnet's *Life*).

16. Bedell, no doubt, found himself in a hornet's nest, when he ventured to oppose the lawyers. He himself called the law his Purgatory, and his journeys to Dublin his returning to Purgatory. He sought to console himself with the words: *Post tenebras spero lucem, et dabit Deus his quoque finem.* — Clogy's *Memoirs,* p. 56. His case was most probably

A further misunderstanding subsequently arose between Ussher and Bedell, which was fanned into a flame by the unkind zeal of Dr. Bernard, the former chaplain of the Archbishop, and now Dean of Kilmore. Bedell had set his face against pluralities, and the Dean had applied for the benefice of Kildromfarten, to hold *in commendam* with his deanery, and had been refused.[17] For this refusal, the Dean seems never to have forgiven Bedell. In a letter to Ussher, dated September 18th, 1630, the Bishop enters at large into Dr. Bernard's action. He had received the communion at the Bishop's hands, and expressed a desire for reconciliation; but still he hankered after the living of Kildromfarten, and got himself presented under the broad seal. But the Bishop refused to act, and this "was the only root of all Mr. Dean despite" against him. Bedell goes on to denounce pluralities in the strongest language. In the diocese of Kilmore and Ardagh there were sixty-six Roman Catholic priests and only thirty-two ministers and curates, "of which also three whose wives come not to the church."

The priests had also the advantage "of the language, the possession of the people's hearts, the countenancing of the nobility and gentry." The Bishop gave as another reason for not granting his request that the Dean was ignorant of the Irish language, and therefore could not preach to the people in their

---

tried by Lord Chancellor Loftus, and if so, he had no chance of mercy. Commenting on the case, Clogy says, "The truth is, my Lord Primate of Armagh gave himself over so much to the search of the Fathers, and all antiquity, and to that apostolic work of praying and preaching the Word, that he had no time scarce once to think of the discipline of the Church, or to regulate any thing that was amiss . . . therefore when he came to die, he earnestly besought the Lord to pardon his sins of omission about things left undone," p. 74–5. Clogy was Bedell's son-in-law.

17. The deanery of Kilmore at this time was a sinecure. Ussher, in his Visitation-book of 1622, says, "The deanery is merely *titular*, nothing belonging to it; but the bishop for the time being made choice of any one of his clergie whom he thought fittest to give unto the name the title of a dean." Bernard afterwards exchanged the deanery for that of Ardagh.

own tongue.[18] As a devoted friend of the English interest, Ussher failed to understand Bedell's desire to perpetuate the use of the Irish language, which he regarded as an obstacle in the way of the closer union of the two countries.

We are here presented with two abuses, which more than anything else contributed to destroy the prospects of a reformation of religion in Ireland — the holding of a number of benefices by a single clergyman, and the continued discountenance of the native language in the public worship of the church.

A few years later, August 18th, 1663, Bramhall, Bishop of Derry, writes to Laud from the Castle of Dublin on the former abuse: "The boundless heaping together of benefices by *commendams* and dispensations in the superior courts, is but too apparent; yea, even often by plain usurpations and indirect compositions made between the patrons, as well ecclesiastical as lay; and the incumbents by which the least part, many times not above forty shillings, rarely ten pounds in the year, is reserved for him that should serve the altar; insomuch that it is affirmed that by all or some of these means, one Bishop in the remoter parts of the kingdom doth hold three-and-twenty benefices with cure.

---

18. See Ussher's *Works,* xv, p. 531–8. Bernard's character maybe pretty well made out from the fact that he managed to be on good terms with both Royalists and Parliamentarians. He set his sails to the winds of prosperity. He writes to Ussher, "My lot is fallen well; blessed be the hand of that divine Providence, . . . I have more than an ordinary habitation, . . . I have a very gentlemanlike assembly, and a rich people, and yet, blessed be God, very tractable, sanctifying the Sabbath with reverence." He goes on to describe his manner of preaching and teaching and adds, "And yet for all this variety I avoid tediousness, which keepeth the people constant who have greatly increased their knowledge, beyond that which I am willing to speak," and more to the same purpose. — Ussher's *Works,* xvi, p. 360–3. Mr. Solley says Bernard was in the pay and employment of Cromwell when he wrote the *Life of Ussher.* — See *Notes and Queries,* 4th series, ii, p. 165.

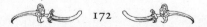

Generally their residences are as little as their livings, seldom any suitor petitioning for less than three vicarages at a time.[19]

The MS. Irish Bible of Bishop Bedell, chiefly through the adverse action of Archbishop Laud, who concurred with Ussher in the views he took on the subject, remained unprinted for fifty years. It was then taken up and published by the patriotic Robert Boyle, who expected £700 for the purpose.[20]

It was only within the last half century that the Church of Ireland awoke to its duty of ministering the Gospel to the Irish people in their native language, and founded the Irish Society for the purpose. If the building of such "castles in the air," as Ussher called preaching and catechising in the Irish tongue, had been prosecuted from the first, we might not now have to deplore the fact that the Reformed Church of Ireland is the Church of the

---

19. Bramhall's *Works,* i, p. 80. Some of the bishops set a bad example in this respect. Bishop Moygne, for instance, Bedell's predecessor "upon the ruins of two stripped bishoprics" (Kilmore and Ardagh); "had founded his family, and purchased a seigniory for his son." — Clogy's *Memoirs,* p. 35; but see W. Monck-Mason's *St. Patrick,* p. 184. Bedell refused to hold the two bishoprics, and got Ardagh transferred to the Rev. John Richardson, "peculiar for a very grave countenance, and his being an extraordinary textuary." Richardson fled to London on the outbreak of the rebellion in 1640, and published some comments on the Annotation of the assembly of Divines. — See Cotton's *Fasti,* iii, p. 184. With regard to the above charge against Bishop Moygne, it is remarkable how many Irish bishops in former days founded noble families. We may notice, for example, Loftus, Archbishop of Dublin, who founded the Ely family; Maxwell, Bishop of Kilmore, the Farnham family; Robinson, Archbishop of Armagh, the Rokeby family; Agar, also Archbishop of Armagh, the Normanton family; Pery, Bishop of Limerick, the Limerick family; Beresford, Archbishop of Tuam, the Decies family; and many others.

20. See Richardson's *Short History, &c.; Brief Sketch* of various attempts to diffuse a knowledge of the Scriptures through the Irish language and Bishop Bedell's Irish Bible in Marsh's Library. Bedell translated the Apocryphal books, but Boyle would not allow them to be published. The original MS. of the Apocrypha is now preserved in the above Library, together with the MS. copy of books, Genesis to the Song of Solomon. The remainder was

minority.[21] This action of the Archbishop is all the stranger when we consider that among his posthumous writings is to be found a tract on the duty of teaching the Holy Scriptures in the tongue of the people. In this treatise *(Historia Dogmatica Controversiae inter Orthodoxos et Pontificos de Scripturis et Sacris Vernaculis)*, Ussher proves conclusively, both from Jewish writers and Greek and Latin Fathers, that for 600 years the practice of celebrating public worship or reading Holy Scripture in a strange tongue was unknown to the Church. He even gives a list of persons who were punished immediately before the English Reformation for reading the Bible in the common tongue; and yet we find him at this time discountenancing the idea of translating the Bible into Irish, for fear of weakening the English connection![22]

---

lost. Sir B. Lee Guinness, when restoring St. Patrick's Cathedral, had the several MSS. bound in two quarto volumes, whole morocco. Two copies of O'Donnell's New Testament, 1602 and 1681, are preserved in the same Library, as also the Book of Common Prayer in Irish, 1608. A manuscript copy of original letters from the Hon. Robert Boyle to the Rev. Narcissus Marsh, D.D., Provost of T.C.D., on the subject of the printing and publishing of the Irish Bible, may also be seen in Marsh's Library *(Class* V. 3. 3. 26). There are also to be found there proposals for printing a Welsh Bible. The letters show the extreme interest taken in the work by Boyle, and the liberality with which he pursued it. Many copies of Bedell's Bible were sent to Scotland, as the Bible in Irish was intelligible to those familiar with the Gaelic tongue. — Clogy's *Memoirs,* p. 125 (note); see Ussher on these two languages, *Works,* vi, p. 103, and Reeves' *Andamnan,* p. xxxviii–ix. Bedell's MS. Hebrew Bible was rescued from the Irish insurgents in 1641, and is now in Emmanuel College, in accordance with his will. — Wharton Jones' *Life,* p. 193.

21. According to a document quoted by O'Connell in his *Memoir of the Irish People,* the English language, at the opening of the Reformation in Ireland, was spoken only in half the counties of Meath, Dublin, Louth, Wexford, and Kildare, and even in these half counties Irish was the language of the mass of the people, with the exception of the cities and walled towns. — See Kelly's *Dissertations,* p. 94 (note).

22. In the reign of Queen Elizabeth, the King of Denmark applied for an Irish scholar to translate Irish MSS. in his possession; a suitable person was

The misunderstandings between these two good men were not rectified till a year later, when Bedell visited the Primate at Termonfechan. He afterwards wrote, "I cannot easily express what contentment I received at my late being with your Grace at Termonfechin. There had nothing happened to me, I will not say since I came to Ireland, but, as far as I can call to remembrance, in my whole life, which did so much affect me on this hand as the hazard of your good opinion."[23]

Strange to say, this business of translating the Bible into the Irish tongue could not be carried on without creating further unpleasantness between the Archbishop and his suffragan. Some years later, Ussher commended a certain Mr. Murtagh King (an Irish native and a convert to Protestantism) to the Bishop as useful for his purpose. Bedell was so pleased with Mr. King's assistance that he gave him a living.[24] His enemies, however, represented King to the English Primate as a man unfit for his profession. The Bishop was compelled to appeal to the Lord-Deputy Strafford, and referred to Archbishop Ussher, the Bishop of Meath, and others, for a good character for his protege. A candidate came forward for Mr. King's living, and got possession under the great seal.

---

discovered for the work, and was ready to undertake it, when a member of the Council interfered on the ground that it might be prejudicial to the English interest. — Anderson's *Historical Sketches,* p. 26 (note). It is strange that with all his linguistic accomplishments, and his interest in the antiquities of his native country, Ussher seems to have had but a very slender acquaintance with the Irish language. — See King's *Early History of the Primacy of Armagh,* p. 50; O'Donovan's *MS. Letters* on the ordinance survey in the Irish Academy, under "Fore," in county Westmeath; Stokes' Article on St. Fechan, *J.R.S.A.,* 5th series, ii, p. 1–12; and Elrington's *Life of Ussher,* p. 29 (note): On the other hand, Ussher's uncle, Henry Ussher, Archdeacon of Dublin, was recommended for the Primacy as "very perfect in the Irish language." — *Calendar of State Papers,* 1592–6, p. 311.

23. Ussher's *Works,* xv, p 531.

24. With this Murtagh King was associated a Mr. James Nangle. — Bedell's *Life of Bedell,* p. 95.

Bishop Bedell cited and excommunicated him, for which he was cited in his turn before the Prerogative Court, and declared contumacious. Ussher throughout refused to interfere, and allowed all this trouble to fall on the head of the Bishop.[25] As for the unfortunate Mr. King, now an old man, on the verge of eighty, we are told how he was "trailed by the head and feet to horseback," and so carried off to Dublin, where he languished in prison till his death.[26]

Tanta molis erat, to give the Irish people, the Irish Bible![27]

---

25. The inconsistent conduct of Ussher is difficult to understand. It is suggested that the strong prejudices he formerly entertained against the use of the Irish language had suddenly revived. — See Clogy's *Memoirs*, p. 118.

26. Bedell to Strafford, Dec. 1st, 1638, Burnet says the whole business was "a deep fetch to possess reformed divines with jealousy and hard thoughts of the work." — See Anderson, as before, p. 64 (note), where interesting information is given about predecessors of Bedell in the same work — Kearney, Walsh, Donnellan, and O'Donnell. O'Donnell, who translated the Book of Common Prayer into Irish and printed it at his own expense, was one of the first scholars of Trinity College, Dublin, one of the earliest elected Fellows, and if not the first, the second who received the degree of D.D. from the University. He died Archbishop of Tuam. It is part of the irony of history that the Irish types sent over by Queen Elizabeth to print the New Testament should have been stolen and carried off to Douay, where they were used by the Jesuits for, proselytizing purposes. From the Shirley *Letters*, p. 317, we learn that the Queen paid £66 13s. *4d.* to the Irish "Bushoppes for making of caracts for the Testament in *Irishe*"; unless "they presently put the same in print her Majesty may, be repaid £90." Oct. 27th, 1567. Elizabeth was the only English Sovereign who ever attempted a knowledge of the Irish language. — See Olden's *Church of Ireland*, p. 332–3.

27. If truth is to be spoken, Bedell seems to have got more credit than he really deserved for the Irish Bible. The fact is, he was largely assisted by others, and, more especially, by Denis Sheridan, a converted Roman Catholic priest, to whom he gave the livings of Killasher (Florence Court). — See King's *Lough Erne;* and Clogy's *Memoirs*, p. 125 (note). Bedell died in Sheridan's

Nero watches the city of Rome burn while he sings . . . but who would he blame for his own act of madness? And how would these victims of faith meet their deaths at his cruel hands? Page 869, *The Annals of the World*.

Read more about
James Ussher's
The Annals of the World
www.nlpg.com/annals.asp

house at Drumcorr. This Sheridan was of the same family with William Sheridan, Swift's friend of later days, and Richard Brinsley Sheridan, whose granddaughter was mother of the present Marquis of Dufferin. In his "Notes on the Sheridans," Lord Dufferin attributes the translation of the Irish Bible entirely to Denis Sheridan. He speaks of him as a devoted disciple of the saintly Bedell, Bishop of Kilmore, under whose direction he translated the English version of the Bible into Irish. Denis Sheridan's son succeeded Bedell as Bishop of Kilmore. Another son became Bishop of Cloyne. — See Introduction to *Songs, Poems, and Verses of Lady Dufferin*, p. 5–6; see also T. Wharton Jones' *Life and Death of Bedell*, ch. xx.

CHAPTER XIV

ARCHBISHOP USSHER AND LAUD; CORRESPONDENCE; THE NATURE OF SACRAMENTAL GRACE; APPOINTMENTS TO THE PROVOSTSHIP OF TRINITY COLLEGE

B oth Ussher and Laud (with whom the Primate had now [1629] begun, a voluminous correspondence) had at this time passed through grievous sickness. "It is true, my Lord," writes Laud to the primate, "God hath restored me even from death itself, for I think no man was further gone and escaped." A little later, we find Ussher writing to his friend, Dr. Ward, that God had brought him "even unto the pit's brink." He had suffered from "an excessive bleeding of many days together." "As Abraham had received his son from the dead, so," writes Dr. Ward, hearing of his recovery, "we all, even God's Church, have received your Lordship in the like manner *a faucibus orci*."[1]

---

1. Ussher's *Works,* xv, p. 499.

Still, Ussher is busy with literary work. He writes to Mede from Armagh, August 10th, 1632, that he has in hand a treatise, De *Britiannicarum Ecclesiarum Primordiis,* and also a work on the Chronology of the Scriptures. He sends Vossius certain MS., including his history of Gottescalcus, and the predestination controversy (already noticed), and we find he has been busy on a large censure of the Epistles of St. Ignatius. He asks for a transcription of the Latin MS. of Ignatius in Caius College. In a subsequent letter, August 9th, 1632, he acknowledges a receipt of the transcript which "served him to a singular good use." He also says he has got a good large fragment of the beginning of Clement's genuine Epistle to the Corinthians."[2] Ussher is anxious, if possible, to get some Irish preferment for the learned John Gerard Vossius, and mentions to Laud for the purpose the Deanery of Armagh. Laud replies that he will do what he can in the matter.[3]

It is observable that the abstruse theological questions that occupy our attention today were just as rife in Archbishop Ussher's time. The subjects of predestination, election, perseverance, baptismal regeneration, were as warmly discussed then as now.

"Not only divines," writes Dr. Ward, "but lawyers and women meddle with these points."[4] Into questions of the sort we find Ussher, Bedell, Downham, Davenant, Ward; and others plunging with characteristic fervour. Ussher writes to Ward on "the efficacy of baptism of infants" as "an obscure point," and desires to be instructed. The Bishop of Derry has a book on the subject adapting St. Augustine's opinion — *Sacramenta in solis electis hoc vere efficiunt quod figurant.* Dr. Ward, writing

---

2. Ussher's *Works,* xv, p. 559.

3. Vossius did not get the Deanery. In 1623, he was made Professor of History in the University of Amsterdam. He died some years later from injuries received by falling from his library ladder.

4. Ussher's *Works,* xvi, p. 520.

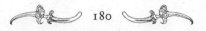

to the Archbishop, says his views are those of Hooker, proving that already the authority of this great English theologian was well established: "The instrumental conveyance of the grace signified to the due receiver is as true an effect of a sacrament, when it is duly administered, as obsignation, and is pre-existing in order of nature to obsignation."[5] Bedell, joining in, says, "I think the nature of sacraments to be not as medicines, but as seals to confirm the covenant, not to confirm the promise immediately"; but he writes on this subject "in exceeding hot haste."[6]

Ward replies in favour of infants receiving "spiritual ablution of original guilt" in baptism, "since they cannot interpose any impediment to hinder the operation of the sacrament"; and he thinks the definition of a sacrament in the Catechism "a good and sound definition."[7] Bedell next points out that infants in their baptism do receive a benefit, inasmuch as they are received thereby into the visible Church, which is "a comfort to the parents and an honour and profit to themselves." There is presently granted them an entrance into covenant with God, wherein God promises pardon of sin, and life eternal upon their faith and repentance, to which they have a present right, though the accomplishment may be deferred. If God takes them out of this world in a state of expectation, it is pious to believe that He takes the condition for performed. The mystery of redemption by Christ is revealed to them most probably, and faith granted to them. All that come to the sacrament, elect or non-elect infants alike, receive the pardon of sin, original and actual, sacramentally, and whoever performs the conditions of the covenant has the fruition of what has been already sealed to him.

---

5. Ditto, xv, p. 506.

6. Ditto, p. 509.

7. Ussher's *Works*, xvi, p. 511. Fuller says of Ward, he was "a Moses, not only for slowness of speech, but otherwise meekness of nature." — Hist. *Univ. Cambridge*, p. 234.

"This conceit of sacraments to make them medicines," thinks Bedell "is the root of all error in the matter."[8]

On May 29th, 1630, a son was born to the King, and a messenger of the Court, "an officer of honour" specially selected for the purpose, was sent to Dublin with a royal letter to announce the event to the Lords Justices, who forthwith requested the Primate to preach the thanksgiving sermon which he did on the text, "Instead of thy fathers shall be thy children, whom thou mayest make princes in all the earth."

The Primate was also requested to see that the day should be duly notified to all the Clergy, that on that day there be "public prayers, thanksgivings, and sermons, in all the churches," and that the said prayers be then publicly read in the time of divine service; and that afterwards ringing of bells, making of bonfires, and all other expressions of joy may be made to testify the general joy and gladness of that day."[9]

On April 30th, 1634, Ussher announces to Ward the death of the good Bishop of Derry (Dr. Downham), and "ye Dr. Bramhall,"

---

8. Ussher's *Works,* p. 520. Though Bedell was in some respects a Puritan, he was no bigot. His acquaintance with Father Sarpi had not been thrown away on him. In the last letter written by him and addressed to Daniel Swiney, the Roman Catholic Bishop of Kilmore, as "My reverend and loving brother," he says, "There is the difference of our way of Church worship — I do not say of our religion, for I have ever thought and published it in my writings that we have one common Christian religion." — See Article "Bedell" in. *Dict. Nat. Biog.* In this respect, Bedell has his counterparts in Bishop Jebb of Limerick and Bishop Law of Killala. The latter, in a pastoral letter to his clergy in 1793, said, "I look on my Roman Catholic brethren as fellow-subjects and fellow Christians; believers in the same God; partners in the same redemption. Speculative differences on some points of faith are with me of no account. They and I have but one religion — the religion of Christianity. Therefore, as children of the same Father, as travellers in the same road, and seekers of the same salvation, why not love each other as brothers?" — Stanley's Essays on *Church and State,* p. 325.

9. Ussher's *Works,* xv, p. 529–30.

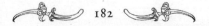

he writes, "is likely to succeed Him in that bishopric, which is absolutely the best in the whole kingdom."

To keep up the continuity of our story, we must now glance at the successive appointments made to the Provostship of Trinity College, after the promotion of Bedell — a matter in which Archbishop Ussher was naturally much interested. Laud writes to him to say the King would fain have a man who would go on where Mr. Bedell leaves [off]. "I am engaged for none. I heartily love freedoms granted by charter, and would have them maintained."[10] By Laud's advice, the King consents that the Fellows' petition, that they might be allowed to elect their own Provost, should be granted, provided they elect a man serviceable to the Church and to him,[11] but the election must not be carried through without submitting the name of the new Provost to his Majesty, for his royal approval.

The Fellows thereupon elected Dr. Robert Ussher, the Primates cousin. The Archbishop writes to Laud, August 10th, 1629: "Dr. Ussher is indeed my cousin-german, but withal the son of that father at whose instance, charge, and travel, the charter of the foundation of the college was first obtained from Elizabeth. . . . To his learning, honesty and, conformity unto the discipline of the church, no man, I suppose, will take exception." His ability in government had been already shown during his Vice-Provostship. He means to go on where Bedell left off, and the Archbishop promises that if his cousin is appointed he will hold himself strongly engaged thereby, "to have a special eye to the government of that college."[12] Robert Ussher was accordingly appointed (October 3rd, 1629), the sum of £10 having been paid into the King's Exchequer for the royal letter authorising the Fellows to carry out their own statute. The new Provost showed himself very anxious to further his predecessor's ideas on the subject of instruction in the Irish

---

10. Ditto, p. 443.

11. Ditto, p. 445.

12. Ussher's *Works*, xv, p. 449–50.

tongue. He directed that a chapter of the Irish Testament should be read by a native each day during dinner.[13]

Ware says of him, "He was an enemy to all theatrical representations, and would not admit them in the college until he was in a manner commanded by the Lords Justices."[14]

Robert Ussher, who was thus elected a second time to the office, proved himself an unsuccessful head. He wanted the character and decision required to rule the disorderly spirits who then made mischief within the walls of the college. In this difficulty, the Primate, who had pledged himself for the good governance of the college, applied to Laud as to what was best to do. He suggests that the Provost should be removed, as being one "who was of too soft and gentle a disposition to rule so heady a company." Ussher also asks Laud to use his influence to procure new statutes which would invest the Provost with additional powers. The difficulty was removed by inducing Robert Ussher to accept the Archdeaconry of Meath in lieu of the Provostship, and shortly afterwards he was made Bishop of Kildare.

Laud now recommended William Chappel, Dean of Cashel, and formerly Fellow of Christ's College, Cambridge, for the office. In his earlier years, Chappel had acted as Dean and Catechist in that College, where he had among his pupils John Milton.[15] There is some interest attaching to Chappel, owing to the belief that he

---

13. Stubbs' *History,* p. 62.

14. Ware's *Works,* i, p. 392.

15. Stubbs' *History,* p. 30; *Rawdon Papers,* p. 109. Chappel was esteemed "a rich magazine of rational learning, and a most painfull careful tutor." He disputed on one occasion before James I, on points of controversy between Protestants arid Roman Catholics, the King himself entering into the arena. He was accused of the awful sacrilege of having whipped the future author of *Paradise Lost* while his pupil at Christ College. After his flight to England on the outbreak of the Rebellion in 1641, he suffered many grievous things from the Parliamentary party. Chappel's *Life* of himself, written in Latin verse, is printed by Hearne in Leland's Collection, v, p. 261–8. — See Masson's *Life of Milton,* i, p. 128, 159–61; Cooper's *Annals of Cambridge*; and the Article in the *Diet. Nat.*

is the original of the "old Damaetas" of Milton's *Lycidas*.[16] The Lord-Deputy Strafford accepted the nomination, and true to his policy of "thorough," at once proceeded to carry it out: "I went to the College myself recommended the Dean to the place, told them I must direct them to choose the Dean, or else to stay until they should understand his Majesty's pleasure, and in no case to choose any other. They are so, as on Thursday next he will be Provost, and your Grace shall not need to trouble the King about it."[17]

From his Latin *Life* of himself, it would appear that Chappel accepted the office with reluctance, and then went to London to ask Laud to excuse him. Chappel was no exception to his predecessors; he seemed as little able to maintain discipline within the College walls. A great difficulty was experienced in filling up a Senior Fellowship, the three Fellows at the head of the Seniors being irreligious men who neglected the chapel services. The surplice difficulty again arose. To one of them, Nathaniel Hoyle, this "rag of Popery" was so distasteful that he refused to wear one till immediately before the election. Chappel and the two Senior Fellows, on their own authority, proceeded to repeal as much of the statute as required the vote of four Senior Fellows to elect to the Board. For this act, the two Seniors, Newman and Conway, were expelled and the Provost censured. The proceedings were communicated to Laud, who wrote back to Strafford. In his reply, the Lord-Deputy acknowledges the differences between the Provost and Fellows "are

---

Biog. It may be observed that the "Lycidas" of Milton was Edward King, son of Sir John King, Knt, an Irish Privy Councillor. King was a pupil of Chappel, and was drowned on his way to Ireland in 1637.

16. See Stubbs' *History*, p. 67 (note). Chappel was likewise reputed to be the author of *The Whole Duty of Man, Rawdon Papers*, p. 51. The authorship is discussed in Nichol's *Lit. Anecdotes*, ii, p. 597–604. There were at this time six Senior Fellows of the College whose Fellowships were worth £9 a year with diet, and eight Junior Fellows with a salary of £3 a year and diet; sixty poor scholars, whose scholarships were only worth their diet, and about fifteen Fellow Commoners.

17. Strafford to Laud, August 23rd, 1634.

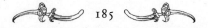

grown very high." The Archbishop regrets that "so great differences should be revealed in view of so many Romanists as swarm there, and cannot but look upon it with joy."

To Chappel, the Provostship proved anything but a bed of roses. He was attacked on all sides — "*Ruunt facto agmine In me profana turba, Romae Genevaeque.*" Eventually he was found to give so much trouble that those who had the interest of the College at heart were glad to get rid of him at any cost, and a place was found for him in the See of Cork. The King, however, seems to have stood by him, and granted him leave to hold the Provostship for eighteen months in commendam with the bishopric. He also won the approval of the Lord-Deputy, who wrote, "I have so great an opinion of his government and integrity that I am putting my son thither under his eye and care, by which you will judge I purpose not to have him one of Prynne's disciples."

Ussher and Chappel do not seem to have hit it off. Chappel hints that the Primate was not pleased with him because he had not gone down to wait on him at Drogheda as his predecessor had done on his appointment, and he goes on to attribute most of the College troubles to Ussher's interference.

One of the "charges brought against Chappel was that he was "an Arminian," which probably meant that he was too much of a Churchman. Another was that he was an "Irish Canterbury."[18] On his resignation, the Provostship was conferred in 1640 on Richard Washington, B.D., Fellow of University College, Oxford, and thus the long reign of Cambridge Provosts was broken, although the choice still remained in favour of an English divine to rule over an Irish university.[19] Washington was only a short time Provost,

---

18. This was a favourite phrase used towards obnoxious Churchmen. Bramhall, amongst others, enjoyed the title; he was also dubbed by the Presbyterians, "Bishop Bramble." — Dict. *Nat.Biog.*

19. Fuller brings the charge against the College that it was perpetually "Cantabrising" in its appointments. — Church *Hist.*, iii, p.137. He had previously spoken of the University as "a colony of Cambridge." — Ditto, p. 134.

as he fled from Dublin in the following year, on the outbreak of the Rebellion, and returned to Oxford, where he was re-elected a Fellow. He saved himself from ejection by turning Cromwellian.[20]

Probably a less understood prelate never existed than Laud, Archbishop of Canterbury. There is almost no enormity of which he has not been accused. Erastianism is a favourite charge brought against him, and the statutes he succeeded in getting drawn up for the better government of Trinity College, Dublin, have been put down to his desire to Erastianise that institution, and place the appointment to the Provostship entirely in the hands of the Crown. It has also been said that he desired to crush out Puritanism, and establish High Churchism within the walls of the College. Now none of these charges can be proved. The fact is, they are very far from the truth. Laud was not the original mover in the matter of the new statutes, and he was very unwillingly dragged into the controversy. He had enough on his hands without being troubled with the internal affairs of the University of Dublin.

Archbishop Ussher was anything but an extreme Churchman, as it was at his solicitation that Laud, much against his will, accepted the Chancellorship. "I advised them," writes Ussher to the English Primate, "to pitch upon no other but yourself, which they did with all alacrity. If your Grace will deign to receive that poor society under the shadow of your wings, you shall put a further tie of observance not upon that only, but upon me also, who had my whole breeding there."[21]

Laud did not wish for the office, and wrote back to Lord Strafford, "As for the College, I am very sorry they have chosen me Chancellor, and if they will follow the directions I have given them by my Lord Primate, I hope they will send me a resignation that I may give it over, and your Lordship be chosen, being upon the place and able to do them much good." It was only on the receipt of a second and pressing letter from Archbishop Ussher,

---

20. Walker's *Sufferings of the Clergy,* p. 135.

21. Ussher's *Works,* xv, p. 572.

representing the disorganised condition of the University, that Laud consented to take the Chancellorship. Now as to Laud's share in the new statutes. It was not the first attempt to revise the original and necessarily imperfect statutes of Queen Elizabeth. Bedell had already attempted something of the kind, and when Ussher pressed the Chancellorship on Laud, it was with a view partly to give the College a body of new statutes for its better government. *"Miserere domus labentis"* writes Ussher. The new statutes were as a matter of fact modeled on those drawn up by Bedell. The principal change made by Laud in the internal affairs of the College was making the Fellowships tenable for life instead of for seven years; and he likewise took steps to promote the study of the Irish language.

"There is no doubt," says the latest historian of the University of Dublin, "of the wisdom which is conspicuous in Laud's emendation of the statutes, and of the excellent fruit which it afterwards produced in the growth and success of the College."[22] The expression on the part of Laud that "the Romanists" should hear of the wranglings going on inside of the College walls, proves how little the Primate's sympathies lay in that direction, although his enemies never tire of asserting that Laud was in heart a Roman Catholic. This was not the only occasion when Laud referred in hostile terms to the "Romanists." Congratulating Ussher on the termination of the meeting of Convocation a short time later, he wrote, "If you should have risen from this Convocation in heat, God knows when or how the Church would have cooled again, had the cause of differences been never so slight. By which means the Romanists, which is too strong a party already, would both have strengthened and made a scorn of you."[23] This surely is not

---

22. Stubbs' *History*, p. 78.

23. Ussher's *Works*, xvi, p. 7. "It was Laud's constant effort to prove that Irish Catholicism need not be Roman, and in this Strafford was of one heart and mind with him." — Hutton's *Laud*, p. 168.

the language of a Romaniser! What really moved the English Primate was the disorganised state of Trinity College.

"For that College, as your Lordship has often acknowledged unto me," writes Laud to the Lord-Deputy Strafford, "both by letter and otherwise, having been as ill-governed as any other in Christendom, or worse, will never be able to recover, and to settle to be a good seminary for that Church, if both the power and the credit of the Provost be not upheld by his superiors; and should a Provost that is otherwise vigilant and careful err in some circumstantial business, it is far better for the publick, if not to maintain his errors, yet to pass by them rather than to give countenance and encouragement for such young heads as seek for no other liberty than that which may make way for licentiousness."

"My Lord, upon this ground I could heartily wish the heats which, I doubt not, have been in this business had been forborne, or that yet, your lordship could bring it to that temper that both parties would lay down the cause and not put me to give a public decision, which, as this case stands, may do some hurt which way soever the justice of the cause, upon full evidence, shall sway my judgment."[24]

It is evident from this that Archbishop Laud did not thrust himself into the affairs of Trinity College, but was a most unwilling arbiter of the differences which unhappily existed at the time. As to the charge of Erastianising, it is sufficient answer to point out that the change was merely a nominal one, since the Sovereign had interfered more or less with every nomination to the office since the founding of the University.

---

24. Strafford's *Letters,* Vol. ii, p. 36; Laud's true character has been defended by no one more eloquently than Mr. Gladstone, who says of him, "He was the patron not only of the saintly and heroic Bedell, but on the one hand of Chillingworth and Hales, on the other of Ussher, Hall, and Davenant, groups of names sharply severed in opinion, but unitedly known in the history of ability and learning." — Lecture at Oxford, Oct 24, 1892; see also Hutton's *Laud,* p. 152; and, for a similar (Presbyterian) opinion of Laud, Tulloch's *Rational Theology,* ii, p. 352–3.

CHAPTER XV

ARCHBISHOP USSHER'S PERSONAL APPEARANCE AND CHARACTER; PRIVATE LIFE IN DROGHEDA; "RELIGION OF THE ANCIENT IRISH"

Archbishop Ussher has been described as moderately tall, and of upright figure with brown hair and rich complexion. The gravity and benevolence of his countenance commanded respect and reverence.[1] His manners were those of a courteous gentleman, free from pride on the one hand, and too much softness on the other.

---

1. Parr's *Life,* p. 74. An original portrait of Ussher by Zuccheri, 1654, can be seen in the Provost's House, T.C.D. There is a copy of it in the Examination Hall, and an engraving in Elrington's *Life,* as also in the present volume. Eight engraved portraits of Ussher by different hands may be seen in the Library, T.C.D., presented by Edmund Bewley, LL.D. (E. U. 27). A bust of Ussher also stands in the Library. According to Parr, Ussher's face was "hard to hit." He never saw but one picture like him, and that was painted by [Sir Peter] Lely. This portrait, which was preserved by Sir T. Tyrrel at Shotover, gives the Archbishop an anxious, care-worn expression as if he felt the pressure of the times. It was sold about 1855, and its present locality is unknown.

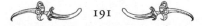

His fine constitution, which was temperately nourished, enabled him to endure long periods of study, which were sometimes protracted from the early hours of the morning to midnight, with intervals only for his episcopal duties, and a small amount of exercise. In his last years, his eyesight began to fail, and as he could only see to read in a strong light, he followed the sun from room to room, book in hand carrying on his studies.[2] Ussher's temper was mild and philosophic, and at the same time deeply affected by Christian principles. He used say, "If good people would but make goodness agreeable and smile instead of frowning in their virtue, how many would they win to the good cause!" According to his chaplain and biographer, Dr. Parr, "If he perceived any whom he accounted truly religious, sad and melancholy, he would often ask them why they were so, and if anything really troubled them? If not, he would proceed thus: 'If you have entirely devoted yourselves to the service of God, what reason have you to be melancholy, when (if you will seriously consider) none have more cause to be cheerful than those who live a holy and a virtuous life? By this your dejection you may bring an evil report upon religion; for people seeing you always sad will be apt to think 'tis that occasions it, and that you serve a hard Master, whose yoke is heavy and commands grievous, which will deter others; and scare them from the ways of piety and virtue, which you ought by no means to do, for sincere Christians may and ought to rejoice, and to show themselves cheerful; whereas the vicious and wicked have the greatest reason to be sad'; and as he advised others, so he himself was always of an even, cheerful temper, seldom troubled or decomposed."[3] At his palace in Drogheda, the Archbishop lived a homely and studious life.[4] He preached regularly every Sunday

---

2. Several references to his failing eyesight occur in Ussher's later correspondence. — See Vol. xvi, p. 562, 586; see also Bernard's *Life*, p.102.

3. Parr's *Life*, p. 84.

4. Ussher lived in Drogheda because he had no palace at Armagh, the city and cathedral having been burnt down by O'Neill in 1566 (the latter lest

morning, and in the afternoon one of his chaplains repeated the sermon in the private chapel to the servants and retainers, and any of the townspeople who chose to come in.

He had prayers four times a day, at 6 A.M. and 8 P.M., and chapel service before dinner and supper. He prized the Prayer-book, and left it in record that "he had a reverent and very high esteem for it, and that he should at any time have called it an idol was a shameless and most abominable untruth."[5] His entertainments were such as became his high station — "good and plenteous, but nothing curious or excessive." His chief recreation lay in walking or riding. He was fond of "telling stories, or relating the wise or witty sayings of other men, or such things as had occurred to his own observation; so that his company was always agreeable, and for the most part instructive; but still he would conform himself to the genius and improvement of those he conversed with, for, as with scholars he would discourse of matters of learning, so could he condescend to those of meaner capacities."[6]

He gave some useful hints to young students, which may well be reproduced here. He advised them to read the Fathers in chronological order, and then Church history, and to avoid thy schoolmen, as for the most part puzzling and unprofitable.

---

it might become a barrack for Saxon soldiers). Ussher uniformly uses the corrupted English form of the word "Tredagh." Englishmen, probably, have found it difficult to compass the Irish name. Drogheda — i.e., "the Bridge of the Ford" — was then one of the most important seaport towns in Ireland. The Deputies frequently resided there, at that time. The original charter was granted to the place by King John, with a right to bear his crest or half-moon and star, with the motto *Deus prasidium mercatura decus.* — See *Dublin Penny Journal,* p. 161, 356.

5. Parr's *Life,* p. 85. The form of words used in the ordination of priests by the Church of England: "Receive the Holy Ghost," &c., "whosoever sins," &c., was much approved of by Ussher. — Bernard's *Clavi Trabales,* p. 55. "He so much approved of set forms of prayer in public that he always kept himself to one constant short pathetical prayer before his sermon with little alteration." — Ditto.

6. Parr's *Life,* p. 85.

We are told that he was particularly averse to the introduction of new terms into theology, and to this end quoted the saying, *Qui nova facit verba, nova gignit dogmata.*[7] According to Ussher, solid and useful learning would be best promoted, first, by learned notes and illustrations of the Bible; secondly by censuring and inquiring into the ancient councils and works of the Fathers; thirdly by the orderly writing and digesting of ecclesiastical history; fourthly by gathering together whatsoever may concern the state of the Jews from the destruction of Jerusalem to the present age; fifthly by collecting of all the Greek and Roman histories and digesting them into one body.[8] We get a most interesting insight into the life and doings of the Archbishop at this time (1634) from a small volume of travels believed to have been written by Sir William Brereton, of Cheshire, during that year. On July 8th he finds himself at Tredaugh (Drogheda). He speaks of the town as one of the largest and best built he has seen in Ireland. The quay is like that of Newcastle, and the water channels remind him of those he has seen in Dutch towns.

The corporation and townspeople he notes as "popishly affected." The Lord Primate's palace is near the east gate, and "a neat, handsome, and convenient house," built by Primate Hampton.[9] It is four square, of wood, rough cast and not high; a handsome, plain, though long and narrow hall; two dining rooms; one little neat gallery which leads into the chapel . . . there is a little pair of organs therein." "Here Ussher preached constantly every Lord's

---

7. Parr's *Life*, p. 97.

8. Ditto, p. 96.

9. The Archbishop had two residences, one in Palace Street, Drogheda, the other at Termonfechan (the church-land of St. Feighan), a few miles distant, and of which some ruins may still be seen, which are called the "Bishop's Castle." Several interesting antiquities, including holy wells and a "baptizing stone," may be seen in the neighborhood. — See O'Donovan's *Letters on the Ord. Survey of Ireland, Roy. Irish Academy,* under "Louth," p. 66–7. The palace in Drogheda ceased to be an episcopal residence in Primate Boulter's time, and no trace of it now remains.

Day in the morning." One of the dining rooms has the arms of the See and bishopric, together with Hampton's own arms, and underneath is the inscription, *Fac tu similiter.* There is a pretty neat garden, and cut in a grass bank the words, "O man, remember the last great day." Such is a picture of an episcopal residence in Ireland in the seventeenth century. We learn that at the time there were two churches in Drogheda.

The Archbishop was in the habit of preaching in "the great church."[10] The communion-table was placed "lengthwise in the aisle." The chancel not being used, was "wholly neglected and in bad repair." Arriving in Dublin, he finds that Ussher preaches every Lord's Day when in town in St. Owen's (Audoen's) Church at eight A.M. He hears him preach, and thinks of him as "the most excellent able man and most abundantly holy gracious man" he has ever heard. He also dines with him. "Dr. Ussher is a tall, proper, comely man, about fifty-six years of age; a plain, familiar, courteous man, who spends the whole day in his study except meal-time. . . . He is a most holy, well-affected Bishop, a good companion, a man of good discourse." Being asked as to the *Book of Sports*, published by authority of James I and afterwards republished by order of Charles I, he said there was no clause therein commanding the ministers to read the book, but if were published in the church by the clerk or churchwardens, that was enough.

The writer meets at dinner Dr. Richardson, Bishop of Ardagh, and his wife, "a tall, handsome, fat woman."[11] On

---

10. This was St. Peter's, one of the finest ecclesiastical buildings of that time in Ireland. Here, numerous Synods were held. The steeple was reputed to be the highest in the world. It was blown down by a storm in 1548, and replaced by a wooden one, which lasted till Cromwell fired the church, when it is said 2,000 perished by fire and sword. No vestige of the original building remains. — See *Dublin Penny Journal*, i, p. 357–8; O'Donovan's *Letters,* &c., as above, p. 45–8.

11. "Ussher," says his biographer, Dr. Parr, "fed heartily on plain wholesome meat without sauce, and was better pleased with a few dishes than with great varieties. . . . He liked not tedious meals, and it was a weariness to him to sit long at table." — *Life,* p. 83.

July 12th, he again hears the Archbishop preach, and repeats his praise that he is "a most holy and heavenly man, and as pregnant witted as any he has ever heard. He tells us how the Archbishop's study in Dublin, (his town house; as we have seen, was on Hoggan Green, now College Green) was placed at a good distance so as to prevent distraction from visitors. He sees no one except from eleven to one and about supper-time. The rest of the day, from five in the morning until six in the evening, is usually spent in his study.[12] Such was Ussher as painted by a contemporary, at once the Christian prelate, the learned and thoughtful scholar, a lover of hospitality, a lover of good men.

We must now return to the outward life of Ussher; and consider the part he played in the great controversies that were still troubling the times he lived in. Ever mindful of the importance of vindicating the position of the Reformed Church of Ireland as the true inheritor of primitive and scriptural doctrine, we find him in 1631 in London, publishling a second

---

12. Sir William Brereton's *Travels,* p. 134–40. The original MS. had a strange experience, and passed through many hands. Among others, it was seen by Sir Walter Scott, who thought highly of it, and advised its publication. Eventually the Chetham Society issued it from the press. Sir William Brereton visited Ussher in Drogheda in 1634. Four years later, the Archbishop entertained an illustrious visitor in the person of the Lord-Deputy Strafford, who in a letter to Archbishop Laud, Nov. 27th, 1638, details some of his experiences: "I was one night with his Grace at Drogheda, where his Lordship made me a very noble welcome, found there the best house I have seen in Ireland, built by Primate Hampton; yet not so much as a communion table in the chapel, which seemed to me something strange. No bowing there I awarrant you." — Strafford's *Letters,* ii, p. 249. Laud writes back to Strafford: "Truly I would wonder that the chapel should have never a communion-table in it, save that I knew that some divines are of opinion that nothing belonging to that Sacrament is aught *extra usum,* and do therefore set the table in any corner (good enough for it), save only at the time of administration." — Ditto, p. 263. The same abuse existed in Christ Church Cathedral. — See Heylin, quoted by Urwick, *Early Hist. of T.C.D.,* p. 86.

and enlarged edition of his valuable essay on *The Religion of the Ancient Irish and Britons.*[13]

In the dedication to his "very much honoured friend," Sir Christopher Sipthorp, one of the Justices of the King's Bench in Ireland, he declares he was "induced to publish the work with the hope that a true discovery of the religion anciently professed in this kingdom might prove a special motive to induce his poor countrymen to consider a little better of the old an and true way from whence they been hitherto misled." The work was intended to point out to the Irish Romanists in particular that the Papal

---

13. Ussher's *Works,* Vol. iv. It was while collecting materials for this work that Ussher came on the famous *Book of Kells,* now in the Library of Trinity College, Dublin. The MS. has the following note written by Ussher: "Aug. 24th, 1621 — I received the leaves of the booke, and found them to be in number 344. He who reckoned before me counted six score to the hundred, — Ja. Ussher [Episcopus], Midensis Elect." The monastery of Kells, where this famous MS. was preserved, was surrendered to Henry VIII by its last abbot, Richard Plunket, in 1539. The MS. afterwards came into the hands of Gerald Plunket, harbour-master of Dublin. — Gilbert's *Cal. Anc. Records* ,ii, p. 44–5; *Nat. MSS. of Ireland; p.* 12–21. From him it came to Ussher. Among other valuable MSS. acquired by Ussher, and now for the most part in the Library of Trinity College, may be enumerated the *Codex Usserianus,* a MS. of the Gospels, probably of the sixth century, an old Latin text of the Hiberno-British recension *(Class* A. 4. 15). It shows, some interlineations in small Irish characters, and entries in the hand of Ussher. — See *Evangeliorum Versio Antehieronymiana ex Codice Usseriano,* &c. Edited, with preface, by Dr. Abbott, Professor of Hebrew, T.C.D. An imperfect copy of the *Crede Mihi,* an archiepiscopal Register of the See of Dublin, with a note in Ussher's handwriting attributing it to the year 1295. The *Psalter of Bishop Rhyddmarch,* Bishop of St. David's, who died at the close of the eleventh century. The MS. had belonged to Bedell and bears his autograph. Ussher quotes from it in his "Religion of the Ancient Irish." *The Book of Lecan,* one of the most important survivals of old Gaelic literature, compiled about the middle of the fifteenth century. This MS. has had a chequered history. It came from Ussher to Trinity College, then disappeared, and turned up in the Irish College at Paris. It is now deposited in the Library of the Royal Irish Academy. See also Reeve's *Adamnan,* p. xxvi, xxxviii, 334.

religion was not the old religion, and to meet their objections, that "they followed the religion of their forefathers, and would never depart from it." It is not too much to say that this work, together with his *Answer to a Jesuit*, already noticed, has proved a great storehouse from whence modern controversialists have armed themselves with weapons against the errors and assumptions of the Church of Rome.

Very little of substantial value has since been added to the controversy, and Ussher must be acknowledged to take rank with Laud, Jeremy Taylor, and Isaac Barrow, as one of the most learned and exhaustive of the defenders of the Protestant faith against Romish innovations. The treatise consists of eleven short chapters, into which an enormous amount of matter is clearly and logically condensed. The following are the subjects treated of: (I) The Holy Scriptures; (II) Grace, Free Will, Faith, Works, Justification, Sanctification; (III) Purgatory and Prayers for the Dead; (IV) of the Worship of God, the Public Form of Liturgy, the Sacrifice and Sacrament of the Lord's Supper; (V) of Chrism, Sacramental Confession Penance, Absolution, Marriage, Divorce, and Single Life in the Clergy; (VI) of the Discipline of our Ancient Monks, of Abstinence from Meat; (VII) of the Church and various states thereof, especially in the days of Antichrist; of Miracles also, and of the Head of the Church; (VIII) of the Pope's Spiritual Jurisdiction, and how little footing it had gotten at first within these parts; (IX) of the Controversy which the Britons, Picts, and Irish maintained against the Church of Rome, touching the Celebration of Easter; (X) of the height that the opposition betwixt the Roman party and that of the British and Scottish grew into, and how the Doctors of the Scottish and Irish side have been accounted most eminent men in the Catholic Church, notwithstanding their disunion from the Bishop of Rome; (XI) of the Temporal Power which the Pope's followers would directly entitle him unto over the kingdom of Ireland, together with the indirect power which he challengeth in absolving subjects from the obedience which they owe to their temporal governors. At the end is drawn up a catalogue of some hundred authors cited in the discourse, ranging from Eumenius Rhetor, A.D. 300, to Polydorus Virgilius, A.D. 1530, proving with what conscientious toil the writer pursued his task. As the subject is a very important one, and full of the deepest interest, we shall glance briefly at some of the most valuable conclusions pointed out by Ussher in his work. He first of all shows how the Holy Scriptures were studied by the ancient Irish and British Churches. He quotes Sedulius, Bede, &c., to this effect.

Bede, for example, witnesses of Bishop Aidan that "all such as went in his company, whether they were of the clergy or the laity, were tied to exercise themselves either in the reading of Scriptures or in the learning of Psalms." Proof is also adduced from the same authority of others that from the time of their very childhood they had a care to learn the Holy Scriptures, and that "in those days it was not thought a thing unfit that even children should give themselves to the study of the Bible." Ussher next goes on to prove *more suo* that the doctrines of "Predestination, Grace, Free Will, Faith, Works, Justification, and Sanctification" were all held and enunciated by the ancient Irish, referring to the teaching of Sedulius and Claudius, "two of our most famous divines," in proof of his assertion. The opposite doctrines he notes as first brought into the Church by Pelagius and Celestius, "the greatest depressors of God's grace and the advancers of man's abilities." "Among our Irish, the grounds of sound doctrine in these points were at the beginning well settled by Palladius and Patricius, sent hither by Celestinus, Bishop of Rome. And when the poison of the Pelagian heresy, about two hundred years after that, began to break out among them, the clergy of Rome, in the year of our Lord DCXXXIX, during the vacancy of the See upon the death of Severinus, directed their letters unto them for the prevention of this growing mischief."[14]

As against, the Romish Purgatory, he proves the ancient Irish Church knew of only three states, and quotes to that effect

---

14. Ussher's *Works*, iv, p. 259–60.

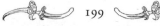

"the book ascribed unto" St. Patrick, *De tribus habitaculis,* in which he says, "There be three habitations under the power of Almighty God: the first, the lowermost, and the middle. The highest whereof is called the kingdom of God or the kingdom of heaven; the lowermost is termed hell, the middle is named the present world, or the circuit of the earth." "The blessed are called to the kingdom prepared for them from the beginning of the world; the cursed are driven into everlasting fire prepared for the devil and his angels."[15] He likewise quotes Sedullus to the effect that after the end of this life "either death or life succeedeth"; and a saying of Claudius, "Christ did take upon himself our punishment and without the guilt, that thereby He might loose our guilt and finish also our punishment."

Reference is also made on this subject to "that ancient canon of one of our Irish Synods," wherein it is affirmed that "the soul being separated from the body is presented before the judgment-seat of Christ, who rendereth its own unto it according as it hath done"; and that "neither the archangel can lead it into life until the Lord hath judged it, nor the devil transport it into pain unless the Lord do damn it." Nor did the early Irish Church offer up prayers for the dead, in the Roman sense, as Ussher plainly proves; although, as he freely allows, it was a universal practice to make eucharistic references in prayer, and especially at the celebration of the Holy Communion, to those "whose souls were supposed at the same instant to have rested in bliss."[16] He quotes Adanman[17] as reporting how Columbkille "caused all things to be prepared for the sacred ministry of the Eucharist when he had seen the soul of St. Brendan received by the holy angels, and that he did the like when Columbanus, Bishop of Leinster, departed this life . . . whereby it appeareth that an honourable

---

15. Ditto, p. 265. This writing is now universally recognised not to be Patrician. — See Todd's *St. Patrick,* p. 485 sq.

16. Ussher's *Works,* iv, p. 269.

17. *Life of St. Columba,* lib. Iii, cap. 15.

commemoration of the dead was herein intended, and a sacrifice of thanksgiving for their salvation, rather than of propitiation for their sins."[18]

On the subject of "the Sacrifice and Sacrament of the Lord's Supper," Ussher proves that the ancient Irish Church "did not distinguish the Sacrifice from the Sacrament, but used the name of Sacrifice indifferently both for that which was offered unto God and of that which was given to and received by the communicant;"[19] and he quotes for the first term the words of Gallus: "My master Columbanus is accustomed to offer unto the Lord the Sacrifice of salvation in brazen vessels"; and for the second expression "of giving the Sacrifice to man," what is noted in one of the ancient Synods of Ireland, that a bishop by his testament may bequeath a certain portion of his goods for a legacy to the priest that giveth him the Sacrifice, and of the receiving of the Sacrifice from the hands of a minister as in that sentence attributed to St. Patrick: "He who deserveth not to receive the Sacrifice in his life, how can it help him after his death? . . ." "The Sacrifice of the elder times," says Ussher, "was not like unto the new Mass of the Romanists, wherein the priest alone doth all."[20]

As to the modern Roman use of giving "the Eucharist in one kind only" to the laity, Ussher shows how their ancestors "in the use of their Sacrament received the Eucharist in both kinds, not being so acute as to discern betwixt the things that belonged unto the integrity of the Sacrifice and of the Sacrament, because in truth they took the one like the other."[21]

The members of the old Irish Church knew nothing of the doctrine of concomitance. They "received the Body of the Lord and sipped His Blood." As for the argument that the ancient writers quoted, all specified to the receiving, not of bread and

---

18. Ussher's *Works,* iv, p. 269.

19. Ussher's *Works,* iv, p. 278.

20. Ditto, p. 278.

21. Ussher's *Works,* iv, p. 279.

wine, but of the Body and Blood of Christ, and that that makes for the doctrine of transubstantiation, Ussher replies, "For as much as Christ Himself at the first institution of His Holy Supper did say expressly, 'This is my Body' and 'This is my Blood,' he deserveth not the name of Christian that will question the truth of that saying or refuse to speak in that language which he hath heard his Lord and Master use before him."[22] The only question is "in what sense and after what manner these things must be conceived to be His Body and Blood." He goes on to show they can only be such "in Sacrament and mystery." The doctrine of Claudius that "the Sacrament is in its own nature bread and wine, but the Body and Blood of Christ by mystical relation was in effect the same with that which long afterwards was here in Ireland delivered by Henry Crumpe, the Monk of Baltinglass, that "the Body of Christ in the Sacrament of the altar was only a looking-glass to the Body of Christ in heaven."[23]

With regard to the term "Mass," now confined by the Roman Catholic Church to the celebration of the Eucharist, Ussher shows that the public liturgy or service of the church was of old named the Mass, even then also when prayers only were said without the celebration of the Holy Communion, so that the last Mass that St. Colme (St. Columbkille) was ever present at is noted by Adamnan to have been *Vespertinalis Dominica nostris missa*, the evening Mass being in all likelihood that "which we call evensong or evening prayer."[24] In the matter of public worship, Ussher shows how independent the Irish Church was until the time of Gilbertus, Malachias and others, the Pope's legates from time to time in Ireland, succeeded in forcing upon the Church the "one Catholic and Roman office."

---

22. Ditto, p. 285.

23. Ussher's *Works*, iv, p. 285.

24. Ditto, iv, p. 276–7. *Cf.* Shakespeare's *Romeo and Juliet*: "Are you at leisure, holy father, now? Or shall I come to you at evening mass?" — Act iv, Scene 1.

The subjection was completed at the Synod of Cashel, when it was enacted that "all divine offices of Holy Church should from thenceforth be handled in all parts of Ireland according as the Church of England did observe them,"[25] the acts of which Synod (presided over by the Bishop of Lismore, as the Pope's legate) were duly confirmed by the authority of Henry II A.D. 1172. How little does the modern Irish Roman Catholic realise the fact that the religion which has so strong a hold upon him, and whose impulses intensify his antagonism towards English rule and English institutions was originally planted in his country by English authority!

In the fifth chapter, Ussher proves that the early Church in Ireland knew nothing of the peculiar doctrines of Rome on the subjects of chrism, sacramental confession, penance, absolution, marriage, divorce, and the celibacy of the clergy. Confession, Ussher allows, was made "upon special occasions both publicly and privately," as well that they might receive counsel and direction for their recovery as that they might be partakers of the benefit of the keys for the quieting of their troubled consciences."

He adds: "In absolving such as be truly penitent, we willingly yield that the pastors of God's Church do remit sins after their manner — that is to say, ministerially and improperly, so that the privilege of forgiving sins properly and absolutely be still reserved unto God alone."[26] In proof of this, Ussher refers to many writers, including Claudius, Bede, &c.

On the subject of enforced clerical celibacy, Ussher points to the decree of "the Synod held by St. Patrick, Auxilius and Isserninus, wherein a special order is taken that the wives of the clergy should not walk abroad with their heads uncovered"; also to the memorable statement of St. Patrick in His "Confession" that he had to his father Calphurnius a deacon, and to his grandfather Politus a priest.[27]

---

25. Acts of the Synod in Giraldus Cambr. *Hib. Exp.* part i, ch. 34.

26. Ussher's *Works*, iv, p. 290.

27. Ditto, p. 294.

The sixth chapter is devoted to proving that the members of the early British Churches eschewed the false sanctity taught by Rome to live in abstinence from meats and drinks. "Their monks fasted indeed, and gave up their worldly goods, but under colour of forsaking all, they did not hook all unto themselves; nor under semblance of devotion did they devour widow's houses. They held begging to be no point of perfection, but remembered the words of the Lord Jesus, how he said, 'It is more blessed to give than take.' " Gildas [A.D. 540] is quoted: "Abstinence from corporal meats is unprofitable without charity.

They are, therefore, the better men who do not fast much, nor abstain from the creature of God beyond measure, but carefully keep their heart within pure before God, from whence they know cometh the issue of life, than they who eat no flesh, nor take delight in secular dinners, nor ride with coaches or horses, thinking themselves hereby to be, as it were, superior to others, upon whom death hath entered through the windows of haughtiness."[28]

The seventh chapter is devoted to a consideration of the true Church and it's Head, and Claudius is appropriately quoted: "The famous place (Matt. Xvi, 18) whereupon our Romanists lay the main foundations of the papacy Claudius expoundeth in this sort: *'Upon this rock I will build My Church';* that is to say, upon the Lord and Saviour, who granted unto His faithful knower, lover, and confessor the participation of his own name, that from petra (the rock) he should be called Peter. The Church is builded upon Him, because only by the faith and love of Christ, by the receiving of the Sacraments of Christ, by the observation of the commandments of Christ, we come to the inheritance of the elect and eternal life; as witnesseth the Apostle who saith, 'other foundation can no man lay beside that which is laid, which is Christ Jesus.' "[29] Claudius Scotus flourished A.D. 815.

---

28. Ussher's *Works,* iv, p. 308.

29. Ussher's *Works,* iv, p. 315.

Claudius indeed acknowledges a kind of primacy for St. Peter, but "he addeth withal that St. Paul also was chosen in the same manner to have the primacy in founding the Churches of the Gentiles." Gildas holds that "to every true priest it is said, 'Thou art Peter, and upon this rock I will build my Church,' " and that "unto every holy priest it is promised, 'Whatsoever thou shalt bind on earth shall be bound in heaven,' " &c. "The good priests of Britain do lawfully sit in the chair of St. Paul, but the bad with unclean feet, they usurp the seat of the Apostle Peter." As to the titles and prerogatives which the Pope II now peculiarly challengeth unto himself, they have been previously shared by other bishops, e.g., the Bishop of Kildare — "honoured by Cogitosus with the style of *Summus Sacerdos* and *Summus Pontifex.*"[30]

In the eighth chapter, Ussher carefully goes into the consideration of the Pope's spiritual jurisdiction, and proves how little his authority was recognised in the early ages of the Irish Church.

It is plain that he accepts the tradition (by no means established) that St. Patrick received a legation from the Pope, but goes onto say there was no further instance of papal interference with the affairs, spiritual or temporal, of Ireland until the time of Gillebert. "We read of sundry archbishops that have been in this land betwixt the days of St. Patrick and of Malachias; what one of them can be named that ever sought for a pall from Rome?"[31]

As to appeals made from time to time to the See of Rome to settle vexed questions, Ussher candidly acknowledges that if he himself had lived in St. Patrick's days, for the resolution of a doubtful question he would as willingly have listened to the judgment of the Church of Rome in those days of its integrity as to the determination of any Church in the whole world. That

---

30. Ussher's *Works,* p. 315–8.

31. Ussher's *Works,* iv, p. 320.

the Irish doctors of ancient times were wont to consult with the Bishop of Rome, Ussher freely allows, but that they "received his resolutions as oracles of truth" is the point, he says, "we would fain see proved."[32]

It was originally, as Ussher shows, through the Ostmen sending over their bishops to Canterbury for consecration, for the Danish settlements in Dublin, Waterford, and Limerick, since they despised Irish orders, and afterwards through the English Conquest under Henry II, that the Church of Rome effectually established her influence over the Church of Ireland. It is to the developing of this point that the last three chapters of the work are devoted. The difference between the early British and Irish Churches and that of Rome in the matter of observing the festival of Easter is one incontrovertible evidence of the original independence of these communions of the See of Rome. A black-letter poem of one Taliessyn, honoured with the title of Ben Beirdth — that is, "the chief of the bards" — is given by Ussher to prove the warm antagonism which existed in those early times to the papal claims:

> Wo be to that priest, y born
> That will not cleanly weed his corn
> And preach his charge among.
> Wo be to that shepherd (I say)
> That will not watch his fold alway,
> As to his office doth belong.
> Wo be to him that doth not keep
> From Romish wolves his sheep
> With staff and weapon strong.

---

32. Ditto, p.330. On the subject of appeals to Rome, Fra. Puller's able work, *The Primitive Saints and the See of Rome,* should be consulted. The above deliverance of Ussher has been frequently taken advantage of in a garbled form by Roman Catholic writers. See, for a striking example, Archbishop Moran's *Essays,* p. 121.

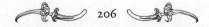

With great acuteness, Ussher traces in the closing pages of this treatise the steps taken by the Church of Rome to hand over Ireland with her Church to the authority of England, that through the rule of the latter kingdom, now completely subjugated to her spiritual power, she might gain a similar ascendancy over the national and hitherto independent Church of Ireland. "In the year of our Lord 1155, the first Bull was sent unto him [Henry II], the sum whereof is thus laid down in a second Bull, directed unto him by Alexander III, the immediate successor of the other. 'Following the steps of reverend Pope Adrian and attending the fruit of your desire, we ratify and confirm his grant concerning the dominion of the kingdom of Ireland, conferred upon you, reserving unto St. Peter and the Holy Church of Rome as in England, so in Ireland, the yearly pension of one penny out of every house.' " At the national Synod held, as we have shown above, at Cashel, the heads of the Irish Church, now thoroughly corrupted by English gold and influence, most ignominiously consented to the bargain, and so passed away at the same moment the primitive purity and independence of Ireland's Church. It is a chapter in the history of the country that the modern Roman Catholic Church in Ireland would do well to study; she would then see that she owes to the England against whom she has perpetually warred, that very unreformed faith to which her sons and daughters cleave with such tenacity.

It was, in fact, the Church of England, at that time ruled by Rome, that was then established in Ireland. The Bull of Pope Innocent VIII, dated February 1484, constituting the collegiate church of Galway, enacts that the College shall consist of "one warden and eight presbyters, all civilised men, and duly holding *the rites and order of the Church of England* in the celebration of Divine service"; and this, in consequence of the resistance still offered to the Roman ritual by the "wild Irish highland men," outside the town, who refused to conform.[33]

---

33. See Hardiman's *Galway,* p. 681; and O'Flaherty's *Far Connaught,* p. 167, where the original is given.

At the close of his work, Ussher adds an interesting note, mentioning the principles on which he had wrought throughout, inviting all his authorities to be examined by his opponents, and saying that his intention has been "to deal fairly, and not to desire the concealing of anything that may lead to the true discovery of the state of former times, whether it may seem to make for him or against him."

Another work from the prolific pen of the Archbishop was published in the following year, 1632. It is his *Veterum Epistolarum Hibernicarum Sylloge,*[34] a collection of letters with learned notes thereon, treating of Irish ecclesiastical matters, from the time of Gregory the Great to the end of the fifth century. Some of the notes bear the name of Bedell, who had evidently assisted Ussher in compiling the volume.[35] Three poetical effusions of Columbamus will be found in the collection, which is of extreme interest to all students of ancient Irish Church history.[36]

---

34. Ussher's *Works,* iv, p. 385–572.

35. Ussher had a high opinion of Bedell's attainments. It is on record that on one occasion, when several of the Bishops were being entertained at Strafford's table in Dublin, one of the party said, "We are all talking, but my Lord Kilmore saith nothing," to whom Dr. Ussher replied, "Broach him, and you will find good liquor in him." Bedell was then asked some questions on the subject of "faith," when he so puzzled them that they all fell a laughing, except Bedell himself, "and no man did ask him any more questions." — See Clogy's *Memoirs of Bedell,* p. 151; Bayle's *Dict.,* iii, p. 139.

36. On the *Sylloge,* see Dr. Stokes' *Ireland and. the Celtic Church,* p. 209–10.

CHAPTER XVI

USSHER AND THE PRESBYTERIANS; THE QUESTION OF EPISCOPACY; AN EIRENICON

The relation of Archbishop Ussher to the Presbyterians, now becoming an important colony in the North of Ireland, has been the subject of much discussion. On one side it has been attempted to be proved that Ussher recognised the orders of the Presbyterian Church, and was anxious that its ministers should be retained in the benefice which they held. The opposite view is as strongly maintained by others, who assert that the Archbishop has been quite misrepresented. The contradictory statements made on each side render it difficult to arrive at the exact truth, but the facts of the case seem to lean toward the view that Ussher was prepared at one time to recognise the validity of Presbyterian orders, and to sanction the occupation of incumbencies in the North of Ireland by Presbyterian ministers. One of these latter — a Mr. Blair — was hospitably entertained by Ussher at his palace in Drogheda, and, if we are to believe him, enjoyed the approval of the Archbishop, who lamented the differences that kept them apart.

It required a letter from Laud, then Bishop of London, to the Lord-Deputy Strafford, to inaugurate a severer *regime*, and so defeat the bold bid on the part of Scottish Presbyterian ministers for the benefices of the Church of Ireland by recalling Ussher to his obligation to maintain episcopal discipline in the Church. He writes to say that the King's pleasure that Ussher would see the jurisdiction of the Church established in Ireland, to be maintained both against the Recusants and all other Factionists, and that he should do his best endeavor to stop all such rumours as may dishearten the Bishops in God's service and his.[1]

Sir James Hamilton and other Scottish settlers in the North of Ireland had acquired along with their lands the patronage of certain benefices, to which they nominated Presbyterian ministers, and it will be readily seen how action of this kind was likely to introduce disorder into the Church. Unfortunately, the two Bishops who the presided over the dioceses of Down and Connor, and Raphoe respectively — Drs. Echlin and Knox, themselves of Scottish extraction — were not averse to making things as easy as possible for their countryman.

After a manner these ministers submitted to episcopal ordination, but their hearts did not go with their acts. Among those who thus accepted orders to qualify for their livings were Edward Brice,[2] Prebendary of Kilroot; James Glendinning, Vicar of Carmoney; Robert Cunningham, Rector of Holywood and Craigavad; Robert Blair, Rector of Bangor; James Hamilton, Rector of Ballywater; Josias Welsh, Rector of Templepatrick; Andrew Stewart, Rector of Kilbride; George Dunbar, Rector of Larne; and John Livingston, Rector of Killinchy. Of these, Blair

1. Strafford's *Letters*, I, p. 82.

2. Edward Brice was the first Presbyterian minister to settle in Ireland. In 1614, he had been deprived of his benefice in Scotland on the charge of adultery, but Bishop Echlin either disbelieved or condoned the offence, as he admitted him to the cure of Templecurran or Broad Island. His tomb may still be seen at Ballycorry in the county of Antrim. — See *Dist. Nat. Biography*, vi, p. 311; King's *Ch. Hist.*, p. 869.

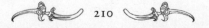

alone seems to have come into personal contact with Ussher, who sent for him with a view to obtaining information as to the state of the Church in the North of Ireland. If we are to believe Presbyterian authorities, these clergymen never really discarded their Presbyterianism, and only submitted to the form of episcopal ordination to secure their livings.

When Blair objected, Bishop Echlin said to him, "I must ordain you, else neither you nor I can answer the law, nor enjoy the land."[3] After repeated irregularities, Blair and Livingstone were suspended from the benefices. In the records of the Prerogative Court in Dublin for 1634 may be seen the names of the above ministers, with the date of their ordination as deacons and priests, and the names of the Bishops who ordained them.[4]

As to Ussher's personal feelings on the subject, we know he had a desire to deal gently with the Presbyterian party. He wrote to Bishop Echlin desiring him to "relax his erroneous censure," when the latter was inclined to bear severely on the irregular ministrations of these men, and he only forbore to throw his shield over them when the Lords Justices interfered by order from the King.[5]

---

3. See Grub's *Eccl. Hist. Scot.*, ii, p. 341; Mant's *Ch. Hist. Ireland*, i, pt. ii, p. 454. For the Presbyterian view, Reid's *Hist. Presb. Church Ireland*, i, p. 137, &c.; Adair's *Narrative*, p. 25, &c.; Killen's *Eccl. Hist. Ireland*, ii, p. 11–16, may be consulted.

4. Grub's *Eccl. Hist. Scot.* i, p. 343 (note). Grub mentions how Blair endeavoured to prevent Lord Claneboy and his lady kneeling to receive the Lord's Supper. As to the controversy between the Bishops and the Presbyterian ministers, especially on the point of kneeling to receive the Holy Communion, see Reid's *History*, i, p. 523–42.

5. Mant's History as above, p. 463–4. Bishop Leslie, who succeeded Echlin in 1635, went so far in his efforts to conciliate the Presbyterian ministers as to allow them to substitute the best translation they could find for the Scripture passages in the Prayer-book, and read from the Chronicles, the Song of Solomon, and the Revelation, and omit the lessons from the Apocrypha, if they only subscribed, which they refused to do. — See under "Brice," in *Dict. Nat. Biog.*, vi, p. 311.

At a later date, when it was going hard with the King, and Presbyterian influence was in the ascendant, Ussher took a leading part in seeking to bring about a reconciliation by drawing up an *eirenicon*, which he hoped might be accepted on both sides. Doubts have been thrown on the genuineness of this treatise, but Elrington so far recognises its claim that he publishes it in the twelfth volume of the Archbishop's collected works.[6] Ussher's plan was proposed in 1641, and seven years later, when matters were *in extremis* between the Royalists and the Parliamentarians, we shall find that he proposed his plan for a second time, with the approval of the Presbyterians, who accepted it as being as much as they could expect. The King was also won over to the same view, and even at the late hour the compromise might have been carried, except for the antagonism of the Parliamentary Commissioners, who were inexorable in their determination to abolish episcopacy altogether.

If we are to accept as genuine what is related of the Archbishop by Baxter, as well as by Dr. Bernard, Ussher's chaplain, he was certainly prepared to recognise the validity of the Presbyterian orders on the Continent. The later, in his *Life of Ussher*, gives the following extracts from a reply made by the Archbishop to a query on the subject: "Touching Mr. — I cannot call to mind that he ever proposed to me the question in your letter enclosed, neither do I know the Dr. who hath spread the report; but for the matter itself, I have declared my opinion to be that *Episcopus et Presbyter gradu tantum differunt non ordine*, and, consequently, in places where Bishops cannot be had, the ordination of Presbyters standeth valid.[7] Yet, on the other side, holding as I do that a Bishop hath the superiority in degree over a Presbyter, you may easily judge that the ordination made by such Presbyters as have severed themselves from those Bishops unto whom they had sworn canonical obedience, cannot

---

6. *Works*, xii, p. 527 sq.

7. This was the view of Cranmer, who went so far as to maintain that ordination might be effected by princes or even a congregation. — See Tulloch's *Rational Theology*, i, p. 47–9.

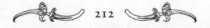

possibly by me be excused from being schismatical; and howsoever I must needs to think that the Churches which have no Bishops are thereby become very much defective in their government, and the Churches in France, who, living under a Popish power, cannot do what they would, are more excusable in this defect of the Low Countries that live under a free State; yet for testifying my communion with these Churches (which I do love and honour as true members of the Church Universal), I do profess that with like affection I should receive the blessed Sacrament at the hands of the Dutch ministers if I were in Holland, as I should do at the hands of the French ministers if I were in Charentone."[8]

We must not suppose from this, however, that Archbishop Ussher was indifferent to, or unmindful of, the claims of episcopacy, as the primitive and apostolic form of Church government. Quite the contrary; and, therefore, acting as he did, we may judge how intense was his desire to see peace established in the midst of the Commonwealth, and what sacrifices he was ready to make, with this object in view.

"Like Jonas, he was ready to be cast overboard for the stilling of the tempest."[9] No one was readier at a later date to defend episcopacy, with all the vast learning he had at his command, which is proved by his two tracts, one *The Original of Bishops and Metropolitans briefly laid down,* and the other, *A Geographical and*

---

8. Bernard's *Judgment of the Archbishop on Ordination,* p. 123–27. Ussher seems to have drawn a curious difference in this matter between foreign and home Presbyterian orders. Says Collier: "This learned prelate seems to have an overbalance of affection for the foreign Protestant Churches. This put upon him some strain to vindicate their orders and make their ministrations valid. For this purpose he revived the novelty of some of the schoolmen and made no scruple to affirm the office of Bishop and Presbyter was the same as to substance, and only different degrees of the same order. . . . But notwithstanding this charitable bias, Ussher made no difficulty to censure the practice of the English and Scotch Presbyterians. He would neither allow their orders nor communicate with them." — *Eccl. Hist.,* ii, p. 868.

9. Preface to *Clavi Trabales.*

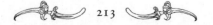

Historical Disquisition touching the Asia properly so called. The first of these he wrote at the request of Bishop Hall[10] and proves therein, from the Christian writings of the second and third centuries, how the Episcopate may be traced back to apostolic times.[11] According to Ussher, the angels of the Seven Churches represent "seven singular Bishops who were the constant presidents over the Churches." In the second tract, he proves that the Asia of the New Testament, and more particularly these Seven Churches, lay within the limits of Lydia, and that each of the seven cities was a metropolis, and were seats of the principle Churches in accordance with the civil arrangements of the Empire.

A third tract was a confirmation of the Judgment of Dr. Rainoldes touching the original of episcopacy, "more largely confirmed out of antiquity." All these tracts are published in Vol. vii of the Archbishop's works.

"The ground of episcopacy," Ussher maintains, "is derived partly from the pattern prescribed by God in the Old Testament, and partly from the imitation thereof brought in by the Apostles and confirmed by Christ himself in the time of the New. The government of the Church of the Old Testament was committed to the priests and Levites, unto whom the ministers of the New do now succeed, in like manner as our Lord's Day hath done unto their Sabbath, that it might be fulfilled which was spoken by the prophet touching the vocation of the Gentiles, "I will take of them for priests and for Levites, saith the Lord."[12] The writers

---

10. See Bishop Hall's letter to Ussher, making the suggestion. — Lewis, *Life of Hall,* p. 317. It was to be a Tractarian movement of the seventeenth century. Laud, Morton, and Davenant were to represent England, Bedell and Leslie, Ireland. Some of the Scottish Bishops were also able to help. The movement fell through, Ussher and Hall alone taking part in it.

11. "To do the Bishops justice and support the government of the Church, Archbishop Ussher published a seasonable tract to combat the Root, and Branch Bill; and prove episcopacy of apostolic institution." — Collier's *Eccl. Hist.,* ii, p. 808.

12. *Works,* vii, p. 43.

to whom Ussher appeals in favour of his thesis are Ignatius, Justin Martyr, Dionysius, Hegisippus, Irenaeus, Tertullian, Polycrates, and Clemens. "From St. John's time," says Ussher, "we have this continued succession of witnesses."[13]

As the Archbishop's treatise alluded to above, and which we have ventured to call an *eirenicon,* is not generally known, we will lay a few of its principal points before our reader.[14] The purpose had in view in drawing it up is clearly notified on the title-page: "The reduction of episcopacy unto the form of Synodical Government received in the ancient Church; proposed in the year 1641 as an expedient for the prevention of those troubles which afterwards did arise about the matter of Church Government."

"The original," says Dr. Bernard, in his address to the reader, "was given me by the most reverend Primate, some few years before his death, written throughout with his own hand, and of late have found it subscribed by himself and Doctor Holsworth, with a marginal note at the first proposition, which I have also added. In writing it," continues his chaplain, the Archbishop was "far from the least suspicion to be biassed by any private ends, but only aiming at

---

13. Ditto, p. 70.

14. In 1670, Archbishop Leighton drew up a somewhat similar scheme entitled "Defence of a Moderate Episcopacy." Bernard says Ussher's plan "was proposed in the tempestuous violence of the times as an accommodation by way of a prevention of a total shipwreck." — Clavi *Trabales,* p. 54. See also Bishop Andrewes on Church government, continued and enlarged by Archbishop Ussher in *Clavi Trabales,* p. 95–136. Andrewes gave his MS. to Ussher in 1640. In 1659, Edward Stillingfleet tried his hand on the same question from a Broad Church point of view, and published his *Irenicum: A Weapon-Salve for the Church's Wound; or the Divine Right of Particular Forms of Church Government, Discussed and Examined according to the Practice of the Apostles and the Primitive Church, and the Judgment of Reformed Divines, whereby a Foundation is laid for the Church's Peace, and the accommodation of our Present Differences.* These were all "Home Reunion" efforts of the seventeenth century. The Irenicum is very fully examined by Tulloch in his *Rational Theology,* i, ch. vii.

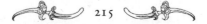

the reducing of order, peace and unity, which God is the author of and not of confusion." Ussher thus introduces the subject:

Episcopal and Presbyterial Government conjoined — By order of the Church of England, all Presbyters are charged to administer the doctrine and sacraments and the discipline of Christ as the Lord hath commanded, and as this realm hath received the same; and that they might the better understand what the Lord hath commanded therein; the exhortation of St. Paul to the elders of the Church of Ephesus is appointed to be read unto them at the time of their ordination: "Take heed unto yourselves and to all the flock among whom the Holy Ghost hath made you overseer, to rule the congregation of God, which he hath purchased with His blood." Of the many elders who in common thus ruled the Church of Ephesus, there was one president whom our Saviour in His Epistle unto this Church in a peculiar manner styleth the angel of the Church of Ephesus, and Ignatius, in another epistle written about twelve years after, unto the same Church, calleth the bishop thereof. Betwixt the Bishop and the Presbyter of that Church, what an harmonious consent there was in the ordering of the Church government, the same Ignatius doth fully there declare; by the Presbytery, with St. Paul, understanding the community of the rest of the presbyters or elders, who then had a hand not only in the delivery of the doctrine and sacraments, but also in the administration of the "discipline of Christ." For with the Bishop, who was the chief President, the rest of the dispensers of the word and sacraments joined in the common government of the Church; and therefore where in matters of ecclesiastical judicature, Cornelius, Bishop of Rome, used the received form of "gathering together the presbytery," of what persons that did consist, Cyprian sufficiently declareth when he wished him to read his letters "to the flourishing clergy which there did preside," or "rule with him"; the presence of the clergy being thought to be so requisite in matters of episcopal audience that in the fourth Council of Carthage it was concluded that "the Bishop might hear no man's cause without the presence of the clergy, and that otherwise the Bishop's sentence should be void unless it were confirmed by the presence of the clergy"; which we find also to be inscribed unto the Canons of Egbert, who was Archbishop of York in the Saxon times, and afterwards unto the body of the Canon law itself.

True it is, that in our Church this kind of presbyterial government hath been long disused, yet seeing it still professeth that every pastor has a right to rule the Church (from whence the name of rector also, was given at first unto him), and to administer the discipline of Christ as well as to dispense the doctrine and sacraments, and the restraint of the exercise of that right, proceedeth only from the custom now received in this realm; no man can doubt but by another law of the land this hindrance may be well removed. And how easily this ancient form of government, by the united suffrages of the clergy might be revived again, and with what little show of alteration the synodical conventions of the pastors of every parish might be accorded, with the presidency of the Bishops of each diocese and province the indifferent leader may quickly perceive by the perusal of the ensuing propositions.

Then follows Ussher's plan — "How the Church might synodically be governed, Archbishops and Bishops being retained."

I. The rector, churchwardens, and sidesmen were to constitute a tribunal of discipline for every parish, with powers to present those which cannot be reclaimed to the next monthly Synod: and meanwhile the Pastor might debar such "from access to the Lord's table."

II. An old statute of Henry VIII, revived in the first year of Queen Elizabeth, might be put in force creating suffragans to equal the number of the rural deaneries, who would be what the Chorepiscopi were to the ancient Church, and who might summon a Synod of all the rectors monthly. This Synod would possess powers of excommunication.

III. The Diocesan Synod might be held once or twice in the year, in which "all the suffragans, and the rest of the rectors or incumbent pastors, or a certain select number of every deanery within the Diocese," would have seats, and "with whose consent, or the major part of them, all things might be concluded by the Bishop or Superintendent, call him whether you will; or, in his absence, by one of the suffragans, whom he shall depute in his stead to be moderator of that assembly."

IV. The Provincial Synod was to consist of "all the bishops and suffragans; and such other of the clergy as should be elected out of every Diocese within the province"; and "the Archbishop of either province might be the moderator of this meeting, or in his room some one of the bishops appointed by him." "This Synod might be held every third year; and if Parliament do then sit, according to the act of triennial Parliament, both the Archbishops and provincial Synods of the land might join together and make up a National Council, wherein appeals from inferior Synods might be received, all their acts examined, and all ecclesiastical constitutions which concern the state of the Church of the whole nation established."[15]

---

15. Ussher's *Works*, Vol. xii.

This plan bears the *imprimatur* of the Archbishop and of Dr. Holsworth. "We are of the judgment that the form of government here proposed is not in any point repugnant to the Scriptures, and that the suffragans mentioned in the second proposition may lawfully use the power both of jurisdiction and ordination according to the word of God and the practice of ancient Church."[16]

The early Irish Church in the days of her primitive purity clearly showed an approximation towards the form of Church government sketched above by Ussher, and it was no doubt his intimate acquaintance with her early history that suggested much of this plan.

A record preserved in Wilkin's Councils proves that Ireland originally was full of village bishops, whose office was gradually merged into rural deaneries. Thus a canon of the third Council held at Kells, in Meath, in 1152, enacts that the Churches of Athenry, Kells, Slane, Skyrne, and Dunshauglin, being heretofore bishops' sees, should hereafter be the heads of rural deaneries, with archpresbyters residing therein. In the present Diocese of Dublin rural bishops were to be found established in Swords, Lusk, Finglas, Newcastle, Tawney, Leixlip, Bray, Wicklow, Arklow, Ballymore, Clondalkin, Tallaght, and O'Murthy. Here again we have evidence forthcoming of the Eastern derivation of the ancient Irish Church, such rural sees being a characteristic of the East, where St. Cyril, for example, had under him fifty rural bishops. In the six African provinces there were five hundred of these rural sees.

It will be remarked that throughout this plan, Ussher only deals with the question of Church government. The question of the scriptural sanction and authority of episcopacy is untouched. No one knew better than Ussher from his investigations into

16. At the Restoration, Ussher's plan was brought forward by Calamy and Reynolds on behalf of the Presbyterian ministers, in the hope that it might form a groundwork for reconciliation. — See Collier's *Eccl. Hist.*, p. 871.

the subject, especially in the region of ancient Church history in Ireland, that the grace of the episcopate flows down from the earliest sources.

Ussher was not the man to make shipwreck of fundamentals. As Dr. Barlow, afterwards Bishop of Lincoln, writes of him, he "even found old orthodox truth maintained by him upon just and carrying grounds, where elsewhere he had often sought but seldom found."[17] On the above subject of the powers of the Chorepiscopi, Barlow points out to Ussher that in accordance with the Council of Ancyra, even these might not ordain without licence first had from the bishop. The theory that they were only *simplices presbyteri,* according to the counterfeit Damascus and others, he will not hear of. He conceives that it is demonstrable undeniably from carrying principles in antiquity that they were bishops. It was impossible that the *presbyteri civitatis* might ordain, if that be the meaning of the canon, with licence from the bishops, "it never appearing in antiquity that any presbyter's ordination of a presbyter was canonical." It is unfortunate that we do not possess Ussher's reply to Barlow's query as to the real force of the above canon.[18]

---

17. Ussher's *Works,* xvi, p. 98–100.

18. On the subject of this canon, see Gore's *Church and the Ministry,* Appended Notes D and E, p. 370–7; also Bingham, Vol. i, p. 56–9; Reeves' *Eccl. Antiq. Down and Connor;* and art. "Chorepiscopi," in Smith's *Dict. Of Christian Antiq.* For the institution in Ireland, Ussher's *Works,* Vol. x; Lanigan's *Hist.,* Vol. ii, p. 128, &c.; King's *Hist.,* p. 1,013.

CHAPTER XVII

LORD STRAFFORD AND THE CHURCH OF IRELAND; QUESTION OF PRECEDENCE BETWEEN ARMAGH AND DUBLIN; ARTICLES OF THE CHURCH OF ENGLAND AND NEW CANONS ADOPTED BY THE IRISH CONVOCATION

I n 1633, Lord Strafford had arrived in Ireland to take up the office of Chief Governor of that distressful country.[1] The same year saw his great contemporary Laud advanced to the English Primacy.

Both these remarkable men manifested a deep interest in the spiritual and temporal welfare of the Church of Ireland. The Archbishop's studies in the See of Canterbury did not prevent him advising both Strafford and Ussher on Irish Church affairs.

---

1. He came over to Ireland as Viscount Wentworth, and was not created Earl of Strafford with the title of Lord-Lieutenant till 1640.

One great desire of Laud was to see the Church put into possession of extensive property alienated from her by the rapacity of the landowners, and the fraudulent leases granted by Bishops.

"I pray my Lord to be hearty in this," writes Laud to Strafford, "for I shall think myself very happy if God be pleased to spare my life to see this business ended."[2] He writes again, asking the Deputy to find out from the Lord Chief Justice what steps should be taken to assist the poor vicars out of the impropriations in Ireland.[3] Archbishop Ussher, writing to Laud acknowledges how ready he found Wentworth to do all in his power toward recovering the alienated patrimony of the Church. Shortly after entering on his high office, the Lord-Deputy writes to Laud from Dublin Castle giving a frightful description of the state of the Irish Church, "which I find," he writes, "many ways distempered, an unlearned clergy which have not so much as the outward form of churchmen to cover themselves with, nor their persons anyway reverenced or protected; the churches unbuilt, the parsonages and vicarage houses utterly ruined, the people untaught through the non-residency of the clergy occasioning by the unlimited and shameful number of spiritual promotions without cure of the souls, which they hold by *commendams;* the rites and ceremonies of the Church run over without all decency of habit, order, or gravity, in the course of their service; the possessions of the Church to a great proportion in lay hands; the Bishops alienating their very principal houses and demesnes to their children and to strangers, farming out their jurisdictions to mean and unworthy persons, the Popish titulars exercising the whilst a foreign jurisdiction much greater than theirs." The Deputy also complains of the public schools, endowed with grants by King James, being ill-provided and ill-governed, and their funds sometimes supplied underhand to the support of

---

2. Strafford's *Letters,* i, p. 82.

3. Ditto. In 1634, Laud was able to write "done" in his diary with regard to the matter of impropriations by the Crown.

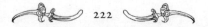

Popish schoolmasters.[4] He likewise refers to the extraordinary fact that baptisms and marriages are nearly always performed in private houses, "and which is odd, they never marry till after supper, and so to bed."[5] He advises that the Irish should be made conformable to the English practice of public marriages, as "more civil and comely." Laud writes back later, Nov. 1623, to the Lord Deputy: "The truth is, a great many Church cormorants have fed so full upon it (the Church), that they are fallen into a fever, and for that no physick better than a vomit if it be given in time, and therefore you have taken a very judicious course to administer one so early to my Lord of Cork. I hope it will do him good."[6]

Again, he writes wisely, "I am glad you will so soon take order that Divine service may be read throughout in the churches, be the company that vouchsafe to come never so few. Let God have His whole service with reverence, and He will quickly send more to help to perform it." Toward the close of the year (Dec. 1633) Strafford writes to Laud showing how he was putting his good advice into practice. He complains of the Bishop of Killala, who had leased the See lands of the value of £500 to Sir Daniel O'Bryan. The Knight did so juggle with the Bishop underhand as that he compounded privately to accept of £26 rent for all the interest of the church. *Si hac fiunt in viridi, in arido quid fiet.* "I got notice of it sent to the Bishop, told him roundly he had betrayed the bishopric, that he deserved to have his rochet (setting the dignity of his calling aside) pulled over his ears, and to be turned to a stipend of four nobles a year, and so warmed his old sides as I made him break the agreement, crave pardon, and promise to follow the cause with all diligence."[7] Another prelate he denounced was the Bishop of Down, who had leased out "the

---

4. Strafford's *Letters*, i, p. 187–8.

5. Ditto.

6. *Strafford's Letter's*, i, p. 156.

7. Ditto, i, p.171.

very demesne and principal house of that bishopric to his own son for sixty years," reserving little or no rent.

Wentworth "made him see his great fault." He has in mind two or three other bishops whom he desires to "trounce" for having alienated Church property.

The condition of the churches in Dublin was also extraordinary. One of them had been given over as a stable to a former Deputy, a second had been turned into a private dwelling-house for a nobleman, and the choir of a third used as a tennis court. The vaults (crypts) of Christ Church Cathedral were used as alehouses and tobacco shops, where the people were "pouring either in or out their drink offerings and incense, while we above are serving the High God."[8]

In the sister Cathedral of St. Patrick's there were also abuses. Lord Cork's monument had been allowed to block up the east end of the Cathedral, "as if it were on purpose to gain the worship and reverence which the chapter and whole church are

---

8. Strafford to Laud, Vol. i, p. 173. Bramhall writes to Laud in a similar strain, Aug. 1633. The vaults were leased to "Popish recusants." "The table," he writes, "used for the administration of the Blessed Sacrament in the midst of the choir is made an ordinary seat for maids and apprentices." — Bramhall's *Works,* Vol. i, p. lxxxix. Among the rules laid down by Bedell for the regulation of his diocese was this: *Ut sacrarium consistorium non convertatur, aut sacra mensa notariis, aut scribis, sit pro pluteo.* — Clogy's *Memoirs,* p. 63. Some of Bedell's episcopal injunctions would seem rather contradictory in these days. He separated the sexes, and made the women sit outside the chancel. He required the minister alone to repeat the Psalms and *Te Deum,* as most in accordance with the rubric. The Puritans, who were against the practice, complained in 1641 that the Church people "did tosse the Psalms like tennis-balls." They petitioned Parliament to restrain those persons "who doe interrupt the minister when he readeth the Psalms by taking every other verse out of his mouth with a hackering confused noise." Indeed, the Westminster divines abolished the Psalter altogether, and substituted for it a metrical version, by Francis Rous, M.P., afterwards Speaker of the Barebones Parliament, and subsequently one of Cromwell's peers. — *Lewis Hewess* (private) MSS., 1,640–1. Burnet's Life of *Bedell,* p. 113–114.

bound to give towards the east."[9] "This being the case in Dublin, your Lordship," he adds sententiously, "will judge what we may expect in the country." The Earl of Cork, in consequence of the agitation raised on the subject, was compelled to have the tomb removed to the south side of the chancel, where it remained a considerable eyesore till finally removed to its present position at the south-west end of the nave on the restoration of the Cathedral by Sir B. Lee Guinness in 1865.[10]

This was not the only bone of contention which Strafford had with the great Earl of Cork. He summoned him before the Council in Dublin Castle, and forced him to pay a fine of £15,000 for illegally seizing on certain advowsons and church properties in Cork and also to surrender the revenues of the Bishopric of Lismore, amounting to £1600 a year, which he had managed to get hold of. The Earl complains in his diary that Lord Strafford had compelled him to disgorge some £40,000, and we need not wonder if afterwards when the unfortunate Deputy was *in extremis,* the Earl of Cork was found to be one of his bitterest enemies.[11]

---

9. Strafford's *Letters,* i, p. 173. It is remarkable that Ussher, writing to Laud on the subject, speaks of "the Cathedral Church of St. Patrick's *in the suburbs of Dublin*" showing that the Cathedral at that time was outside the city. Ussher's *Works,* xv, p. 572.

10. Strafford treated the splendid monument with but little respect. He had it "trundled away in boxes, as if were marchpanes all banqueting stuffs going down to the christening of a young master in the country." — Strafford's *Letters*, i, p. 377.

11. Rusworth's *Trial of Strafford,* p. 23. The Earl of Cork apparently took a strange view of the family motto — "God's Providence is my inheritance." For a different view of the Earl see Cox's *History,* Vol. ii, opening remarks "To the Reader"; and Mason's *Cathedral of St. Patrick,* p; liii–lvii, where some interesting information may be gathered regarding the Boyle family. It must be said that the Earl is found speaking well of Strafford to Laud, praising his "prudence, indefatigable industry, and impartial justice" (Strafford *Letters,* — ii, p. 245), but in his diary is found an entry expressing his great joy at the downfall of his enemy. The founder of the family, Richard Boyle, was born at Canterbury in 1566,

Another noble plunderer of the Church was the Lord Clanrickard of that day, who had disposed of a number of parsonages and vicarages for £4000.

We cannot feel surprised if men like Laud and Wentworth raised up a host of foes against themselves. The Puritan party would naturally be enraged against them for their efforts to strengthen the Church, both in England and Ireland; and the successful attempts made to recover from the hands of the spoilers the ecclesiastical property they had seized exposed them to the unrelenting attacks of such powerful enemies as the Earl of Cork, and prelates like the above Bishops of Killala and Down. "This is so universal a disease" (Church plunder), he writes to Laud, "that I shall incur a number of men's displeasures if he best rank among them." But still he does not flinch. "Have at the ravens," he cries, "if I spare a man of them, let no man ever spare me."[12]

About this time a question arose which had more than once previously disturbed the Church, touching the rival claims for precedence as between the Archbishops of Armagh and Dublin. A Parliament "had been summoned to vote supplies, and it had to be decided which of the two prelates was to have the place of honour.

The dispute had begun so far back as 1182, when the Pope (Lucius III) had granted a Bull of precedence to John Comyn, the Archbishop of Dublin. A series of rivalries followed to the time of the Reformation. In 1337, David O'Heraghty, Archbishop of Armagh, had been summoned to Parliament at St. Mary's Abbey, Dublin, but was obstructed by the Archbishop of Dublin, who

---

and came to Ireland in 1588 with £27 in his pocket. In 1602, he was in a position to purchase the great estate of Sir Walter Raleigh in the south of Ireland. He made such improvement in his property as attracted the notice and commendation of Cromwell. It is an extraordinary fact that his iron-works in the south of Ireland realised for him the enormous sum of £100,000. What has become of these iron ores? — See Earl of Cork's *True Remembrances,* Budgett's *Memoirs,* and Article in *Dic. Nat. Biog.*

12. Strafford's *Letters,* p. 299.

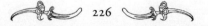

would not permit him to have a cross borne before him as he had intended in asserting the right of precedence of the See of Armagh over that of Dublin.[13] When at the period of the reformation, the Archbishop of Armagh (Dowdal) took the Roman side, and the Archbishop of Dublin (Browne) that of the King, royal letters were issued transferring the Primacy to Dublin.[14]

The state of things was reversed under Queen Mary, but the question remained in suspense.

In June 1634, immediately before the assembling of Parliament, Lord Strafford had the two Archbishops, Ussher and Bulkeley, summoned before him, and the case was finally decided in favour of Armagh and has so continued ever since. The precedence of the Primate over the Lord Chancellor was determined at the same time. It may noticed that Archbishop Hampton, Ussher's predecessor, had previously maintained the rights of his See against Theophilus Jones, Lord Chancellor, and Archbishop of Dublin, and afterwards against Archbishop Bulkeley. All the proofs which he drew up are extant in his own handwriting among the MSS. of Trinity College, Dublin.[15] He

---

13. Gilbert's *Chartularies of St. Mary's Abbey,* i, xlii. A similar contest had raged in the Church of England between Canterbury and York. An attempt was made to settle the question at a Council at Windsor in 1072, but the dispute broke out afresh a century later at a synod held in Westminster, when York incontinently sat in the lap of Canterbury, and was only driven thence at the expense of blows and torn vestments. — See William of Newbury, *De Rebus Ang.* Iii, I; R. De Hoveden, ii, 92; *Cal. Papal Letters,* A.D. 1304, p. 160, where Gregory IX complains that the Archbishops of Canterbury and York "cannot come together to the royal councils on account of the quarrel of carrying the cross."

14. On Aug. 6, 1551, Archbishop Browne writes to the Earl of Warwick that the Archbishops of Armagh claim the Primacy and tythe of the whole realm by the Bishop of Rome's Bulls, but he (Browne) claims the same by the King's Majesty and his most noble progenitors' grants and gifts. — *Calendar of State Papers.*

15. See Reeves' *Ware,* Vol. i, p. 97 (MS. note*).* Hampton always signed himself simply "Armagh" — Ditto.

thus concludes, "I am weary and a little ashamed at spending so much time on matters merely formal. The Archbishop of Dublin hath compelled me. He challengeth that which is not due to him. I defend the long continued right of my See. My defence is necessary; his challenge and encroachments are superfluous and more than needed."[16]

In coming to conclusion at this time, when the question came on again, the Lord Deputy had the advantage of the learned argument drawn up by Archbishop Ussher, and which also is to be found among the MSS. of Trinity College.[17] Curious to say, the like dispute raged between the Roman Catholic occupants of the same Sees, and was only finally decided in 1728, after a successful vindication of the rights of Armagh by MacMahon, the Roman Catholic Primate. According to this authority, Archbishop Bulkeley was very keen on the question, and attended the Council accompanied by a crowd of lawyers ("*Causidicorum turba stipatus*").

At the same time that Parliament assembled, the two Houses of Convocation were directed to pass under review the Articles and Canons of the Church of Ireland with a view to bringing the two Churches into closer conformity. On July 14th, Parliament assembled, and an imposing service was held in St. Patrick's Cathedral in the presence of Lord Strafford,[18] when the sermon was preached by Ussher who took for his text the words, "The sceptre shall not depart from Judah, nor a lawgiver from between

---

16. *Class* E. 3. 13.

17. *Class* E. 3. 15. Elrington prints *in extenso* the Lord-Deputy's decision, p. 151–3. See also *Ware*, i, p. 71–80.

18. For an account of the grand procession to and from the Cathedral, see Strafford's *Letters*, i, p. 282. The Lord-Deputy, who loved pomp and order, found the Castle a perfect Augean stable when he arrived in Dublin, and was at much trouble to restore some kind of decent ceremonial in State functions. He was also a splendid entertainer, but would allow of no toasts beyond the usual loyal ones with a view to putting down the drinking habits which were then excessive in the city. — See Mozley's *Essays*, i, p. 24–5.

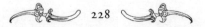

his feet, until, Shiloh come. And to him shall the gathering of the people be."

Archbishop Ussher was President and Lesley, Dean of Down, was chosen Prolocutor of the Lower House. It was the settled purpose of the Lord-Deputy, backed up by Laud to bring the Church of Ireland into as complete conformity as possible with that of England; but there is reason to believe that the project was far from being favourably entertained by Ussher, who clung to the independence of his Church as a distinctly separate and national organisation. On the subject of the Irish Articles, of his own making chiefly, he gave way unwillingly, and with an effort to make the two sets of equal obligation. With regard to the Canons he was more courageous, and succeeded in having separate Irish Canons carried, largely modelled however, on those of the Church of England, and in some respect, superior to them. Ussher had to deal with a very powerful will in the person of Strafford, who in this as in other respects illustrated his own policy of "thorough."[19]

It is more than probable that time has vindicated this policy of the great Deputy, as no doubt much of the strength of the Irish Church in after times was derived from her close alliance with that of England, an alliance, however, which did not save her eventually from disestablishment.

The resistance developed itself in the Lower House of Convocation, where the chairman of the Committee, Dr. Andrews, Dean of Limerick, entered on an independent course criticising the English Canons, allowing some and questioning others. Strafford, who at the time was engaged in the House

---

19. This word "thorough" has been strangely misunderstood as if it implied the principle of absolutism, whereas it only meant straightforwardness and resolute prosecution of an Irish policy as opposed to the fatal tendency to temporise and vacillate. The opposite was understood to be the policy of "Lady Mora." By the latter the Lord Chancellor Weston was meant. — See Strafford's *Letters* i, p. 379–80; and Traill's *Strafford*, p. 99 (note) and 200–1.

of Lords, was under the impression that all things were going fairly for him in the Convocation; great was his astonishment therefore when he found that they were actually going over the English Articles one by one, putting an, A here for "agreed," and a "D" there for *deliberandum*. He sent at once for Andrews and his annotated copy of the Canons, and rated him soundly. He said it was not a Dean of Limerick who sat in the chair, but an Ananias,[20] and that it was not for a few petty clerks to make Articles of faith and laws for the Church without the privity of State and Bishops.

They were no better, he said, than a pack of Brownists. The Lord-Deputy, then taking a high hand, insisted that no question should be put touching the receiving or otherwise of the Articles of the Church of England, but that the question should be put directly for allowing and receiving the Articles of the Church of England, each member to give his vote in writing, saying "Yes," or " No," and without further discussion.[21] Indulging in a grim severity, he had the unfortunate Dean afterward transferred to the See of Ferns and Leighlin, "one of the meanest in the whole kingdom," without any *commendam,* giving him the poor satisfaction that he would die "as a person of some importance, having been a bishop."

It is manifest that Archbishop Ussher was not happy over the business, and entered on it with reluctance.[22] The enacting

---

20. A character in Ben Jonson's *Alchymist.* Ananias is represented as a hypocritical purist who holds a brief for the "Brethren" of those days.

21. See Straffords *Letter to Laud,* Vol. i, p. 342–5. The meeting of the Lower House to consider Strafford's demands was evidently a stormy one. "There were some hot spirits, sons of thunder, amongst them, who moved that they should petition me for a free Synod, but in fine they could not agree amongst themselves who should put the bell about the cat's neck;" — Ditto.

22. The Editor of the *Rawdon Papers* falls into an extraordinary error when he says that Ussher "lent his powerful assistance" to passing of the Articles and Canons. — See R.P., p. 24 (note).

Canon he was commissioned to draw up did not satisfy Strafford, who forthwith prepared one of his own, assuring the Primate that he knew the minds of the members better, and that they would pass the Canon as he had penned it.[23]

The Lord-Deputy, writing to Laud, informs him of the terms in which he addressed the Prolocutor, insisting on his view being carried out, the Upper House being now quite complacent.[24]

"I send you here enclosed the form of a Canon to be passed by the votes of this Lower House of Convocation, which I require you to put to the question, for their consent without admitting any debates or other discourse; for I hold it not fit, nor will suffer that the Articles of the Church of England be disputed. Therefore I expect you to take only the voices consenting or dissenting, and to give me a particular account how each man gives his vote. The time admits of no delay, so I further require you to perform the contents of this letter forthwith, and so I rest your good friend, Wentworth."[25]

---

23. Collier is in error when he says that Ussher drew up this Canon. — See his *Eccl. Hist.,* ii, p. 868; see also Elrington's *Life of Ussher,* p. 172, (note).

24. Of the twenty-two prelates who took part in this Convocation, only two, Ussher and Martin, Bishop of Meath, were educated in Trinity College, Dublin; the rest were English or Scotch. — Ball's *Reformed Church of Ireland,* p. 129 (note). Bramhall says, if there were any of the Bishops who spoke in favour of the Irish Articles, "they were very few and did it faintly." *Works,* Vol. v, p, 81. The following Bishops were all Englishmen: Bulkeley (Dublin), Bedell (Kilmore), Buckworth (Dromore), Downham (Derry), Boyle (educated at Oxford), Gough (Limerick); Steere (Ardfert), Pilsworth (Kildare), Wheeler (Ossory), Ram (Ferns and Leighlin), King (Elphin), Dawson (Clonfert and Kilmacduagh). The following were Scotch: Spotswood (Clogher), Echlin (Down and Connor), Lesley (Raphoe), Hamilton (Cashel), Heygate (Kilfenora), Adair (Killala and Achonry). The Bishop of Killaloe, Lewis Jonas, was a Welshman. — See Cotton's *Fasti.*

25. Laud's *Works,* vii, p. 98.

The result was as the Lord-Deputy anticipated, there being only one non-content — "a Calvinist," says Collier, "who had looked deeper than the rest into the matter." Thus did an English lay churchman of resolute spirit play the chief part in giving a blow to Irish Calvinism, and compel the Church of Ireland to set aside her own Articles of Religion in favour of those of the Church of England.[26]

The enacting Canon declared "we do receive and approve the Book of Articles of Religion agreed upon by the Archbishops and Bishops, and the whole clergy in the Convocation holden in London in the year of our Lord, 1562," &c.[27]

Notwithstanding this ratification of the English Articles in Ireland, Archbishop Ussher continued to require assent and consent to the old Irish Articles as well from all candidates for holy orders, and some of the other Bishops did likewise.[28] The double

26. The change may be seen by comparing the language of almost mathematical precision of the Irish Articles (12 and 14) regarding the definite number of the elect with the cautious and moderate tone of the 17th of the English Articles.

27. Bramhall, who had been consecrated a short time previously (May 26th, 1634) in the Castle Chapel, Dublin, by Ussher and the Bishops of Meath, Down, and Cork, says he was the intermediary between Strafford and the Convocation throughout this business: "I was the only man employed from him to the Convocation and from the Convocation to him." — *Works,* Vol. v, p.83. No doubt, the Bishop of Derry was, next to the deputy, the most determined party in seeing the changes carried out.

28. Ussher represents the state of the case thus in a letter to Dr. Ward, Sept. 15th, 1635: "The Articles of Religion agreed upon in our former Synod, A.D. MDCXV, we let stand as they did before. But for the manifestation of our agreement with the Church of England we have received and approved your Articles also." — *Works,* xvi, p. 9. This seems a halting way of putting it. Bramhall is much more decisive. He says, "If any Bishop had been known to have required any man to subscribe to the Irish Articles after the English were received and authorised under the great seal of Ireland, he would have been called to account for it." — *Works,* v, p. 81. Bramall says on the authority of Bernard, that Bedell

assent and consent only ceased altogether at the restoration of the monarchy.[29]

Bishop Jeremy Taylor, preaching in 1663 at the funeral of Archbishop Bramhall, represented the gain to be derived by both Churches from the acceptance of a common code of Articles, that thereby they became "*populus unius labii,* of one heart and one lip, and removed the shibboleth that made the Church lisp too indecently, or rather in some degree speak the speech of Ashdod, and not the language of Caanan."

The question of the Articles having been thus decided, Bramhall moved that the English Canons of 1604 should henceforth be accepted as the Canons of the Church of Ireland. Ussher again resisted, and with greater success. The matter ended by a compromise, Irish Canons to the number of 100 being drawn up, founded more or less on the English ones, but differing from them occasionally in some important respects. Writing to Laud, the Lord-Deputy acknowledged that Ussher was hugely against the business, which was merely a point of honour . . . lest Ireland might become subject to the Church of England as the province of York is to that of Canterbury; needs forsooth we must be a Church of ourselves, which is utterly lost, unless the Canons here differ, albeit not in substance, yet in some form from yours in England; and this crotchet put the good man into such an agony as you cannot believe so learned a man should be troubled withal."[30]

One cannot but sympathise with the Irish Primate in his efforts to preserve what he thought to be some shreds of independence for

---

examined a candidate for orders, Thomas Price, afterwards Archbishop of Cashel, in the Irish Articles subsequent to 1634; but this must be a mistake, as Price was in priest's orders, and sat as Archdeacon of Kildare in the Convention of that year. — See Bramhall as above and notes p and q.

29. They were then practically abolished, "as if they had never existed." — Smith's *Life,* p. 73.

30. Strafford's *Letters*, i, p, 381.

his Church, and his chagrin when he found that those efforts were in vain. At the same time, that Church could scarcely be regarded as very independent which was ruled, as was the case at this time with the Church of Ireland, almost entirely by bishops of English or Scottish extraction. Both Bishop Mant and Dr. Elrington are at some trouble to compare the respective sets of Articles, and wherein they agree or differ. The twelfth Irish Article, which is believed to have embodied Ussher's instructions, requires the heads of the Catechism to be divided into as many parts as there are Sundays in the year, and so explained in the parish churches.[31]

Canon 19 received an addition to the effect that every parish clergyman in the afternoon before the celebration of the Holy Communion, should give notice by the tolling of the church bell or otherwise, "to the intent that if any have any scruple of conscience, or desire the special ministry of reconciliation, he may afford it to those who need it; and those extremely dull or much troubled in mind are exhorted to resort unto God's ministers to receive from them as well advice and counsel for the quickening of dead hearts . . . as the benefit of absolution."

This part of the Canon gave great umbrage to the Puritan party which the indiscreet zeal of a wild young English curate, named Croxton, sent over to Ireland by Archbishop Laud, further intensified. The English Primate did not himself view the new Canons with much favour. He wrote, "I cannot but think the English Canons entire, with some few amendments, would have done better."[32]

On the subject of the desirableness of conducting public worship in the Irish tongue, where the English language was not

---

31. This was probably done at the suggestion of Bedell, who, when yet a Lecturer in Christ Church Cathedral, used to break up the Catechism into fifty-two parts, on which he preached every week. Before he did this, Ussher was in the habit of using a private Catechism of his own for the purpose. — See Clogy's *Memoirs of Bedell,* p. 31–2.

32. Laud to Ussher, Ussher's *Works,* xvi, p. 7.

understood, Ussher had now seen reason for changing his mind, and he accordingly seconded Bishop Bedell, in proposing and carrying the eighth and eighty-sixth Canons, both of which gave facilities for the purpose.

On the other hand, Bishop Bramhall opposed, founding his objection chiefly on the statute of the 28th of Henry VIII, passed in 1537.[33]

Visit www.nlpg.com/annals.asp to discover more fascinating history from *The Annals of the World*

---

33. Anderson's *Historical Sketches,* p. 61. This absurd and mischievous statute ran as follows: "If any spiritual promotion within this land at any time become void, such as have title to nominate shall nominate to the same such a person as shall speak English, and none other, unless there can be no person as can speak English will accept it; and if the patron cannot within three months get any such person that can speak English he shall cause four proclamations to be openly made at four several market days in the next market town adjoining the said spiritual promotion, that if any fit person that can speak English will come and take the same he shall have it; and if none come within five weeks after the first Proclamation, then the patron may present any able honest man, albeit he cannot speak English." Severe penalties were to be inflicted in cases where the statute might be violated.

CHAPTER XVIII

FRESH LITERARY LABOURS; "THE ANTIQUITIES OF THE BRITISH CHURCHES"; THE EPISTLES OF ST. IGNATIUS

The enacting of the English Articles and the drawing up of new Canons was not the only business that engaged the attention of Convocation. The state of the Church was also passed under review, and provision was made to abate many abuses. A petition was addressed to the King, signed by the Archbishops of Armagh and Cashel, representing the miserable condition of the rural clergy, who were reduced to "extreme contempt and beggary," in consequence of "frequent appropriations, *commendams,* and violent intrusions into their undoubted rights in times of confusion; their churches ruined, their tythes detained, their glebes concealed and by inevitable consequence a system of non-residence forced on them."

The petition represents to the King the advantage that would accrue to Church and State if a resident clergy were provided, "endowed with competence to serve God at his alter," not to speak of the general protection of the Almighty which it would most assuredly bring on his Majesty and kingdom. Barbarism

and superstition would be expelled, the subject would learn his duty to God, and true religion would be propagated. The petition goes on pray that the King would settle those appropriations which were in the Crown, and not yet disposed of, upon a "rural and resident clergy."[1]

But the evil condition of the Church at this time was not confined to its temporalities. The clergy, in many instances, were not realising their high responsibilities. We find Lord Strafford addressing Archbishop Ussher and the other Ecclesiastical Commissioners in 1636, urging them to stir up the clergy to their duties. "Whereas," the Lord Deputy writes, "we cannot but take notice of the general non-residence of clergymen to the dishonour of God, the disservice of their cures, the vain expense of their means in cities and corporate towns, and the great scandal of the Church, we do hereby require and authorise you to proceed instantly with all severity to the reformation of this great abuse, and to cause all those whom you shall find to live idly about this city of Dublin, or other cities or corporate towns, or upon their farms, to repair instantly to their parish churches to attend that charge, whereof they owe an account both to God and man; and if they shall disobey your command in this respect, to sequester their livings for a year, and if they be still negligent, to deprive them; purposing on our return into this kingdom (if it shall so please God and his Majesty) to take strict account of your proceedings and good endeavours in each of these particulars."[2]

Whatever opinion we may form of Strafford, we are compelled to acknowledge that this was the language of one who had at heart the highest and most important interests of the Church of Ireland. And here we may bring under final review the principles that underlay and directed the ecclesiastical policy of the two great men with whom Ussher was brought into such

---

1. Collier's *Ecclesiastical History,* ii, p. 763, quoted by Mant, *Church of Ireland,* i, part ii, p 484–5.

2. Strafford's *Letters,* Vol ii, p. 42.

close contact during his Archiepiscopal reign in Ireland, and whose names have been so prominently before us in these pages — Laud and Strafford. The principles that influenced them may be said to have contemplated throughout the social, moral, and spiritual elevation of the Church of Ireland. There was scarcely a beneficed clergyman at the passing of the Irish Church Act who had not reason to thank his stars that Laud and Strafford had lived and worked for the Church of Ireland in the seventeenth century, for his annuity was in a large degree the fruit of the ceaseless and courageous efforts of these men.

By their labours, an annual income of £30,000 was, recovered for the Church, "an incredible sum for that day,"[3] representing as it did more than £240,000 a year in our present currency — in a word, about half of the income of the Irish Church at the time of its disendowment. The whole of the tithes impropriated by the Crown were then restored, and, as we have seen, in addition, more than one noble and more than one right rev. robber of churches were made to disgorge their share of the spoil. In addition to these services, Strafford had in his mind a project, which he was not able to carry out, for restoring or rebuilding all the cathedral churches in Ireland,[4] and he was specially interested in giving the diocese of Down a cathedral worthy of its growing importance.

To touch on another and delicate subject, Laud and Strafford may be blamed by some as having unduly interfered with the doctrinal symbols of the Church of Ireland, and deprived her of her Articles of Religion. But what salvation was wrought thereby!

Who can doubt that if the Irish Articles (which indeed were not in themselves of a national character at all, but largely modelled on the theology of Geneva) had been retained, the result would have been disastrous to the best interests of the Church? "The awful and immoral system of John Calvin"[5] would have

---

3. Mozley's *Essays*, i, p. 31.

4. Ditto, p. 32.

5. Aubrey Moore in *Lux Mundi*, p. 99.

been stereotyped in the Irish Church, and spiritual life dwarfed and starved in proportion. Laud's great effort was to pull the Church together, and save it from becoming a mere Puritan sect, a poor echo of continental Protestantism.[6]

To do this, he saw that it was necessary to draw the two Churches closely together. He was fighting the same battle in England and Ireland, and in this latter country he found a ready helper in Strafford. Freedom of thought, a wider and more tolerant theology, respect for ancient learning and ancient precedents, these things lay at the foundation of what they did. Laud was one of those few men who see before their times; he had the courage to face great risks and great difficulties in the prosecution of his purposes. As has been well said: he was *one* man with a *view* in those temporising days, and he pursued that view through good report and evil report, through all the tangled mazes of Court life.

He had read and thought, and besides, he was a man of action. He never lost sight of the great enterprise he had put before him alike in England and Ireland, and although at the time that policy seemed to perish, it was only for a season. Out of his ashes came renewed vigour for the Churches he loved and served so well, and today we are reaping the fruits of his labours. In the words of Holy Writ, his purpose was "to build the old waste places, to raise up the foundations of many generations, to be the repairer of the breach, the restorer of paths to dwell in."

But to return to our story. Hardly had Convocation ceased to sit when Ussher was invited to take part in the Commencements in Trinity College, July 1635. Writing to Ward, he speaks of his weariness after long attendance in Parliament and Convocation, and then being called upon to moderate in the Divinity Act, and assist in the making of doctors of divinity. He returns, however,

---

6. A predestinarian theology like that set forth in the Lambeth Articles could in no sense be regarded as of native growth; on the contrary, its characteristic features are entirely foreign to the Celtic way of looking at the facts of religion, and can find no counterpart in our primitive national theology.

with fresh zeal to his studies, and publishes under the title of *Immanuel, or the Mystery of the Incarnation*[7] the substance of a series of sermons preached by him at Drogheda.

Judging from this work, we would conclude that the Archbishop's audience had been trained to expect very solid food; they are scarcely sermons which would be listened to now with ordinary patience. The volume is dedicated to Lord Strafford — *Grati animi qualecunque testimonium.*

Another swing of the pendulum now took place, as the King was urgent for supplies, directions were issued to the Archbishops and Bishops of the Irish Church to make matters more comfortable for the Roman Catholics. In pursuance of these injunctions, Archbishop Ussher addressed a letter to his brother prelates instructing them that, until they received directions to the contrary, they should suspend all proceedings against recusants "for their clandestines," and "in a quiet and silent manner" withdraw them.[8]

A more ambitious work than the above was the next fruit of the Archbishop's pen, *The Antiquities of the British Churches*, which was published in August 1639, and an early copy of which he presented to his friend Dr. Bramhall, the learned Bishop of Derry. The book had been commenced at the suggestion of James I, who, as we have seen, gave permission to Ussher to study in England for the purpose of its production. After an interval of twenty years it appeared, with dedication to Charles I.[9]

---

7. Ussher's *Works*, iv, p. 573–617.

8. Ussher's *Works*, xvi, p. 532.

9. *Britannicarum Ecclesiarum Antiquitates,* printed in Dublin, quarto, 1639, and reprinted 1677. — Ussher's *Works*, v–vi. The closing chapter (xvii) is full of authorities on the early history of Christianity in Ireland. It sets forth at large the traditions of St. Patrick's visit to Rome, and commission by Pope Celestine. An elaborate chronological index will be found at the close of the work. Ware, in his day, wrote, "This work is so great a treasure of British and Irish ecclesiastical antiquities that all who have since written with any success on this subject cannot avoid owning how much they are indebted to his labours." — *Works*, i, p. 108.

There are indications that Ussher was likewise labouring over his great task of a critical edition of St. Ignatius. He is seeing the light more clearly in separating the genuine from the spurious. Writing to Dr. Ward from Drogheda, March 10th, 1637, he says, "The M.S. copy of *Ignatius* in Caius College Library hath this singular in it — that in the genuine epistles . . . those passages are wanting which are excepted against, as institutions and oppositions by our writers, and that the place touching the Eucharist cited by Theodoret out of the Epistle to the Smyrnaeans, which is wanting in all other books, is to be found in this. But I intend ere long to publish *Ignatius* myself, as considering it to be a matter of very great consequence to have a writer of his standing freed (as much as maybe) from those interpolations of later times."[10] Several years later, he writes from Oxford, June 1640, telling a correspondent that he is searching for a Syriac copy of the Epistles. He is sure such a copy is to be found in Rome.[11] If he could get "either a Syriac, or an Arabic, or an, Armenian, or a Persian translation," it would serve him "to exceeding good purpose."[12] Eventually the work is published in 1644, and he sends complimentary copies to various friends, including Dr. Hall, Bishop of Norwich, who writes back expressing his thanks in a Latin epistle, congratulating the Archbishop of the conclusion of his work, and saying it was a cause of thankfulness to himself and it the entire Christian world.[13]

"To the critical genius of Ussher," says another great student in the same field, "belongs the honour of restoring the true

---

10. Ussher's *Works*, xvi, p. 34. It is to be observed that in earlier years, when composing his *Answer to a Jesuit*, Ussher quoted from the Long Recension without any misgivings.

11. In 1845, Cureton, as is well known, discovered three of the Ignatian Epistles in Syriac version in the British Museum.

12. Ussher's *Works*, xvi, p. 64–5; see also his letter to Ravius, of November 1639 (ib., p. 53).

13. Ditto, p. 92; also his letter to Salmasius, of May 31, 1644 (ib., p.72).

Ignatius."[14] If the Archbishop had sent forth no other effort of his brain, this alone would have been enough to have stamped him as one of the greatest and most independent scholars of his own or any age.

The story of the discovery of the Latin text, by which Ussher was enabled to publish an edition of the Epistles free from corruption and interpolation, is of absorbing interest, and goes far to prove the extraordinary penetration of this remarkable man. We may be excused, therefore, if we enter a little fully into the matter here.[15]

Ussher had been led to observe that the quotations from the Epistles of Ignatius in the writings of three English divines — Robert Grosseteste, John Tyssington, and William Wodeford — the first-mentioned being Bishop of Lincoln, and the two latter members of the Franciscan convent at Oxford; while they differed from the Greek and Latin versions, known as the "Long Recension," agreed with the quotations from St. Ignatius to be found in the writings of Eusebius and Theodoret. Ussher accordingly came to the conclusion that there must be hidden somewhere in the libraries of England MSS. of a version containing this earlier and sounder text. He directed a search to be made, and before long his critical judgment was rewarded with complete success.

Two MSS. of such a version were discovered, the first now known as *Caiensis,* and which was presented to Gonville and Caius College by a former Fellow, Walter Crome, D.D., A.D. 1444, as is testified in the fly-leaf in Crome's handwriting. The entire MS., which is a large one, is also the work of Crome, and contains, in addition to the Epistles of Ignatius, the Epistles of Dionysius, and some writings of St. Ambrose. The transcript from this MS., for the use of Ussher, is now preserved as one of its most cherished treasures in the library of Trinity College, Dublin, and contains

---

14. Bishop Lightfoot, *Apostolic Fathers,* Part II, Vol. i, p. 231.

15. For what follows we are much indebted to Bishop Lightfoot's interesting notes. — See his *Apostolic Fathers*, Part II, Vol. i, p. 76 and ff, p. 226 and ff.

on the second page a manuscript note in the Archbishop's handwriting, to the effect that the MS. was transcribed from the Caius College copy above mentioned, and was collated by him with another MS. obtained from the library of Richard Montague, D.D., Bishop of Norwich.[16] This second MS. was afterwards lost, and the attempts made to recover it have proved fruitless. "I, too, have angled for it," says Bishop Lightfoot, "in many waters, but inquiries made in all likely quarters have failed."

Very probably, as the Bishop surmises, it was lost among the confusions and depredations of the Parliamentary regime. Out of these Latin versions, with the aid of the Long Recension, Ussher produced his edition in 1644. There was only one flaw in it, but it was a serious one. Led astray by St. Jerome, who misunderstood a term in Eusebius, and imagined that the historian was speaking of one letter, when in reality he was referring to two — the Epistle to the Smyrneans and that to St. Polycarp — Ussher was induced to reject the latter as spurious, and discarded it from his edition of *Ignatius*. "It was the one blot," as Lightfoot says, "on his critical scutcheon." However, with this exception Ussher succeeded in producing a genuine text, and "those who have since attempted to reinstate the Long Recension have beaten their heads against a stone wall."[17] The investigations which led to such happy results were a remarkable evidence of the application to critical science of the principles of the Baconian philosophy which were already taking possession of men's minds.

---

16. "The old Latin version of *Ignatius*, Ussher published out of two MSS. found in England, noting in red letters the interpolations of the former Greek." — Ware, i, p. 110. A copy is preserved in the Library T.C.D. *(Class* GG. h. 8). The Latin transcript may also be seen *(Class* D. 3. II).

17. Bishop Lightfoot as above. Jerome blundered over a Greek word (by which Eusebius meant in a separate epistle"), supposing him to speak of only one letter. "This ignorance," says the Bishop, "might have been pardoned if it had not misled the greatest of Ignatian critics" — Apost. *Fathers,* Part II, Vol. i, p. 148 (note).

"A faculty of wise interrogation," as Bacon had said some time before, "is half a knowledge."[18]

Nor was Ussher's penetration exhibited only in these discoveries; he also came to the conclusion from certain delicate evidences that would have escaped a less observant mind, that Grosseteste was himself the translator of the first-mentioned M.S., a conclusion the correctness of which has been all but demonstrated by subsequent critics. With equal penetration he anticipated the discovery of an Armenian version,[19] and his forecast was abundantly justified in 1783 by the publication at Constantinople of an Armenian text supposed to be of the fifth century, which was reprinted in 1849.[20]

To Ussher, therefore, belongs the distinguished honour of having produced the first edition of the genuine writings of this apostolic Father, equally removed from the Syriac or Short Recension published by Cureton in 1845, and the Long Recension now universally acknowledged to be spurious.

It speaks volumes for the self-repression of the man, that in 1641,[21] while composing his tract on "The Original of Bishops," &c. for Bishop Hall and quoting from St. Ignatius, he says not a word about the great work on which he was then engaged. It is to be observed also that he was careful to confine all his extract to the correct text. In this respect, he was in marked contrast with Whitgift, Hooker, and Andrewes, who freely quoted from the interpolated form. Among others whom Ussher's reticence imposed upon was Milton, who in fiery language maintained that if God had ever intended we should learn anything from this writer, He would not "have

---

18. *Adv. Of Learning*, Pt. ii, p. 95.

19. *Works*, xvi, p. 65.

20. Notwithstanding all these labours bestowed on the Epistles of St. Ignatius there are still living, scholars who refuse to believe their genuineness. — See, e.g., Killen's *Ancient Church*, period ii, sect. ii, ch. 2 and 3; Bury's *Student's Roman Empire*, p. 456 (note).

21. He had begun to print his *Ignatius* in September 1640 (*Works*, xv, p. 64).

so ill provided for our knowledge as to send him to our hands in this broken and disjointed plight."[22] The great Puritan little knew that even then Ussher was providing for him the fuller knowledge.

The only thing required to complete the triumph of Ussher and prove him to be one of the keenest and most sagacious of theological critics, was the discovery of a genuine Greek text, which, strange to say, followed almost immediately. Two years after Ussher's publication,[23] Isaac Vossius published his celebrated edition, taken from a MS. discovered in the Medicean Library at Florence, which contained, in the Greek, six out of the seven genuine Epistles, wanting only that to the Romans, which was lost, the MS. being imperfect at the end. This latter Epistle was found fifty years later, and published by Ruinart in Paris, A.D. 1689, and thus Ussher's triumph was perfected.

As may well be supposed, the Archbishop's work met with the strongest opposition from the Presbyterian leaders, who had taken their cue from Calvin. That remarkable man had, with a bold stroke, thrown over all the Ignatian Epistles without exception, as impudent forgeries. "Nothing," he had written, "could be more disgusting than those silly trifles which are edited in the name of Ignatius."[24] It was felt that the seven genuine letters contained passages as inconsistent with the Presbyterian system as anything to be found in the Long Recension, and therefore the hard word went forth to put them all out of court.

22. Milton's *Prelatical Episcopacy, Works*, vol. iii, p. 72 and ff. Milton's language was utterly unworthy of him, and justifies the criticism of Dr. Johnson, that he had adopted "the puritanical savageness of manners." In his eyes, Ussher was a dunce-prelate." Equally, violent language may be seen in other writings of the day. — See, e.g., Prynne's *Canterbury's Doom*, p. 14.

23. *Dissertatio de Ig. et Pol. scriptis.* — Ussher's *Works*, p. 87–295.

24. *Inst.* i, ch. xiii, sec. 29. "Extremes meet. Calvin has found a counterpart in our day in the author of *Supernatural Religion*, who says the whole of the Ignatian literature is a mass of falsification and fraud," i, p. 269. Quoted by Lightfoot in his Essay on that work, p. 62.

"The new letters," wrote Claude Salmasius, Professor of History at Leyden, "are as much interpolated as the most reverend and learned Ussher has shown the old to be. They are the false lies of an impostor in the days, perhaps, of Marcus Aurelius."[25] David Blondel, successor to Vossius in the Chair of History at Amsterdam went even further in his condemnation of Ussher's work. Another able opponent was Daille. At the Archbishop's request, Dr. Hammond answered some of these objections, while Daille was ably handled sometime later by Pearson.[26] An intention which Ussher had of including the Epistle of St. Barnabas was prevented by a fire which destroyed his manuscript.

As might be expected, the importance of Ussher's great discovery was duly recognised by scholars, and one of the first learned bodies to honour him was the University of Oxford. A decree was passed at a Convocation held on March 10th, 1645, that a portrait of the Archbishop should be executed at the expense of the University, with a suitable inscription, and prefixed to his work. The engraving eventually appeared in his treatise *De Symbolo,* with an inscription signed by the Vice-Chancellor, Robert Pink.[27] Ussher himself, it may be observed,

---

25. See, on the other hand, Ussher's graceful letter when sending a copy of his book to Salmasius. — *Works,* xvi, p. 72.

26. For his pains, Dr. Hammond was dubbed by the Presbyterians "Sir Knave." Ussher writes to him: "I have read with great delight and content your accurate answer to the objections made against the credit of Ignatius his Epistles." We learn from his letter that Dr. Hammond received a second nickname, being "rudely requited with the bare appellation of Nebulo for his assertion of episcopacy." This was done with a view to creating the impression that "the defence thereof was now deserted by all men." — Ussher's *Works,* xvi, p. 135 and 156. Capellus had recently written a book at Sedan, with this object in view.

27. The following is the "Eulogium": "James Ussher, Archbishop of Armagh, Primate of all Ireland, skillful of primitive antiquity, the unanswerable defender of the orthodox religion, the maul of errors, in preaching frequent, eloquent, very powerful, a rare example of all unblamable life." — Wood's *Fasti Oxon.* Pt. i, p. 427. The Latin original is given in Elrington's *Life,* p. 236.

was resident in Jesus College, Oxford, at the time, pursuing his studies. He was now a D.D. *ad eundem* of the University.[28]

Having sent forth his *Ignatius*, Ussher speedily published a further fruit of his pen in an essay on the Apostles' Creed, and other formularies of the faith, Eastern and Western. The work, which is dedicated to Vossius, whose opinions he was controverting, shows that the latter clauses of the Nicene Creed are older than the Council of Constantinople.[29]

That to his other attainments Ussher added an appreciation of mathematics, and took an interest in astronomical science, is plain from his correspondence. Thus we find the learned Davenant communicating with him on the subject of "Spherical Triangles" and "Eclipses"; and Dr. Gilbert writes an elaborate essay on the planetary system, in which he anticipates the modern speculation of "the plurality of worlds."[30]

---

28. Elrington's *Life,* p. 235 (note).

29. Ussher's *Works*, vii, p. 297–342. Ussher relied chiefly for his view of the matter on the Nicene Creed as recited by Epiphanius in his *Anchoratus,* a book written seven years before the Council of Constantinople was held, "where in the clauses referring to the Holy Ghost, &c, supposed to have been first added by that Council, are to be found." — See Ussher's *Works,* xvi, p. 82, 84, 87–9.

30. Ussher's *Works*, xvi, p. 41–5. The letter of Dr. Gilbert, addressed to Ussher from Dublin, Dec. 11th, 1638, is a remarkably eloquent production, and in some respects reminds the reader of some famous essays on the same subject two centuries later. He enlarges on the infinitude of the stellar system, and asks why we should suppose that we alone are an intelligent portion of it, and goes on to say "so might the spider nested in the roof of the grand seignior's seraglio say of herself: all that magnificent and stately structure, set out with gold and silver and embellished with all antiquity and mosaic work, was only built for her to hang up her webs and toils to take flies. We, the glorious ants of this earth, magnify ourselves upon this mole-hill here to be the great and sole end of the world's workmanship, whilst we consider not how little and nothing we are of it." Another learned correspondent of Ussher's was Henry Briggs, Savilian Professor of Astronomy at Oxford, 1596–1620. He became

In Parr's catalogue of Ussher's MSS., which were never printed, mention is made of a tract on planetary mathematics. Among other MSS. in Trinity College, Dublin, may be found a catalogue in Ussher's handwriting of fifteen stars of the first magnitude and other astronomical papers.[31] If Ussher had not devoted himself so entirely to the study of theology and ecclesiastical history, there is evidence to show that he might have distinguished himself in the higher walks of mathematical and astronomical science.

---

acquainted with Ussher in 1609. Briggs was much taken up with "the noble invention of logarithms," and visited Napier of Merchiston, the discoverer. He was a great opponent of the pursuit of astrology, which he pronounced "a system of groundless conceits." — See Ussher's *Works*, xv, p. 90; *Dict. Nat. Biog.*, under "Briggs."

31. *Class* D. 3. 15 and D. 3. 24.

CHAPTER XIX

USSHER IN ENGLAND; DEATH OF STRAFFORD; REVOLUTIONARY CHANGES IN CHURCH AND STATE

Return we now to the public life of the Archbishop. It was his painful duty about this time to take part in the degradation and sentence of a brother bishop, John Atherton, Bishop of Waterford and Lismore, who had been found guilty of unnatural crime and sentenced to death. Ussher was much concerned about his fate, and his chaplain, Dr. Bernard, was most assiduous in visiting him in prison, in the Castle of Dublin. Atherton showed signs of true penitence, and Bernhard preached a sermon afterwards entitled "The Penitent Death of a Woeful Sinner," in which this fact was set forth with great power.[1]

---

1. Bernard's sermon, which was dedicated to Archbishop Ussher, was long a popular chap-book in Dublin. Lord Strafford had taken up Atherton and made him Prebendary of St. John's, Dublin, in 1630. In 1635, he became Chancellor of Christ Church and in 1636, Bishop of Waterford and Lismore. In 1640, he was put on the capital charge, and degraded and hanged in Dublin, Dec. 5th of that year. His body, by his own desire, was buried in an obscure part of St. John's churchyard. Carte is responsible

 251

The last important engagement of Ussher, previous to leaving Ireland, never to return, was discharged when he preached before Parliament in March l640, being then in his fifty-ninth year. Immediately afterwards, he crossed with his family to England, and proceeded to Oxford, where he first took up his quarters at Christ Church.[2]

Ussher had previously waited on the King in London, who received him with much graciousness.[3] Dark days were now in store for Church and State. The first mutterings of the storm that was shortly to break over the country, and before which crown and mitre were alike to go down, were heard, and the King had

for the theory that Atherton attracted the enmity of the Earl of Cork by suing for some of his lands, and that falling a victim to his hostility he had this charge trumped against him, but this cannot be proved, and the Bishop acknowledged to his guilt. His execution was witnessed by an immense crowd, his last words being interrupted by a wretch who sat astride on the top of the gallows and derided the unhappy man. Bernard's sermon was preached at the Bishop's burial, the night after his execution, in St. John's Church, Dublin. — See Wood's *Athen. Oxon.,* ii, p. 892; Cotton's *Fasti Eccl. Hib.;* and Bernard's *Penitent Death,* &c.

2. There is a tradition, which has no support beyond the gossip of one of Robert Wodrow's correspondents, published in a collection of anecdotes, that Ussher took Scotland on his way in order that he might make the acquaintance of Rutherford, and that he preached in his church. First, all the biographers agree that Ussher travelled to London on this occasion accompanied by his family. Secondly, summoned over for consultation on important State business, it is not likely that Ussher would have allowed himself to have been delayed so long by a tedious and troublesome journey via Scotland and the North of England. If he did take this route, it is incomprehensible that none of his many biographers knew anything about it. — See Wo*drow's Analecta,*ii, p. 364 and iii, p. 133–4. The apocryphal character of the story is further proved by the fact that the episode about the "eleven" commandments is also told on the occasion of Ussher's supposed shipwreck on the coast of Ireland. There is no record of his having ever been shipwrecked. — See Elrington's *Life,* p. 280–1 (note).

3. According to Ware, Ussher was invited over by some eminent persons on account of the then difference between the King and Parliament. — *Works,* i, p. 108–9; also Smith's *Life,* p. 71. We learn from a letter addressed to him by Laud, that he was to be put up by the King's permission at the

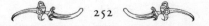

need of wise councillors. Ussher was called into the royal presence, and his advice sought on the question of the Church of Scotland. A spurious tract had been issued at the time, bearing as its title "The Directions of the Archbishop of Armagh concerning the Liturgy and Episcopal Government." Ussher at once disowned the publication, and applied to the House of Commons to have it suppressed, which was done, although it was republished by the Puritans a short time later as a genuine work and with the malicious addition on the title-page: "Being thereunto requested by the Honourable the House of Commons, and then presented in they year 1642." This was not the only pamphlet that was improperly fathered upon Ussher, a fact which goes to prove how much he was thought of at the time, and how great was the desire of opposing factions to represent him as being on their side.[4]

Bishop Bramhall, who remained behind in Ireland was now in trouble with the authorities. Such high quarry as Archbishop Ussher having escaped the enemies of the Church turned on Bramhall. On March 4th, 1641, articles of high treason were brought against him in the Irish Parliament. In his distress, he appealed to Ussher from his prison in Dublin Castle on April 25th, 1642. The Archbishop successfully interceded on his behalf with the King, and the proceedings were stayed. "I assure you," wrote Ussher, "my care in soliciting your cause never slackened at Court with as great vigilancy as if it did touch my own proper person."[5] While these two men differed much in temperament and the way in which they viewed some things, they maintained an unbroken friendship to the last.

Dean of Westminster lodgings, where he was to spend the winter. There was some difficulty about the keys of the chambers, but Laud says, "I will do all that lies in me to accommodate your Grace." In a postscript, Laud alludes to the coming troubles. "Two thousand Brownists had raised disturbance at St. Paul's, crying out that they would have no Bishops nor High Commission." — Ussher's *Works*, xvi, p. 536–7.

4. See Elrington's *Life of Ussher*, p. 223–4 and 248–50.

5. Bramhall's *Life in Anglo-Cath. Lib. App.*, p. xxi.

"Although," says his biographer, "the former (Bramhall) was a man of active zeal and hasty temper and devoted heart and soul to the restoration of the Irish Church in a way Archbishop Ussher opposed, and upon principles with which he did not sympathise, in times, too, of strong excitement and violent party feeling, yet there ever existed between them a most friendly and, even affectionate intercourse."[6] In his "Discourse on the Sabbath," speaking of Ussher and his suffragans, Bramhall says, "We were like the Candles in the Levitical temple, looking one towards another and all towards the stem."[7]

We have already drawn attention to the *eirenicon* proposed by Ussher with a view to a reconciliation between Episcopalians and Presbyterians. It would seem as if under pressure of the times Ussher did for a moment contemplate the possibility of reducing episcopacy to a kind of moderatorship — the Bishops to be deprived of their orders and proper jurisdiction, and reduced to the level of superintendents or presidents of Ecclesiastical Council. But if this were so, it was only a temporary aberration, for some time later he produced those tracts on the apostolical origin and authority of the episcopate already referred to.

His action, contradictory as it may appear, may be fully explained by his strong desire to preserve in a great crisis some shadow of episcopal government. "If we can save it here," he writes to Bramhall "(for which I can tell you we are put to our utmost), there will be no need to fear anything that moveth from thence" — referring to the anti-episcopal agitation likewise proceeding in Ireland.[8] At the time it was made a question of life and death between the King and his enemies, and accordingly we find that during the royal imprisonment in Carisbrook Castle some years

---

6. Bramhall's *Life.*

7. Bramhall's *Works,* Vol. v, p. 74.

8. "Sir John Clotworthy hath presented a far larger petition to the House of Commons for the abolishing of episcopacy in Ireland than that which you sent unto me and signed with a huge number of hands." — Ussher to Bramhall, *Rawdon Papers,* p. 82.

later (1648), a conference was called at the intervention of the Presbyterians, who had fallen out with the Independents, at which the King sought the advice of some of the bishops, and amongst others of Archbishop Ussher. The Irish Primate would not hear of the plan for abolishing bishops, but once more proposed the scheme he had advanced in 1641, and which now obtained the acceptance of the Presbyterian ministers who were present.

The King, in a temporising mood, went so far as to undertake that the exercise of the episcopate should be suspended for three years, and that episcopal ordinations should be performed only with the consent of presbyters, and that all episcopal jurisdiction should be carried on subject to authority of King and Parliament. The Puritan party, however, were determined on the total suppression of the episcopal order and would listen to no compromise, and so the conference fell through. Matters went so far that some of the enemies of the bishops had the audacity to threaten the King that if he would not consent to "the utter abolition of Episcopacy he would be damned."[9]

A more invidious task had been put before the Archbishop sometime previously, when called upon to decide as to the justice or otherwise of consenting to the death of his friend and former coadjutor in the Irish Government, Lord Strafford.

The Earl had been impeached and condemned for high treason by Parliament, and his death sentence was now awaiting the Royal signature. In this emergency, Charles asked "the counsel of the Bishops of London, Durham, Lincoln, and Carlisle, together with that of Ussher. The meeting was held on Sunday, and, as Ussher

---

9. See Elrington's *Life of Ussher,* p. 256 (note). For an account of this Conference, see Fuller's *Ch. Hist.,* iii, p. 556–562, and Neal's *Hist. of the Puritans,* ii, p. 68–74. Butler, in his *Hudibras,* catches the spirit of the time: "The oyster women locked their fish up,
And trudged away to call 'No Bishop!'
Some cried the Covenant instead
Of pudding, pies and ginger bread." — Canto ii.
See also Fuller's *Ch. Hist.,* iii, p. 431; and Walker's *Trials of the Clergy,* p. II.

was preaching in St. Paul's, Covent Garden, he said he could not be present. He attended, however, the second meeting held in the evening. There seems to have been a large amount of Jesuitical casuistry over the question, and a straightforward answer was not forthcoming. The episcopal advisers of his Majesty's conscience could not agree. It is alleged that Ussher gave a reluctant assent.[10]

Later in his life, and when supposed to be dying, according to Dr. Parr, Ussher made the following statement: "I never gave nor approved of such advice as that the King should assent to the Bill against the Earl, but, on the contrary, told his Majesty that if he was satisfied by what he heard at his trial that the Earl was not guilty of treason, his Majesty ought not in conscience to consent to his condemnation." After it was reported that Ussher was dead, the charge that he had consented to the death of Strafford was repeated in the royal presence, when Charles, according to Dr. Parr, repudiated the truth of the accusation in the strongest manner, and declared that Ussher had come to him with tears in his eyes, exclaiming, "Oh, Sir, what have you done? I fear that this act may prove a great trouble to your conscience, and pray God your Majesty may never suffer by the signing of this Bill."[11]

Be this matter how it may, and it does seem unlikely that Ussher counselled the signing of the death warrant, the King selected Ussher to bear his last message to his devoted servant. That message contained the rather equivocal announcement,

---

10. See, among other authorities who take this view, Dr. Littledale in *Encyc. Brit.*, under "Ussher." He speaks of it as one blot on Ussher's memory, "that being one of the five prelates whom Charles I consulted as to whether he could conscientiously assent to the Act of Attainder against the Earl of Strafford after having pledged his word to him for his safety, Ussher joined in the casuistical advice given by all except Juxon, who alone told the King that his word could not be lawfully broken." Lord Campbell also, in his *Lives of the Chancellors*, Vol. ii, p. 485–6, inculpates Ussher. Elrington indignantly denies the truth of the charge, as do also Bernard and Parr. On this side likewise is Gardiner, *Hist. Fall Charles I*, ii, p. 173. The question is discussed in *Notes and Queries*, First Series, Vol. iv.

11. Parr's *Life*, p. 61.

"That if the King's life only were hazarded thereby, he would never have given passage to his death, and that the execution, without extreme danger, could not be deferred."[12] There is reason to believe that the prelate who induced the King to consent to the Earl's death was, Dr. Williams, Bishop of Lincoln.[13]

A further and apparently convincing reason for believing that Ussher did not act with such incredible baseness, is the fact that he waited on the Earl in his last moments, an office of affection and even danger he could scarcely have fulfilled had he counseled his death. He accompanied Strafford to the scaffold, where he knelt and prayed beside him at the block. Ussher afterwards told the King "he had seen many die, but never saw so white a soul return to his Maker." Writing to Bishop Bramhall, he likewise expressed his admiration of the hapless Earl, as ending his sufferings after a most Christian and magnanimous fashion — *Ad stuporem usque.*[14]

Ussher had not long left Ireland when the rebels pounced upon his property in Drogheda. His houses in the country were

---

12. Memorandum by Ussher preserved in his Almanack. — Elrington's *Life,* p. 214–15.

13. See Clarendon's *History,* Vol. i, p. 147. Williams made a Jesuitical distinction between the "public" and "private" conscience of the King.

14. See the Rawdon Papers, No. xxxiv.; Smith's *Life of Ussher,* p. 80–1; Parr's ditto, p. 46, 61; and Sanderson's *Hist. of the Reign of Charles,* under date 1641. It was disgracefully charged against Ussher that he could never find it in his heart to forgive Stafford for his action with regard to the Articles of the Church of Ireland in the convocation of 1634, and he took his revenge by voting for his death (Heylin, in his observations on *L'Estrange's Hist. of the Reign of Charles I,* p. 240–1). It was said that Ussher carried "a sharp tooth" against Strafford on this account. But, as Bramhall nobly says, the good Primate was not "of such a vindictive disposition (vindictive is too low an expression; I might more aptly call it diabolical) as to write discontents in marble, and, like another Haman, to give bloody counsel upon private disgusts." Any one who lived in Ireland "could not choose but see what mutual and cordial respects passed daily between these two great persons from the first day of their acquaintance to the last." Bramhall goes on further to gather many instances of their constant friendship, and ends thus: "Lastly, which

plundered, his rents withheld, his cattle maimed and killed, and it was only a vigorous defence that saved his house in Drogheda, with its matchless collection of books and manuscripts.[15]

Through all his troubles, the Archbishop's serene temper never failed him. He had learned, as his biographer Dr. Parr says, "in whatsoever state he was, therewith to be content." The King, to make up in some degree for his losses, had presented him to the See of Carlisle *in commendam;* but he was shortly deprived of the scanty revenues of the bishopric when the Parliamentarians sequestered all episcopal revenues.[16] Some time after his arrival in England, Ussher was requested to take part in a committee called

---

weigheth more with me than all the rest, the choosing him (Ussher) to be his ghostly father and spiritual adviser at his death, and his receiving Absolution and the Holy Sacrament of the Body and Blood of Christ from his hands when he had chaplains of his own in the city, doth convince me and all ingenuous persons that there was no dissatisfaction of either party against the other." — *Works,* v, p. 83–4.

15. The news reached London in a strange way, as we gather from an insertion in the *Calendar of Domestic Papers* of 1640 (Rolls Series), where we learn how one James Smith, apothecary to Dr. Langham, was at dinner at the house of Mr. Clay, grocer or druggist, of Lombard Street, London, when he mentioned that he had received certain news out of Ireland to the effect that after the Lord-Lieutenant left the country the Irish utterly razed and pulled down Ussher's dwelling-house, and that the Archbishop was himself coming from Ireland to England for succour, "by reason there is a rebellion in Ireland like to the rebellion in Scotland." The house referred to must have been the palace at Termonfechan, as the Archbishop's house in Drogheda was saved as we learn from Bernard's history of the siege. He writes, "One of the chiefest cares that lay upon me was that great treasure of my Lord Primate's library. . . . We heard of the daily rudeness of the vulgar in burning and cutting in pieces the papers and books of such of the clergy already made a prey of," and he especially notices the libraries of Lord Conway and the Bishop of Meath. — *History of the Siege,* p. 9.

16. Story, in his *Cathedrals,* under "Carlisle," seems to say that Ussher resided for a time in that city, but we can find no proof of it elsewhere. We find in a Carlisle correspondence, published in Wood's *Ath. Oxon.,* iv, p. 799, a writer saying, "I do not find, or have ever heard, that he [Ussher] was here in person."

together by the House of Lords to see if they could come to some compromise whereby the Church might be saved from the dangers that surrounded it. At the head of the committee sat Williams, Bishop of Lincoln. Nothing came of it. It met for about a month, but when it took in hand the cathedral establishment, and proposed to do away with deans and chapters, it melted away.

Archbishop Laud, now in prison, thus refers its meetings: "A committee for religion settled in the Upper House of Parliament. Ten earls, ten bishops, ten barons — so the lay votes will be double to the clergy. The committee will meddle with doctrine as well as ceremonies. . . . Upon the whole matter, I believe, this committee will prove the national Synod of England, to the great dishonour of the Church. And what else may follow upon it, God, knows."[17]

It would have been impossible for a man of Ussher's reputation to have remained destitute and without employment for his talents, and more than one overture was made to him to transfer himself to foreign parts. The University of Leyden invited him to fill a Chair in that (then) renowned seat of learning, and Cardinal Richelieu invited him to France. Civilities passed between these two remarkable men. The Cardinal presented him with a gold medal, as an acknowledgment of his services to literature, and the Archbishop returned the compliment (it is said) with a pair of Irish wolf-dogs, a sly hit, as has been supposed, at the well-known hunting tastes of the French ecclesiastic.[18]

According to D'Alembert, an authority for the story, the return gift disgusted the Cardinal and prevented further courtesies.[19]

The year 1642 finds Ussher pursuing his studies in Oxford, where he lodged in the house of Dr. Prideaux, Bishop of Worcester, and close to Exeter College. On Sundays, he preached plain sermons to crowded congregations in St. Olave's or Allhallows

---

17. Laud's *Diary,* quoted by Elrington, *Life of Ussher,* p. 229 (note).

18. See Bishop Fitzgerald's article in the *Dublin University Magazine,* xviii, p. 154.

19. D'Alembert, *Works,* ix, p. 224; also Ware's *Works,* i, p. 109.

churches.[20] At the close of the year we find Ussher again in attendance with the King, who receives the Holy Communion at his hands, and takes the opportunity of declaring his unabated devotion to the true Protestant religion "without any connivance of popery."

On the first day of July 1643, the famous Assembly of Divines, whose deliberations and conclusions were destined to affect so materially the future current of theology in these countries, met at Westminster. Ussher, amongst others, was invited to attend the Assembly, which was convened by Parliamentary authority, but without the consent of the King, who refused to sanction the Bill passed to summon it. Ussher not only refused to be present, but preached against it as an illegal and schismatical gathering.

In return, the House of Commons had the meanness to confiscate the Archbishop's library, which had been brought over from Drogheda and deposited in Chelsea, College. The books would have been sold and dispersed had not Dr. Featley interfered, and with the assistance of Mr. Selden, also a member of the Assembly, succeeded in protecting them.[21] There had been some disputing as to whether the members should admit Ussher into the Assembly at all. "They had as good inquire," said Seldon, "whether they had best admit Inigo Jones, the King's architect, to the company of mouse-trap makers."[22] In the Assembly, Dr. Featley alone stood up for episcopal Church government. He afterwards wrote to Ussher saying what part he had taken, and asking for preferment. The letter was intercepted, and laid before the Assembly, who forthwith expelled Featley, sequestered his benefice, seized his books, and cast him into prison, where he languished till his death.[23]

---

20. Parr's *Life*, p. 48. It was while resident in Oxford that his daughter Elizabeth was married to Sir Timothy Tyrrel of Shotover and Oakley.

21. Parr's *Life of Ussher*, p. 50; Elrington's ditto, p. 230–2.

22. See Todd's *Walton*, i, p. 181 (note).

23. Clarendon's *History*, ii, p. 228–9. Featley was charged with being "a spy and intelligencer to Oxford." — See *Calendar of State Papers,* 1643, p. 489.

It is a marvellous illustration of the intellectual detachment of Ussher, and of his power to rise above external circumstances, that it was during these convulsions in Church and State he perfected and published his edition of the Ignatian Epistles. He also published a short time afterwards (1647), an appendix, in which he notices some objections to his work;[24] he likewise contemplated an edition of the Epistle of Barnabas, but the manuscript was, as already mentioned, unfortunately destroyed by fire in a printer's office.

Not only English but Irish questions were now pressing on the attention of the King. The Irish Privy Council had sent a deputation to England urging the King to withhold toleration from his Roman Catholic subjects in Ireland. Sir Charles Coote, one of the most violent and harsh of the Protestant leaders, charged Ussher with counselling moderation.[25] Later on, when summoned to meet this charge before the Court of Examiners established by Parliament, Ussher declared that neither Sir Charles Coote nor any other party had communicated with him on the subject, but that he had advised the King to make no concessions to the Roman Catholics without his advice.

It is likely that Ussher, conscious of the excesses committed on both sides, was anxious to moderate between the contending parties. He spoke for peace and for the exhibiting of the practical fruits of Christianity. What little chance there was of such principles prevailing in any part of the kingdom at this time, is plain from the violent pamphlets that were now sown broadcast. Among the most bitter of these pamphleteers was Prynne, who had got hold of this charge of Coote against the Archbishop, and had strangely distorted it. Ussher's advice he characterised as "a very strange speech for a saint-seeming Protestant Archprelate.

---

24. *Appendix Ignatiana;* see also *Praefationes in Ignatium*; Ussher's *Works,* vii, p. 273–295.

25. Coote was cruel and vindictive all round. He harried alike Roman Catholics, Episcopalians, and Presbyterians. — See Leland's *History,* iii, p. 146; Reid's *History,* ii, p. 239.

The very best and learnedest in all the whole pack of prelates, even the Primate of Armagh, hath extremely degenerated in his Christian zeal for the Protestant religion since he turned Royalist and Cavalier. The God of heaven deliver us from such an hypo-critical, false archiepiscopall generation of vipers."[26]

That Ussher's close communication with the King while the Court remained at Oxford, had drawn him towards his afflicted and perplexed Sovereign is highly probable. He seems to have been called on to solve the very difficult question how far a peo-ple would be justified in taking up arms against their King, and to have decided it largely on the side of "passive obedience."

The archbishop's views may be seen at large in his treatise on "The Power of the Prince," an essay composed at the request of Charles, but not published till after Ussher's death. It appeared in 1660, with a dedication to Charles II and a preface by Bishop Sanderson.[27]

Matters had now become so serious in Oxford that Ussher, by the advice of his friends, determined to seek safer quarters. The entire town had been turned into a camp, and soldiers were billeted on all the colleges. He left accordingly for Bristol in the escort of the Prince of Wales. The King remained for some time longer in his quarters in Christ Church College, where he attend-ed daily prayers in the Cathedral. From Bristol, Ussher went on to Cardiff, which was held for the Royalists by his son-in-law, Sir Timothy Tyrrel. Here he worked for a year among his books, and went on with his *Chronological Annals*. It was not long before he was rejoined by the King, who had left Oxford after the battle of Nasbey. They lodged together in the same house.

An interesting memento of this sojourn still exists, in the shape of a small volume in the Bodleian Library, containing a metrical version of the 100th and 101st Psalms by Sir Philip

---

26. *Canterbury's Doom*, p. 14, quoted by Elrington, p. 237. The Puritans had a remarkable facility for calling names.

27. Ussher's *Works*, Vol. xi.

Sydney, with a marginal note by Ussher: "I delivered a copy of this to the King at Cardiffe, Aug. 4th, 1645, having preached there unto him the day before."[28]

Cardiff did not long remain a safe halting-place for the much troubled Archbishop. As soon as the King had left and withdrawn the garrison, Ussher was again compelled to change his quarters. He had not far to go on this occasion, as Lady Stradling invited him to take shelter in her castle at St. Donate's, a small village in Glamorganshire on the northwest coast of the Bristol Channel, overlooking the mouth of the Severn. Here there was a fine collection of books, of which Ussher took full advantage. His visit was not made without considerable danger and loss, as the party were attacked on their journey by a band of wild Welshmen, who pillaged their baggage and scattered the unfortunate Primate's books and papers. He was happily rescued out of their hands by some English gentlemen, who, coming up at the moment, discovered who they were. His losses were subsequently advertised over the country, and by degrees he recovered most of his literary treasures. Some things however, were irretrievably lost, including, most probably, the Medicean MS. of Ignatius.

He also lost the Oxford Readings of the New Testament which he had copied out.[29] Dr. Parr, who was with him at the time, writing afterwards of the annoyance that thus came to the Archbishop, says, "I must confess that I never saw him so much troubled in my life; and those that were with him before myself said that he seemed not more sensibly concerned for all his losses in Ireland than for this, saying to his daughter and those who were endeavouring to comfort him, 'I know that it is God's hand, and I must endeavour to bear it patiently, though I have too much human frailty not to be extremely concerned, for I am touched in a very tender place, and He has thought fit to take from me at once all that I have been gathering together above

28. See Elrington's *Life*, p. 243 (note).

29. Ussher's *Works*, xvi, p. 174.

these twenty years, and which I intended for the advancement of learning and the good of the Church.' "[30] Ussher was a real connoisseur of books. "There was scarcely a choice book or MS. in any of the libraries," says Dr. Parr, "but was known to him. Nor was he conversant in the libraries of our own nation alone, but also knew most of the choice pieces in the Vatican, Escurial, and Imperial Library at Vienna; as likewise in that of the King of France, of Thuanus at Paris, and Erpinius in Holland, as still appears by the catalogues he had procured of them, many of which I have now in my custody."[31]

---

30. Parr's *Life of Ussher,* p. 59–60; Ware's *Works,* i, p. 111–112.

31. Parr's *Life,* p. 99.

CHAPTER XX

USSHER IN LONDON; STRAITENED MEANS; CROMWELL AND USSHER; THE DEATH OF CHARLES I

Always alive to the studies that interested him most, Ussher was now spending much of his time on valuable additions to his great work, *The Antiquities of the British Churches*, enlarging it by illustrations drawn from ancient Welsh sources, materials for which he found in the library at St. Donate's. In the midst of these labours he was prostrated by a serious illness, and thought his end had come. The report, indeed, was circulated that he had died. Calling to his bedside his chaplain, Dr. Parr, he delivered through him solemn injunctions to all his friends to remember their latter end, saying "It was a dangerous thing to leave all undone till their last sickness." To a member of Commons, a relative of Lady Stradling, he said, "They have dealt very injuriously with the King."[1] Contrary to all expectations, the attack passed off, and the Archbishop recovered.[2]

---

1. Parr's *Life of Ussher*, p. 60–1.
2. So sure were some of his friends that Ussher's death had taken place that one of them, John Greaves, then Savilian Professor of Astronomy, drew up an inscription for his monument. — Elrington's *Life*, p. 246.

Ussher's nest was now again to be stirred up. The tide had set strongly against the Royalist cause, and his position at St. Donate's was no longer a safe one. Like other prominent men, he was contemplating flight to the Continent, and had actually chartered a vessel to convey him to France. Before he could sail however, a fleet under the command of the Parliamentary Admiral Molton drew down on Cardiff, and there was some danger of Ussher being taken prisoner. In the emergency, he received a kind invitation from the Dowager Countess of Peterborough to seek shelter at her house in Covent Garden, London. His means, which had been much crippled by all his losses, were inadequate to the expenses of the journey, but some friends came forward with a spontaneous offer of help, and he set out for London in the month of June 1646.[3]

As soon as his arrival at the capital became known, he received a summons from the Court of Examiners, who were sitting in the interests of the Cromwellian party, to appear in person before them. They refused to accept a deputy. Coote's charge was brought up against him, which he denied in general terms. He was then dismissed with a warning that he should take the "negative oath," which, however was not enforced. The enfeebled Prelate now retired with his patron to her country seat at Reigate, where after a while he regained some of his old strength, and began to preach with much of his wonted vigour to all who came to hear him.

While Ussher was seeking an asylum in Wales, a hyper-Calvinistic work entitled *A Body of Divinity, or the Sum and Substance of the Christian Religion*, had been published under his name by one Downham. It was at once repudiated by Ussher,

---

3. On his way, Ussher stopped at Gloucester, and endeavoured without success to convert Biddle, the famous anti-Trinitarian. — "Either he was in damnable error, or else the whole Church of Christ, who had worshipped the Holy Ghost had been guilty of idolatry." Biddle afterwards published twelve Questions against the commonly received opinion touching the Divinity of the Holy Spirit. "Biddle was several times fined and imprisoned for his heterodoxy and finally died under his sufferings." — Edwards' *Gangraena,* iii, p. 87; Wood's *Aht. Oxon.,* iii, p. 593.

who stated that it was printed from a common-place book wherein he had taken down expressions from Cartwright and others. In divers places he declared it differed from his own judgment, and could not be owned by him.[4]

Notwithstanding this disclaimer, the book continued to be published up to a recent date, as if it represented his mature opinions. Elrington refused, though requested to do so, to publish it among Ussher's recognised works. In the catalogue of the Archbishop's printed works in the Library of Trinity College there is a note to this effect: "The *Body of Divinity* is spurious, having been expressly disowned by Ussher. See his *Life*, by Elrington, in the collected works, Vol. i, p. 248."[5]

In 1647, we find Ussher discharging the duties of Lecturer at Lincoln's Inn, to which honourable position he had been elected by the Benchers. He was at first unwilling to assume the office in consequence of the opposition of Parliament,[6] and only accepted it through the intervention of his friend and admirer, Matthew Hale, the eminent jurist, and afterwards Chief Justice of England.

Hale and Ussher had shared in the friendship of Strafford and Laud, each of whom had enjoyed the advantage of Hale's able advocacy.

Among Ussher's constant hearers in Lincoln's Inn was the famous Royalist, John Selden. Another drawn to listen to him was

---

4. Parr's *Life,* p. 74.

5. Strange to say, it is quoted in the Gorham case as if it reflected the opinions of Ussher. Dean Goode also quotes it as an authority in his *Infant Baptism,* p. 312–13. Bernard, in his *Life of Ussher,* says the Archbishop "permitted" the publication of it, though displeased at its being published without his knowledge, because he heard it had done some good. — *Life*, p. 41–2. There is a MS. copy in the Library T.C.D., Class D.3.7. It is thus annotated in the MS. Catalogue: "Had been collected by the author in his younger years for his own use, and was printed through the importunity of friends to whom it was lent. However, this copy is spurious, for the transcriber has omitted all the passages that reflect on the Church of Rome."

6. See *State Papers,* Feb. 1647.

the chatty John Evelyn. This he enters in his Diary, under March 25, 1649: "I heard the Common Prayer (a rare thing in these days) in St. Peter's, at Paul's Wharf, London; and in the morning the Archbishop of Armagh, that pious and learned man Ussher, in Lincoln's Inn Chapel." Again, March 29, 1652: "I heard that excellent Prelate; the Primate of Ireland (Jacob Ussher) preach in Lincoln's Inn on 4 Heb.16, encouraging penitent sinners."[7]

Here Ussher continued to preach for eight years, resigning at the end of that period owing to increasing infirmities of sight and articulation. With the exception of this duty, the Archbishop had now withdrawn entirely from public life, but he never ceased to protest against Cromwell's policy. By permission of the Benchers he had taken up his quarters at Lincoln's Inn, and had collected about him what remained of his library. He also preached occasionally in the Chapel.

He preached November 5, 1654, before the Society of Gray's Inn, of which he had been made member some thirty years earlier.[8] In this year, his lifelong friend John Selden died, and was buried in the Temple Church, when Ussher preached the funeral sermon. In the course of it, the Archbishop gave expression to the regard with which he had always held the deceased. He looked upon him "as so great a scholar that he himself was scarce worthy to carry his books after him." Ussher had visited and ministered spiritual consolation to Selden, and "absolved" him before his death."[9] The last sermon the Archbishop preached was delivered in Hammersmith church on Michaelmas Day 1655, and a year later his own end had come.

---

7. Evelyn's *Diary*, Vol. i, p. 236–263.

8. The following is an extract from the admission-book of Gray's Inn, fol. 811: *"Jacobius Usherius Divinia providentia dominus episcopus Methensis in regno Hibernia, admissus est in societatem, hujus hospitii vicessimo sexto die Januarii, in Anno Dom: 1623."*

9. Rawlinson MS., B. clviii, fol. 75. Macray's *Annals Bod. Lib.*, p. 77 (note). It was reported at the time that Selden had refused to see a clergyman.

In the beginning of the year 1648, Ussher had exhibited another instance of his versatile genius by publishing a dissertation on the change from Solar to Lunar months made by the Macedonians about the year 334 B.C., an essay full of remarkable chronological and astronomical knowledge.

By certain calculations, he attempts to fix the martyrdom of St. Ignatius for March 26, 169. He also gives rules for finding Easter for ever. Other curious lore is to be found in this treatise.[10]

Ussher had now dropped the empty title of Archbishop and Primate from the title-pages of his books; he continued, however, to sign himself in his private letters by his ecclesiastical title, sometimes introducing the surname. A correspondent is distressed almost to tears at the omission and writes (we give a plain rendering of the Latin): "What, I said within myself, has become of the Archbishops and Primate of all Ireland? Alas! And can you suffer your honours to be thus taken from you with so much patience and without resistance? But I perceive how it is, you think it has been by your many and admirable books, composed alike in English and Latin, that no region is so remote that it does not understand, and no age so backward that it does not recognise the fact that the title of Armagh prefixed to your works is not confined to the place, but is an essential part of your honour and dignity, and rightly your judge: 'It is necessary to obey; For what can one do when a madman compels, and he, too, The stronger?' "[11]

It may be asked what were the resources of Ussher, deprived as he now was of the emoluments of his See, and robbed of nearly all his private property. These resources were almost nil, and Parliament, recognising his great claims, had voted him the sum of £400 a year, but it had been irregularly paid. Cromwell

---

10. Elrington gives a brief analysis of the work. — *Life of Ussher*, p. 253–4. He points out in a footnote that Pearson refuted Ussher's calculation, and fixed the death of St. Ignatius on March 26, 147.

11. *"Parere necesse est; Nam quid agas, quum te furiosus cogat, et idem Fortior."* — *Fuv. Sat.* ii, 90: Ussher's *Works*, xvi, p. 124–5.

renewed the grant, and in this way the Archbishop was saved from absolute penury.[12]

Later on, according to Dr. Bernard, Cromwell settled upon Ussher the profit of certain deodands; but his other biographer, Dr. Parr, says the favour was a promise to grant him a lease of twenty-one years of certain lands belonging to the See of Armagh, a grant which the Archbishop did not enjoy, and which was refused to Lady Tyrrel and her husband after his death, on the ground of "malignancy."[13]

However, the Irish Parliament, in 1662, granted Lady Tyrrel an annuity of £500.[14] Ussher was now a widower. Lady Tyrrel appears to have been no exception to the proverbial longevity of annuitants. According to some authorities, she lived to be 106, but this must be a mistake, as the inscription on her monument in Oakley church, Berks, proves. She left behind her a family of twelve children — four sons and eight daughters. The inscription, which mentions her death in 1693, speaks of her as "an excellent wife and most indulgent mother, and highly charitable to the poor." This last characteristic was shared by Sir Timothy

---

12. Dr. Parr states that the "Independent faction getting the upper hand, soon put an end to the payment." — *Life of Ussher,* p 74. The original order for the payment, extracted from the London Rolls Office, may be seen in Elrington's *Life,* p. 251–2. See also *Notes and Queries,* Second Series, Vol. vii, p. 193. Storey, in his *Cathedrals,* says, "Oliver Cromwell, like Buonaparte, feigned respect for great learning, talents and virtues." Hallam, in his *Constitutional History,* draws out a parallel between these two men. — See Macaulay's *Essays,* i, p. 82–3.

13. Parr's *Life,* p. 74.

14. The grant was moved for in the House of Commons on June 16, 1662, by Sir Paul Davys, Knt., the King's Principal Secretary of State. — Mont. MSS., p. 99 (note). Ussher closes a letter to Lady Tyrrel, written from London, July 27, 1654, "in great haste," with the following reference to Mrs. Ussher and his grandchildren: "I am now in London to see your mother who is indifferent in her health, and remembereth herself very kindly to my son and yourself and all the little ones, as doth also your most loving father." — Ussher's *Works,* xvi, p. 297.

Tyrrel, whose monument in the same church records that he was "an indulgent husband, a kind father, and a good master; just in his dealings, and highly charitable to the poor."

Cromwell and Ussher came into personal communication on more than one occasion toward the close of their lives. The Protector was wise enough to recognise the influence of the Archbishop, while he admired his learning, which he felt to be an honour to their common country. On the other hand, Ussher had little confidence in Cromwell. He frequently expressed the opinion that his usurpation was like that of some of the Grecian tyrants, and would have a similar fate; as it began with an army, so it commonly ended with the death of the usurper.[15] He never recognised the lawful authority of the Protector, who had been so prominent an agent in dragging down alike Church and Crown; and when in 1649, after the execution of Charles, he sent for Ussher, the Archbishop at first refused to appear. Four years later, Ussher was again in his presence, and sought some concessions under his hand on behalf of the persecuted clergy. Cromwell was suffering at the time from an ulcerous tumour, and was in the hands of the surgeon. "If this core were out," he said to Ussher, "I should, soon be well"; to which Ussher replied, with great boldness of speech, "I doubt the core lies deeper; there is a core in the heart which must be taken out, or else it will not be well."

"So it is indeed," replied the Protector with a sigh.[16] Cromwell refused to grant the Archbishop's request of more favourable terms for the clergy, and so he left his presence; and returning to his rooms, according to his chaplain and biographer, broke out into an expression of indignant anger. "This false man hath broken his word with me, and refuses to perform what he promised; well, he will have little cause to glory in his wickedness, for he will not continue long; the King will return, though I shall not live to see it; you may." According to Dr.

15. Smith's *Life of Ussher,* p. 109; Elrington, ditto, p. 266.

16. Parr's *Life,* p. 75.

Gauden, afterwards Bishop of Exeter, Ussher said, "he saw that some men had only guts and no bowels *(intestina non viscera).*"[17] This was the last occasion on which these remarkable men met.

A few years before this, two events had happened which left an indelible impression on the mind of Ussher, and no doubt had intensified at once his monarchical and ecclesiastical sympathies. On January 10, 1645, his friend of many years' standing, and who had so frequently counselled him on Irish Church matters — Strafford — had fallen before the storm, and laid his head on the block.

Four years later, on January 31, 1649, Ussher saw his Sovereign led forth to execution. From the roof of the Countess of Peterborough's house, close to Charing Cross, he witnessed the solemn tragedy. "When he came upon the leads, the King was in his speech; the Lord Primate stood still and said nothing, but sighed, and lifting up his hands and eyes (full of tears) towards Heaven, seemed to pray earnestly; but when his Majesty had done speaking, and had pulled off his cloak and doublet, and stood stripped in his waistcoat, and that the villains in vizards began to put up his hair, the good Bishop, no longer able to endure so dismal a sight, and being full of grief and horror for that most wicked act now ready to be executed, grew pale, and began to faint; so that if he had not been observed by his own servant, and some others that stood near him (who thereupon supported him), he had swooned away."[18] They carried down the aged prelate and laid him upon his bed, where he prayed with tears for his Prince. Ever afterwards Ussher kept the day a private fast. His strong opinion was that the deed would further the designs of the Church of Rome in England.

17. Wood's *Athen. Oxon.,* iii, p. 614. "The poor orthodox clergy have passed a Sunday in silence. The old Bishop of Armagh has been with Cromwell but to little purpose, though he had some court holy-water, a dinner, and confirmation of leases in Ireland." — *State, Papers,* April 1, 1656.

18. From the narrative of an eyewitness, related by the Archbishop's servant to his grandson, Mr. James Tyrrel. — Parr's *Life,* p.72.

CHAPTER XXI

PERSECUTION OF THE CHURCH; USSHER'S FRESH LITERARY LABOURS; CORRESPONDENCE; DECLINING HEALTH AND DEATH; HISTORY OF HIS BOOKS AND LIBRARY; CONCLUSION

The fortunes of the Church of England were now at their lowest ebb. Episcopacy had been abolished throughout the three kingdoms and no other form of Church government could be said to have taken its place. The clergy who refused to accept the solemn League and Covenant had been driven from their dioceses. The "great Idol of the Service Book" as the Prayer-book was called, was silenced in favour of the "Directory of Public Worship." The "Calves Coop" as the prayer desk was called, was put away. Any minister using the Book of Common Prayer, either in public or private, was liable to be fined five pounds for the first offence, and ten pounds for the second; or refusing to use the

Directory, forty shillings for each offence. "Master presbyter was left to do as his pickle brains would suit him."

The worship of God was left "to chance, in deliberation, and a petulant fancy." Only here and there did a faithful priest of the Church of England, like Taylor or Sanderson, dare to minister in holy things. When the Prayer Book was used at all, it was from memory. The charge was brought against the learned Pococke, of Oriental fame, that he used part of the Prayer book; that he began his service with the words "Almighty and most merciful Father" and that he said "Praise ye the Lord." He was charged with using the entire of the "Confession" and the substance of the "Absolution."[1] Bishop Sanderson, in his effort to escape the letter of the law, drew up a MS. prayer-book fashioned on the language of the Book of Common Prayer.[2] Other grievous charges were brought against the clergy, involving the most outrageous attacks on their moral character, and the English language was scarcely full enough for the opprobrious terms leveled at them.

A Presbyterian scheme of Church government had been voted by the General Assembly, after thirty days' debate, creating lay elders and deacons for every parish, with congregational provinces and national assemblies; but the Independent party overthrew it.

A grand committee for religion and to try the "malignant" clergy was then established, before whom suspected clerics were summoned. Puritanical ministers were placed in the benefices from which the malignants — that is, the Royalist clergy — were driven. Nor did things fare better with the universities. Dr. Hammond was expelled from his sub-deanery of Christ Church and imprisoned; Dr. Sanderson was driven from his Chair as Regius Professor of Divinity, and forced to retire into the country. Nearly all the Masters and Fellows of Cambridge were ejected, and the revenues of the Colleges sequestered. The Primate and the

---

1. See Twell's *Life of Pococke,* p. 151, &c.

2. Sanderson's *Liturgy* edited and published by Dr. Jacobson, Bishop of Chester, in his Edition of Sanderson's Works.

Bishops of Ely and Bath and Wells were thrown into the Tower. Twelve of the other bishops for a time shared their imprisonment. Bishop Hall, by no means an extreme prelate, tells us in graphic language how it fared with him — his goods sold, his rents withheld, and his cathedral ransacked; all the organ-pipes, vestments, copes, surplices, with the service books and singing-books, carried to the fire in the public market-place, "a lewd wretch walking before the train in his cope, trailing in the dirt, with a service book in his hand, imitating in an impious scorn the tune, and usurping the words of the Litany used formerly in the Church."[3]

Nor did the other cathedral churches fare better. The Parliamentary soldiers wreaked their will on Canterbury, spreading destruction on every side, tearing alike surplices, gowns, and Bibles, and mangling the Books of Common Prayer. Cromwell, we are told, "did most miserably deface the Cathedral of Peterborough."[4] It was a hideous orgie in the name of religion.

The aged Archbishop must have seen and heard many things at this time to make his heart ache, and lead him almost to despair of Church and State. There was an ominous outburst of all kinds of fanatical excesses at the same time that the Church services were entirely suppressed. The Quakers alone of the sects received no toleration, and, strange to say, they filled the jails during the entire period of the Commonwealth.[5] John Evelyn, in his Diary, under date December 25, 1655, tells us what he felt at the prevailing famine of the Word of God. "I went to London where Dr. Wild preached the funeral sermon on preaching, this being the last day after which Cromwell's proclamation was to take place that none of the Church of England should dare either to preach or administer Sacraments, teach schools, &c., on pain of imprisonment or exile. So this was the mournfullest

---

3. See *Life of Bishop Hall,* by Geo. Lewis, p. 401.

4. *Mercurus Aulicus,* quoted by Archdeacon Perry, *History of the English Church,* Vol. ii, p. 468.

5. See George Fox's *Life* for an account of his several imprisonments.

day that in my life I had seen, or the Church of England herself, since the Reformation, to the great rejoicing of both Papist and Presbyter. So pathetic was his discourse that it drew many tears from the auditory. Myself, wife, and some of our family received the Communion."[6] Again, sometime later we find him recording in his Diary how a few faithful Churchmen ventured to meet in London to keep Christmas Day, and how, during the celebration of the Holy Communion, the church was surrounded by soldiers, and the congregation taken prisoners. As they went up to receive the Communion the soldiers held their muskets against them as if they would have shot them at the altar.[7]

The utter collapse of the Church was only prevented by the courage and faithfulness of men like Hammond, Taylor, Skinner, Sanderson, and Martin (Bishop of Meath), who now and then admitted a suitable candidate to holy orders, and maintained in some measure theological learning by their writings.

Archbishop Ussher, from his retreat at Reigate, viewed this state of things with the utmost alarm. He saw with his usual prescience that the Church of Rome alone would prosper by the general confusion and make capital out of the universal disintegration.[8] It was her interest to set sect against sect, and intensify the Puritan reaction. In a remarkable letter addressed to Ussher by Bramhall about this time (July 1654), the later clearly set forth the nature of the Roman conspiracy. He had learned from the best authority that over one hundred Romish clergy had been sent into England from the Continent, who were to feign themselves to be some Presbyterians, some Anabaptists, and who were to argue for or against the merits of their respective systems. Corroboration of the fact that such a deep plot was being hatched

---

6. Evelyn's *Diary*, p. 297. Dr. Wild had been chaplain to Archbishop Laud. At the Restoration he was made Bishop of Derry.

7. Ditto, p. 309.

8. See Evelyn's *Diary*, Vol. i, p. 294. In Ussher's opinion, "the Church would be destroyed by sectarians, who would in all likelihood bring in Poperie."

at this time to confound all religious conviction in the country, and so make the way easier for a return to the Roman camp, is not wanting; and one of the strongest proofs of the truth of the charge is to be found in the action of the Roman Catholics themselves, who succeeded in suppressing the first edition of Parr's *Life and Letters of Archbishop Ussher*, on the ground that it contained this letter of Bramhall's with its damaging revelation.

But throughout these troublous times Ussher kept steadily at his purpose of enriching the Church with theological and historical contributions. In 1650, he published, as the result of many years labour, the first part of his *Annals of the Old Testament*. Four years later, the second part of the work was given to the public. He contemplated a third part, carrying on the work to the beginning of the fourth century of the Christian era, but he did not live to complete it. A tribute to Ussher's universal sovereignty in the Protestant world may be seen in the fact that his theology has been accepted by nearly all the Reformed Churches. In a Latin letter addressed by Bishop Hall to Ussher, he acknowledges with gratitude the gift of a copy of the *Annals* and expresses his astonishment at the enormous industry of the Archbishop.[9] The learned Arnold Boate[10] likewise writes acknowledging a copy, and expressing his thanks.[11]

Ussher was also occupied during these years in a controversy as to the various readings of the Hebrew text of the Old

---

9. Ussher's *Works* xvi, p. 157–8.

10. Boate was born in Holland and graduated in medicine at Leyden. He became a great student of Rabbinical writings, and was invited to Dublin by Ussher, where he practised among his Dutch countrymen who had settled in the city. He married a daughter of Dungan, Justice of the Common Pleas.

11. Ussher's *Works,* xvi, p. 181. It is alleged on the authority of the Stationers' Registers, under date August 21, 1647, that Fuller translated the *Annales* into English, but if so the work has disappeared. Fuller, in his *History,* acknowledges that his "wares" were from "the storehouse of that reverend prelate the Cape merchant of all learning. Clean through this work, in points of chronology, I have with implicit faith followed his computations,

Testament. It is a remarkable evidence of the regard paid to Ussher's judgment that the two learned men who had engaged in an intellectual duel over the question, both appealed in the most earnest way to the Archbishop to decide between them. "I have great cause to think," writes Boate, "that a full and free declaring of your mind will be a condemning of Capellus in all the main points in the controversy between me and him." Capellus writes in an equally confident strain.[12] The Archbishop, in taking part in the dispute, rejects the attempt to correct the Hebrew text out of the Septuagint or Samaritan Pentateuch, and gives it as his own opinion, from which he says he has never swerved, that the Hebrew text of the Old Testament Scriptures was not less open to errors than that of the New Testament and of all other books, but that for the purpose of ascertaining and correcting these errors the industry of the Massorites was of the greatest avail.

Some variations of the Hebrew text might be obtained from ancient interpreters, but none from the Septuagint or the Samaritan text. It is plain from this that had Ussher lived in these days his sympathies would have been with the Higher Criticism rather than with its opponents. But beyond the glimpses we get from his share in the above controversy, little or no light is thrown on Ussher's attitude on the question of inspiration.

With regard to the Septuagint, Ussher held a peculiar opinion. He maintained that "the Seventy Jews translated only the Pentateuch, and that the rest of the Old Testament was translated in the reign of Philometer, an Alexandrian Jew, to gratify the curiosity of the Gentiles on the subject of the Hebrew religion. Ussher likewise maintained that while the original translation

---

setting my watch by his dial, knowing his dial to be set by the sun." Ussher's *Chronology* has been taken advantage of to show that Colenso's principal objections to the truth of the Pentateuch were anticipated and answered more than two hundred years ago. — See Proctor's tractate on the subject, *Bishop Colenso's Principal Objections*, &c.

12. See the correspondence in Ussher's *Works*, xvi, p. 192, &c. also *Works*, Vol. vii.

perished in the Alexandrine conflagration, several copies had been made, one of which was in the possession of Philo, and was afterwards used by Origen for the completion of his Hexapla.[13]

Ussher's opinion was afterwards controverted by Valesius, who in his address to the Archbishop says, "I am unwilling here to heap up praises of you which neither your modesty nor your friendship allows. In most things which you have written on the subject I agree with you, and greatly admire your wonderful learning and keenness of judgment; but there are some points on which I am reluctantly compelled to differ from you."[14] The theory of the Archbishop mentioned above has, we need scarcely say, been universally discarded. It may be observed that Ussher was the first English scholar who undertook a critical examination of the Septuagint.[15]

Toward the close of his life, Ussher kept up an interesting correspondence on astronomical and theological subjects with Mr. Thomas Whalley.[16] One of the questions discussed with considerable zeal was the strange one of the probable period of Adam's sojourn in the Garden of Eden. Mr. Whalley gives his opinion that "the stay of Adam in Paradise was much longer than most men hold . . . perhaps as long as Christ lived upon earth after His baptism." At the same time, it was a nice point on which he did not care to be too curious.

In a subsequent letter, he gives his reasons for thinking that Adam's sojourn in the Garden was of some duration. He was required to dress it and to keep it, to take notice of and contemplate the natures of the plants and animals; to have the beasts of all kinds presented before him, and give names to a multitude of species; to "visit and search the properties also of so many sorts of herbs and plants," to keep a Sabbath, "lie in a heavy sleep, till

---

13. Ussher's *Works,* Vol. vii.

14. See Elrington's *Life of Ussher,* p. 270.

15. *De Graeca LXX. Interpretum Versione Syntagma,* published 1655.

16. Whalley was a Fellow of Trinity College, Cambridge.

the woman was built, and then take knowledge of her, and give her a name; and further, to enter into a long conference with the Serpent, and both of them to sew for themselves garments of leaves." In a further letter he speaks of "the tree of life by consent of many good divines and schoolmen) as not only a sacrament, but as medicine to defend man's nature in his integrity from injury and mortality."[17] Unfortunately, Ussher's reply to these speculations is not forthcoming. That he did correspond on the subject is plain from Mr. Whalley's letters, in one of which he writes, "Your correspondence of the feast of expiation, on the 10th of Tisri in memory of the first sin, I hold very ingenious"; and in another he refers to the Archbishop's "other conjectures, of Adam's continuance in Paradise, and will be thankful if he will vouchsafe to impart to him his meditations on that or any other subject."[18]

The time was now drawing on apace when Israel must die. The aged Archbishop had seen many changes in Church and State. Strafford, Laud, and his Sovereign had alike fallen on the scaffold; the throne had been cast down, and a Protectorate established in its place; the Church was in ruins, the bishops disheartened and scattered, the clergy persecuted, their flock divided, the Prayer-book silenced.[19] Afar off across the Irish Channel things were in all equally deplorable condition. The Church there likewise had been overthrown, while a fierce and bloody revolution had swept over a large portion of the country. Nearly all the bishops had fled; a few faithful ones, like Parry, Bishop of Killaloe, remained at their posts, and witnessed against the ecclesiastical tyranny of the day.[20]

---

17. Archbishop Whately held the same opinion as to the grace conveyed by the tree of life. — See *Lessons on.Relig. Worship,* ch. x.

18. *Works,* xvi, p. 269–80.

19. It was a remarkable coincidence that the same day that Laud was sentenced to be hanged, Parliament abolished the Book of Common Prayer.

20. See for this Dwyer's *History of Killaloe Diocese* and the manly protest of the Bishop, p. 255–6.

In January 1656, Archbishop Ussher wrote in his Almanac, "Now aged seventy-five years. My years are full"; and below in large letters the word "Resignation." At Reigate, where he went in the following month, having bade farewell to his friends and relatives in London, he attempted to complete his *Chronologia Sacra,* but without success. His sight failed him, and he was contemplating the service of an amanuensis. Dr. Parr, his chaplain and future biographer, visited and preached before him in the following month. He tells us how, when his sermon was over, the Archbishop called him to his side and spoke to him a few earnest words of instruction and encouragement. On March 20, the aged prelate, now fast hastening to the grave, undertook to give spiritual consolation to a lady who lay dying in the same house, but whom the Archbishop himself was to predecease. At suppertime, he complained of pain in his side, and pleurisy set in. The physicians could do little for him, and he calmly prepared for death. He thanked the Countess of Peterborough for all her kindness, and said farewell, commending her to the grace of God. He was then left alone. He was heard to utter the prayer, "O Lord, forgive me especially my sins of omission." Shortly afterwards, at one in the afternoon of March 21, 1656, he quietly "fell on sleep."[21]

Cromwell required that a public funeral should be accorded to the great Archbishop, and that he should be buried with all honours in Westminster Abbey. The spot chosen for his final resting place was in St. Paul's Chapel, close to the monument of his first teacher, Fullerton, and near the steps leading to Henry Seventh's Chapel.

We are told that a large concourse of people met the funeral cortege, including many of the nobility and London clergy. So great was the concourse that a military guard was found necessary. Only on this occasion was the Burial Service of the Church

---

21. Ussher died intestate. His daughter took out letters of administration, May 1656, Wills Dept., Somerset House, fol. III, of that date.

of England read within the Abbey walls during the entire period of the Commonwealth. The sermon was preached by the Archbishop's chaplain, Dr. Bernard, and afterwards published. He took for his text the suitable words, "And Samuel died, and all Israel were gathered together and lamented him, and buried him." No stone marks the spot where the Archbishop sleeps.[22]

The funeral expenses, it may be observed, reached a far higher sum than the £200 voted for the purpose by Cromwell, and the deficit was made good by his family, who could ill spare the expense.[23]

Ussher's public life is thus briefly summed up by Dr. Parr: "He had been fifty-five years a minister, nearly fourteen years a Professor of Divinity in Dublin University, and several years

22. Several errors are to be noted here. Elrington says Ussher was buried in St. Erasmus Chapel. In the *Dub. Univ. Cal.* for 1877, Pt. ii, p. 1892, we read, "The spot where he is interred is marked by a flat stone bearing this inscription: 'James Ussher, Archbishop of Armagh.' " But the fact is, as mentioned above, Ussher was buried in St. Paul's Chapel, beside the grave of James Fullerton, his early instructor, whose "quaint epitaph" says Dean Stanley, "still attracts attention. . . . The statesmen of Charles II erected no memorial to mark the spot." — *Mem. of West. Abbey,* p. 249. Ware in 1734, records: "He hath no monument placed over him." And no monument was subsequently erected to mark the spot. Winstanley likewise is in error in stating that Ussher was buried in Henry VII's Chapel. — *Worthies,* p. 476. Mr. Dixon, in his article on "Distinguished Graduates" *(Book of Trinity College,* p. 246), perpetuates the error as to his place of interment. The following is "the quaint epitaph" referred to above: "Here lyes ye remnant of Sir James Fullerton, Knight, first gentleman of ye bedchamber to King Charles ye first, Prince and King: A gracious rewarder of all virtue, a severe reprover of all vice, and a professed renouncer of all vanite. He was a firm pillar of ye Com'wealth; a faithful patron of ye Catholiq' Church; a faire pattern to ye British court. He lived to ye welfare of his country, to ye honour of his prince, to ye glory of his God. He died fuller of faith than of feare; fuller of resolu'con than of paines; fuller of honour than of dayes." Fullerton, who was a Fellow of Trinity College, Dublin, in 1593, was for some time Ambassador at the Court of France.

23. The original order to pay the £200 to Nicholas Bernard is published by Elrington, *Life of Ussher,* p. 278 (note).

Vice-Chancellor of it; sat as Bishop of Meath four years, and thirty-one years Archbishop of Armagh, being the hundredth from St. Patrick in that See."[24]

Several posthumous writings of Ussher were gathered together, some of which were subsequently published, including a volume of his sermons;[25] a collection of tracts published by Bernard, in which Ussher treats of the extent of the satisfaction rendered by Christ's death, of the Sabbath and Lord's Day, and of Ordination in foreign Churches; the Power of the Prince already referred to; the Chronology; the tracts on Celebrating Divine Service in an unknown tongue, and two dissertations on the Pseudo-Dionysian writings and the Epistle to the Laodoceans; the first establishment of English Laws and Parliaments in the kingdom of Ireland, in which last Ussher shows that all Acts made in England were intended for the government of Ireland likewise; a discourse where and how far the Imperial laws were received by the old Irish and the several inhabitants of Great Britain; and the Divinity Lectures. The *Bibliotheca Theologica,* commenced as early as 1608, was sought for with great interest after Ussher's death. The original MS., a folio of some 600 pages, got into the hands of Bishop Stillingfleet, and is now deposited in the British Museum. Dr. Langbaine Provost of Queen's College, who was named for the task by Ussher "as the only man on whose learning as well as friendship he could rely, to cast it into such a form as might render it fit for the press,"[26] endeavoured to collate and transcribe the MS., as it lay in the Bodleian Library, but found it a most difficult business, as a portion had been eaten away by the rats. Langbaine died from a cold he took in the library while thus engaged, having survived the Archbishop three years.[27]

24. P*arr's Life* p. 77–8.

25. *Works,* Vol. xiii.

26. Parr's *Life of Ussher,* p. 13.

27. See Wood's A*then. Oxon.,* iii, p. 447–8 (note); "Langbaine died of cold taken sitting in the University Library." — *Harl.* MSS., 5,898, f. 291.

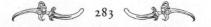

There is, says Elrington, a small thin folio in the library of the University of Dublin, which appears to contain the first sketch of this work.[28]

It will be interesting to know that this library is rich in Ussher MSS., but unfortunately most of them are in imperfect condition. Besides the original matter, there are annotations in Ussher's handwriting on the margin of several MSS. by other hands.

Among the collection are a MS. copy of Hooker's famous sermon on Justification[29] and a MS. containing the Eighth Book of the *Ecclesiastical Polity*. This latter was collated by Archdeacon Cotton, and proved of great use in ascertaining a more perfect text. It was also examined by the late Dr. Todd, Senior Fellow of Trinity College, Dublin, for Keble's edition.[30] There was formerly a second copy as also one of the Seventh Book among the Ussher MSS., but these have disappeared. Ussher also made an analysis of the Eighth Book for his own use, and this is to be found in the library.[31]

Ussher's famous collection of books had for a time a chequered experience. Some valuable works were lost, but the bulk of them was transferred to Chester, and thence to London. Covetous eyes were cast on them shortly after the Archbishop's

---

28. *Class* D. 3. 29. The MS., which is really an oblong octavo, and is written in what Laud calls Ussher's "small close hand" (Strafford's *Letters,* ii, p. 24), contains some curious things. For example, Ussher holds an opinion about the creation of our first parents which does not tally with the modern theory of the development of man. He tells us that Adam was created very wise, and that on the same day on which he was framed, being alone, he spake a language not infused, but of his own making, which language Eve also did understand, and that both she and her husband were spoken to by God, proof texts being given from the opening chapters of Genesis.

29. *Class* A. 5. 6.

30. See Keble's *Introduction to the Eccl. Polity,* p. xxxvii–ix.

31. *Class* D. 3. 3. Six volumes of Ussher's *Collectanea* were given to the Bodleian Library by James Tyrrel, the Archbishop's grandson. Some further Ussher MSS. came to the Library through Laud. — Macray's *Annals Bod.* Lib., p. 102, 125, 318.

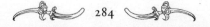

death, and among others the King of Denmark and Cardinal Mazarin made offers for them. Cromwell, however, insisted that they should not be disposed of without his consent.

At a meeting of the Council, at which Cromwell was present, Dr. Owen and two others were ordered to read the catalogue, and see what books might be profitably bought for the State.[32] The City ministers desired to purchase them for Sion College at a price of £2500, to be "disbursed by some private citizens."[33] Eventually the army serving in Ireland was allowed to purchase the entire collection, amounting to some 10,000 volumes, at a cost of £2200, with a view to their being brought back to Dublin.[34] For this purpose they were transferred back again to Chester, and there placed on board the *Kinsale* frigate, and landed in Dublin, August 1657, the captain of the ship, Mr. Robert Phillpott, receiving £9 *6s. 8d.* for the carriage across.

On reaching the city, an embargo was again placed on them, and they were removed to the Castle, where they remained till the Restoration, when Charles II finally surrendered them to the College, but in the meanwhile many valuable works were lost.[35]

From the story we have now told it will not be difficult to gather the chief features in the life and character of Archbishop

---

32. *State Papers*, June 12, 1656.

33. *Tanner MSS.* lii, p. 163, quoted by Urwick in his *Early History of Trinity College*, p. 91 (note).

34. Trinity College *MSS.* Evidently through a misprint in the figures, this sum got enlarged to £22,000, the amount mentioned by Dr. Stubbs in his *History,* following the *Dub. Univ. Cal.* for 1877. Parr and Elrington, in their *Lives,* and Abbott, in his article on the Library, *Book of Trinity College,* p. 149, give the correct figures.

35. *Parr's Life,* p. 102; Elrington's *Life,* p. 303–4. The University of Oxford is rich in Ussher *Collectanea.* According to Evelyn, several of the Archbishop's books and rare MSS. sold to provide him with bread. — *Letter to Pepys,* August 12, 1689. Parr says that Bernard borrowed many of his books and never returned them. Under *Class* D. I. 4. will be found the MS. catalogue of Ussher's books as given to the College

Ussher. His learning was unchallenged; it was the admiration of the age in which he lived. There were few branches of knowledge, as we have seen, with which he had not an acquaintance, and his range in some of them was extensive almost to a phenomenal degree. Perhaps he will never be exceeded in his knowledge of ancient Church history and theology. To the present day, many of his writings are resorted to, as to an unexhausted and inexhaustible treasure-house. No one can be said to be fairly equipped for the controversy with the Roman Church who is not at home in his *Answer to a Jesuit* and his treatise on *The Religion Professed by the Ancient Irish*. As we have seen, he achieved an extraordinary triumph in his successful effort to unravel the mystery of the Ignatian Epistles. His correspondence shows that he was consulted by and that he communicated with

---

Library, Dublin. The portion of the library where they rest bears the inscription: *"Bibliotheca Usseriana ex Dona Serenmissimi Regis Caroli Secundi."* The Ussher MSS. have been rich in finds. For example, there is one *(Class* E. 3. 8. fo1. 163) that contains three letters of Pope Alexander III, addressed to the English King, Henry II, to the Irish bishops, and to the princes and nobles of Ireland respectively, with a view to confirming and strengthening the hold of the English Crown over Ireland. They were originally unearthed by Ussher from "the Little Black Book, of the Exchequer of England in the office of the King's Remembrancer." We learn this from a note in Ussher's handwriting. This work must have been done during one of his many visits to London. In the same way, Ussher unearthed Alexander III's Bull confirming Pope Adrian's gift of Ireland, originally preserved in the *Hibernia Expugnata* of Giraldus, but subsequently suppressed. John Ross, however, the antiquarian and historian of Warwick, who died in 1491, had previously got hold of the Bull and transcribed it into his own *Historia Regum Anglia* (published at Oxford in 1716). It was in Ross's MSS. that Ussher discovered the document, and so was able to restore the text of Giraldus. The Ussher MSS. contain two copies of Giraldus *(Class* E. 3. 31, F. 4, 4). The letters of Alexander III reveal a frightful state of immorality in Ireland, and justify his interference in the direction of bringing a reformation of religion. — See the *Irish Eccl. Record*, Vol. iii, No. 69; King's *Church Hist. of Ireland*, Vol. ii, p. 530 (note); and Hergenrother's *Catholic Church and Christian State*, ii, p. 157. See also Ussher's *Sylloge, Works*, Vol. iv., *Epist.* xlvi, p. 549–50.

all the leading literary men of his time, including many foreign writers of learning and distinction. In private and social life he was all that could be desired — dignified, hospitable, and, with his more intimate friends, affectionate. He was prodigal of his information, and always ready to make others sharers in it. As regards his public life in Ireland, he was frequently placed in circumstances of considerable difficulty. It was needful at times to temporise, and his masters were not always the easiest to serve.

He seems at times to have been of a too gentle and yielding disposition, and perhaps on some occasions did not exhibit a sufficiently resolute spirit. He was a man of peace, and above everything else loved the seclusion of his study. It was his fate to live in times when bishops, and especially a prelate holding the exalted position of the Irish Primate, were compelled to interfere much in affairs of State.

In ecclesiastical matters he became gradually educated from the strict standpoint of his early training, until he was able to defend the doctrine and discipline of the Catholic Church, as one of its most learned supporters. His wide reading broadened his mind and helped him to break through the narrow confinement that came of the Puritan and Calvinistic traditions of his youth. The concessions he was ready at one period to make to the principles of Presbyterianism, were not spontaneous, but were forced from him, as we have seen, by the exigencies of the times and his desire to bring about a peaceful solution, if possible, of a great crisis in the history of his country. His subsequent publications showed that, if anything, his adhesion to Episcopacy as the original and apostolic form of Church government had strengthened with the growth of years.[36]

For Irish Churchmen, Ussher left behind him a great heritage. He left them an example of prodigious industry, showing

---

36. M. Reville, in his *Les Origines de L'Episcopat*, premiere partie, p. 8 (note), places Ussher's name first in the list of those great English divines who defended Episcopacy in the seventeenth century.

itself in vast spaces of learning, and herein he exhibits a model they may well follow at the present day.

It remains to be said that Ussher's published works, including his *Life* by Dr. Elrington, are contained in seventeen volumes, prepared and issued by the University of Dublin at a cost of £3800. The concluding volume, published in 1864, under the joint editorship of the late J.H. Todd, D.D., Senior Fellow T.C.D., and the late Bishop Reeves, contains the notes of three sermons, and most exhaustive indexes to the entire series of volumes, these latter being the admirable work of the Bishop.

Their legendary struggle . . . re-live the final act of defiance by Jewish residents of the citadel of Masada who chose death rather than life under Roman rule of tyranny. Page 881, *The Annals of the World.*

Order your copy of
James Ussher's
The Annals of the World
www.nlpg.com/annals.asp

Appendix

ARTICLES OF RELIGION

Agreed Vpon by THE ARCHBISHOPS AND BISHOPS,
AND THE REST OF THE CLEARGIE OF IRELAND.

In the Conuocation holden at Dublin in the yeare of our Lord
God 1615, for the auoiding of Diuersities of Opinions, and
the establishing of consent touching true Religion. For some
account of the formation and authority of these Articles, see
above, p. 171 seqq.

They are now reprinted from a copy of the original edition
which is appended to Dr. Elrington's *Life of Archbishop Ussher.*

IRISH ARTICLES OF RELIGION.

Of the holy Scripture and the three Creeds.

1. The ground of our Religion, and rule of faith and all sauing
trueth is the word of God contained in the holy scripture.
2. By the name of holy scripture we understand all the Canonicall
Bookes of the Old and New Testament, viz.:

Of the Old Testament.

The 5 Bookes of Moses.
Iosua.
Iudges.
Ruth.

The first and second of Samuel.
The first and second of Kings.
The first and second of Chronicles.
Esra.
Nehemiah.
Esther.
Iob.
Psalmes.
Prouerbes.
Ecclesiastes.
The Song of Salomon.
Isaiah.
Ieremiah, his Prophesie and Lamentation.
Ezechiel.
Daniel.
The 12 lesse Prophets.

Of the New Testament.

The Gospells according to
Matthew.
Marke.
Luke.
Iohn.
The Actes of the Apostles.
The Epistle of S. Paul to the Romaines.
Corinthians 2.
Galathians.
Ephesians.
Philippians.
Colossians.
Thessalonians 2.
Timothie 2.
Titus.
Philemon.
Hebrewes.

The Epistle of S. Iames.
Saint Peter 2.
Saint Iohn 3.
Saint Iude.
The Reuelation of S. Iohn.

All which wee acknowledge to be giuen by the inspiration of God, and in that regard to be of most certaine credit and highest authority.

3. The other Bookes commonly called Apocryphall did not proceede from such inspiration and therefore are not of sufficient authoritie to establish any point of doctrine; but the Church doth reade them as Bookes containing many worthy things for example of life and instruction of maners. Such are these following:

The thirde booke of Esdras.
The fourth booke of Esdras.
The booke of Tobias.
The booke of Iudith.
Additions to the booke of Esther.
The booke of Wisedome.
The booke of Iesus, the Sonne of Sirach, called Ecclesiasticus.
Baruch, with the Epistle of Ieremiah.
The song of the three Children.
Susanna.
Bell and the Dragon.
The praier of Manasses.
The First booke of Macchabees.
The Second booke of Macchabees.

4. The Scriptures ought to be translated out of the original tongues into all languages for the common use of all men: neither is any person to be discouraged from reading the Bible in such a language as he doth vnderstand, but seriously exhorted to read the same with great humilitie and reuerence, as a speciall meanes to bring him to the true knowledge of God and of his owne duty.

5. Although there bee some hard things in the Scripture (especially such as haue proper relation to the times in which they were first vttered, and prophesies of things which were afterwardes to bee fulfilled), yet all things necessary to be knowen vnto euerlasting saluation are cleerely deliuered therein: and nothing of that kinde is spoken vnder darke mysteries in one place, which is not in other places spoken more familiarly and plainely to the capacitie of learned and vnlearned.

6. The holy Scriptures containe all things necessary to saluation, and are able to instruct sufficiently in all points of faith that we are bound to beleeue, and all good duties that we are bound to practise.

7. All and euerie the Articles contained in the Nicene Creede, the Creede of Athanasius, and that which is commonly called the Apostles' Creede ought firmely to bee receiued and beleeued, for they may be proued by most certaine warrant of holy Scripture.

Of faith in the holy Trinitie.

8. There is but one liuing and true God, euerlasting, without body, parts, or passions, of infinite power, wisedome, and goodnes, the maker and preseruer of all things, both visible and inuisible. And in vnitie of this Godhead there be three persons of one and the same substance, power, and eternitie: the Father, the Sone, and the holy Ghost.

9. The essence of the Father doth not begett the essence of the Sonne; but the person of the Father begetteth the person of the Sonne by communicating his whole essence to the person begotten from eternitie.

10. The holy Ghost, proceeding from the Father and the Sonne, is of one substance, maiestie, and glory, with the Father and the Sonne, very and eternall God.

Of God's eternall decree, and Predestination.

11. God from all eternitie did by his vnchangeable counsell ordaine whatsoeuer in time should come to passe: yet so, as thereby no violence is offred to the wills of the reasonable creatures, and neither the libertie nor the contingencie of the second causes is taken away, but established rather.

12. By the same eternall counsell God hath predestinated some vnto life, and reprobated some vnto death: of both which there is a certaine number, knowen only to God, which can neither be increased nor diminished.

13. Predestination to life, is the euerlasting purpose of God, whereby, before the foundations of the world were layed, he hath constantly decreed in his secret counsell to deliuer from curse and damnation those whom he hath chosen in Christ out of mankinde, and to bring them by Christ vnto euerlasting saluation, as vessels made to honor.

14. The cause mouing God to predestinate vnto life, is not the foreseeing of faith, or perseuerance, or good workes, or of any thing which is in the person predestinated, but onely the good pleasure of God himselfe. For all things being ordained for the manifestation of his glory, and his glory being to appeare both in the workes of his Mercy and of his Iustice; it seemed good to his heauenly wisedome to choose out a certaine number towardes whome he would extende his vndeserued mercy, leauing the rest to be spectacles of his iustice.

15. Such as are predestinated vnto life be called according vnto Gods purpose (his Spirit working in due season) and through grace they obey the calling, they bee iustified freely, they bee made sonnes of God by adoption, they be made like the image of his onely begotten Sonne Iesus Christ, they walke religiously in good workes, and at length, by God's mercy they attaine to

euerlasting felicitie. But such as are not predestinated to saluation shall finally be condemned for their sinnes.

16. The godlike consideration of Predestination and our election in Christ is full of sweete, pleasant, and vnspeakable comfort to godly persons, and such as feele in themselues the working of the spirit of Christ, mortifying the workes of the flesh, and their earthly members, and drawing vp their mindes to high and heauenly things: as well because it doth greatly confirme and establish their faith of eternall saluation to be enioyed through Christ, as because it doth feruently kindle their loue towardes God: and on the contrary side, for curious and carnall persons, lacking the spirite of Christ, to haue continually before their eies the sentence of Gods predestination is very dangerous.

17. Wee must receiue Gods promises in such wise as they be generally set forth vnto vs in holy Scripture; and in our doings, that will of God is to be followed, which we haue expressly declared vnto vs in the word of God.

Of the creation and gouerment of all things.

18. In the beginning of time when no creature had any being, God by his word alone, in the space of sixe dayes, created all things, and afterwardes by his prouidence doth continue, propagate, and order them according to his owne will.

19. The principall creatures are Angels and men.

20. Of Angels, some continued in that holy state wherein they were created, and are by God's grace for euer established therein: others fell from the same, and are reserued in chaines of darkness vnto the iudgement of the great day.

21. Man being at the beginning created according to the image of God (which consisted especially in the Wisedome of his minde and the true Holyness of his free will) had the couenant of the lawe ingrafted in his heart: whereby God did promise vnto

him euerlasting life, vpon condition that he performed entire and perfect obedience vnto his Commandements, according to that measure of strength wherewith hee was endued in his creation, and threatened death vnto him if he did not performe the same.

Of the fall of man, originall sinne, and the state of man before iustification.

22. By one man sinne entred into the world, and death by sinne: and so death went ouer all men, for as much as all haue sinned.

23. Originall sinne standeth not in the imitation of Adam (as the Pelagians dreame) but is the fault and corruption of the nature of euery person that naturally is ingendred and propagated from Adam: whereby it commeth to passe that man is depriued of originall righteousnes, and by nature is bent vnto sinne. And therefore, in euery person borne into the world, it deserueth Gods wrath and damnation.

24. This corruption of nature doth remaine euen in those that are regenerated, whereby the flesh alwaies lusteth against the spirit, and cannot bee made subject to the lawe of God. And howsoeuer, for Christs sake there bee no condemnation to such as are regenerate and doe beleeue: yet doth the Apostle acknowledge that in it selfe this concupiscence hath the nature of sinne.

25. The condition of man after the fall of Adam is such that he cannot turne and prepare himselfe by his owne naturall strength and good workes, to faith and calling vpon God. Wherefore we haue no power to doe good workes pleasing and acceptable vnto God without the grace of God preuenting vs, that we may haue a good will, and working with vs when wee haue that good will.

26. Workes done before the grace of Christ and the inspiration of his spirit are not pleasing vnto God, for as much as they spring not of faith in Iesus Christ, neither do they make men meete to receaue grace, or (as the Schoole Authors say) deserue grace of

congruitie: yea rather, for that they are not done in such sorte as God hath willed and comaunded them to be done, we doubt not but they are sinfull.

27. All sinnes are not equall, but some farre more heynous than others; yet the very least is of its owne nature mortall, and without Gods mercy maketh the offender lyable vnto euerlasting damnation.

28. God is not the Author of sinne: hobeit he doth not only permitt, but also by his prouidence gouerne and order the same, guiding it in such sorte by his infinite wisedome, as he turneth to the manifestation of his owne glory and to the good of his elect.

Of Christ, the mediator of the second Covenant.

29. The Sonne, which is the Word of the Father, begotten from euerlasting of the Father, the true and eternall God, of one substance with the Father, tooke mans nature in the wombe of the blessed Virgin, of her substance: so that two whole and perfect natures, that is to say, the Godhead and Manhoode were inseparably ioined in one person, making one Christ very God and very man.

30. Christ in the truth of our nature was made like vnto vs in all things, sinne only excepted, from which he was cleerley voyd, both in his life and in his nature. He came as a Lambe without spott to take away the sins of the world by the sacrifice of himselfe once made, and sinne (as Saint Iohn saith) was not in him. He fulfilled the law for vs perfectly: For our sakes he endured most grieuous torments immediately in his soule, and most painefull sufferings in his body. He was crucified, and dyed to reconcile his Father vnto vs, and to be a sacrifice not onely for originall guilt, but also for all our actuall transgressions. He was buried and descended into hell, and the third day rose from the dead, and tooke againe his body, with flesh, bones, and all things

appertaining to the perfection of mans nature: wherewith he ascended into Heauen, and there sitteth at the right hand of his Father, vntil hee return to iudge all men at the last day.

Of the communicating of the grace of Christ.

31. They are to be condemned that presume to say that euery man shalbe saued by the law or sect which he professeth, so that he be diligent to frame his life according to that law and the light of nature. For holy scripture doth set out vnto vs only the name of Iesus Christ whereby men must be saued.

32. None can come vnto Christ vnlesse it be giuen vnto him, and vnlesse the Father drawe him. And all men are not so drawen by the Father that they may come vnto the Son. Neither is there such a sufficient measure of grace vouchsafed vnto euerie man whereby he is enabled to come vnto euerlasting life.

33. All Gods elect are in their time inseperablye vnited vnto Christ by the effectuall and vitall influence of the holy Ghost, deriued from him as from the head vnto euery true member of his mysticall body. And being thus made one with Christ, they are truly regenerated and made partakers of him and all his benefits.

Of Iustification and Faith.

34. We are accounted righteous before God, onely for the merit of our Lord and Saviour Iesus Christ, applied by faith; and not for our owne workes or merits. And this righteousnes, which we so receiue of Gods mercie and Christs merits, imbraced by faith, is taken, accepted, and allowed of God for our perfect and full iustification.

35. Although this iustification be free vnto vs, yet it commeth not so freely vnto vs that there is no ransome paid therefore at all. God shewed his great mercie in deliuering vs from our former captiuitie, without requiring of any ransome to be payd, or

amends to be made on our parts; which thing by vs had been vnpossible to bee done. And whereas all the world was not able of themselues to pay any part towards their ransome, it pleased our heauenly Father of his infinite mercie without any desert of ours, to prouide for vs the most precious merits of his owne Sonne, whereby our ransome might be fully payd, the lawe fulfilled, and his iustice fully satisfied. So that Christ is now the righteousnes of all them that truely beleeue in him. Hee for them payd their ransome by his death. He for them fulfilled the lawe in his life. That now in him, and by him euerie true Christian man may be called a fulfiller of the lawe: forasmuch as that which our infirmitie was not able to effect, Christs iustice hath performed. And thus the iustice and mercie of God doe imbrace each other: the grace of God not shutting out the iustice of God in the matter of our iustification; but onely shutting out the iustice of man (that is to say, the iustice of our own workes) from being any cause of deseruing our iustification.

36. When we say that we are iustified by faith onely, we doe not meane that the said iustifying faith is alone in man, without true Repentance, Hope, Charity, and the feare of God (for such a faith is dead, and cannot iustifie), neither do we meane that this our act to beleeue in Christ, or this our faith in Christ, which is within vs, doth of it selfe iustifie vs, or deserue our iustification vnto vs (for that were to account our selues to bee iustified by the vertue or dignitie of some thing that is within our selues): but the true vnderstanding and meaning thereof is that although we haue Faith, Hope, Charitie, Repentance, and the feare of God within us and adde neuer so many good workes thereunto: yet we must renounce the merit of all our said vertues, of Faith, Hope, Charitie, and all our other vertues, and good deeds, which we either haue done, shall doe, or can doe, as things that be farre too weake and vnperfect, and vnsufficient to deserue remission of our sinnes, and our iustification: and therefore we must trust onely in Gods mercie, and the merits of his most dearely beloued Sonne, our

onely Redeemer, Sauiour, and Iustifier, Iesus Christ. Neuerthelesse, because Faith doth directly send vs to Christ for our iustification, and that by faith given vs of God wee embrace the promise of Gods mercie, and the remission of our sinnes (which thing none other of our vertues or workes properly doth): therefore the Scripture vseth to say, that Faith without workes; and the ancient fathers of the Church to the same purpose, that onely Faith doth iustifie vs.

37. By iustifying Faith wee vnderstand not onely the common beleefe of the Articles of Christian Religion, and a perswasion of the truth of Gods worde in generall: but also a particular application of the gratuitous promises of the Gospell, to the comfort of our owne soules: whereby we lay hold on Christ with all his benefits, hauing an earnest trust and confidence in God that he will be mercifull vnto vs for his onely Sonnes sake. So that a true beleeuer may bee certaine, by the assurance of faith, of the forgiuenesse of his sinnes, and of his euerlasting salvation by Christ.

38. A true, liuely, iustifying faith, and the sanctifying spirit of God is not extinguished nor vanisheth away in the regenerate, either finally or totally.

Of sanctification and good workes.

39. All that are iustified are likewise sanctified: their faith being alwaies accompanied with true Repentance and good Workes.

40. Repentance is a gift of God, whereby a godly sorrow is wrought in the heart of the faithfull for offending God their mercifull Father by their former transgressions, together with a constant resolution for the time to come to cleaue vnto God and to lead a new life.

41. Albeit that good workes, which are the fruits of faith and follow after iustification, cannot make satisfaction for our sinnes, and endure the seueritie of Gods iudgement: yet are they pleasing to God, and accepted of him in Christ, and doe spring from

a true and liuely faith, which by them is to be discerned as a tree by the fruite.

42. The workes which God would haue his people to walke in are such as he hath commaunded in his holy Scripture, and not such workes as men haue deuised out of their own braine, of a blind zeale and deuotion, without the warrant of the word of God.

43. The regenerate cannot fulfil the lawe of God perfectly in this life. For in many things we offend all: and if we say we haue no sinne, we deceaue our selues, and the truth is not in vs.

44. Not euerie heynous sinne willingly committed after baptisme is sinne against the holy Ghost and vnpardonable. And therefore to such as fall into sinne after baptisme, place for repentance is not to be denied.

45. Voluntary workes besides, ouer, and aboue God's commandements, which they call workes of Supererogation, cannot be taught without arrogancie and impietie. For by them men doe declare that they do not onely render vnto God as much as they are bound to doe, but that they doe more for his sake then of bounden duty is required.

Of the seruice of God.

46. Our dutie towards God is to beleeue in him, to feare him, and to loue him with all our heart, with all our minde, and with all our soule, and with all our strength, to worship him, and to giue him thankes, to put our whole trust in him, to call vpon him, to honour his holy Name and his word, and to serue him truely all the dayes of our life.

47. In all our necessities we ought to haue recourse vnto God by prayer: assuring ourselues that whatsoeuer we aske of the Father in the name of his Sonne (our onely mediator and intercessor) Christ Iesus, and according to his will, he will vndoubtedly grant it.

48. Wee ought to prepare our hearts before wee pray, and vnderstand the things that wee aske when we pray: that both our hearts and voyces may together sound in the eares of Gods Maiestie.

49. When almighty God smiteth vs with affliction, of some great calamitie hangeth ouer vs, or any other waighty cause so requireth; it is our dutie to humble our selues in fasting, to bewaile our sinnes with a sorrowfull heart, and to addict our selues to earnest prayer, that it might please God to turne his wrath from vs, or supplie vs with such graces as wee greatly stand in neede of.

50. Fasting is a with-holding of meat, drincke, and all naturall foode, with other outwarde delights, from the body for the determined time of fasting. As for those abstinences which are appointed by publike order of our state, for eating of fish and forbearing of flesh at certaine times and daies appointed, they are no wayes ment to bee religious fastes, nor intended for the maintenance of any superstition in the choice of meates, but are grounded merely vpon politike considerations for prouision of things tending to the better preseruation of the Commonwealth.

51. Wee must not fast with this perswasion of minde, that our fasting can bring vs to heauen, or ascribe holynesse to the outward worke wrought. For God alloweth not our fast for the worke sake (which of it selfe is a thing meerely indifferent), but chiefly respecteth the heart, how it is affected therein. It is therefore requisite that first before all things we clense our hearts from sinne, and then direct our fast to such ends as God will allow to bee good: that the flesh may thereby be chastised, the spirit may be more feruent in prayer, and that our fasting may bee a testimony of our humble submission to Gods maiestie, when wee acknowledge our sinnes vnto him, and are inwardly touched with sorrowfulnesse of heart, bewailing the same in the affliction of our bodies.

52. All worship deuised by mans phantasie, besides or contrary to the Scripture (as wandring on Pilgrimages, setting vp of Candles, Stations, and Iubilies, Pharisaicall sects and fained religions, praying vpon Beades, and such like superstition) hath not onely no promise of reward in Scripture, but contrariewise threatnings and maledictions.

53. All maner of expressing God the Father, the Sonne, and the holy Ghost in an outward forme is vtterly vnlawfull. As also all other images deuised or made by man to the use of Religion.

54. All religious worship ought to be giuen to God alone; from whome all goodnesse, health, and grace ought to be both asked and looked for, as from the very author and giuer of the same, and from none other.

55. The name of God is to be vsed with all reuerence and holy respect: and therefore all vaine and rash swearing is vtterly to be condemned. Yet notwithstanding vpon lawfull occasions, an oath may be giuen and taken according to the word of God, iustice, iudgment, and truth.

56. The first day of the weeke, which is the Lords day, is wholly to be dedicated unto the seruice of God: and therefore we are bound therein to rest from our common and daily buysinesse, and to bestow that leasure vpon holy exercises, both publike and priuate.

Of the Ciuill Magistrate.

57. The Kings Maiesty vnder God hath the Soueraigne and chiefe power within his Realmes and Dominions ouer all manner of persons of what estate, either Ecclesiasticall or Ciuill, soeuer they bee; so as no other forraine power hath or ought to haue any superiority ouer them.

58. Wee do professe that the supreame gouernement of all estates within the saide Realmes and Dominions in all causes, as well Ecclesiasticall as Temporall, doth of right appertaine to the Kings

highnes. Neither doe we giue vnto him hereby the administration of the Word and Sacraments, or the power of the Keyes: but that prerogatiue onely which we see to haue been alwaies giuen vnto all godly Princes in holy Scripture by God himselfe; that is, that he should containe all estates and degrees committed to his charge by God, whether they be Ecclesiasticall of Ciuill, within their duty, and restraine the stubborne and eiuil doers with the power of the Ciuill swoorde.

59. The Pope neither of himselfe, nor by any authoritie of the Church or Sea of Rome, or by any other meanes with any other, hath any power or authoritie to depose the King, or dispose any of his Kingdomes or Dominions, or to authorise any other Prince to inuade or annoy him or his Countries, or to discharge any of his subjects of their allegeance and obedience to his Maiestie or to giue licence or leaue to any of them to beare armes, raise tumult, or to offer any violence of hurt to his Royall person, state, or gouernement, or to any of his subjects within his Maiesties Dominions.

60. That Princes which be excommunicated or depriued by the Pope may be deposed or murthered by their subiects or any other whatsoeuer is impious doctrine.

61. The lawes of the Realme may punish Christian men with death for heynous and grieuous offences.

62. It is lawfull for Christian men, at the commandement of the Magistrate, to beare armes, and to serue in iust wars.

Of our duty towards our Neighbours.

63. Ovr duty towards our neighbours is to loue them as our selues, and to do to all men as we would they should doe to us; to honour and obey our Superiours, to preserue the safety to mens persons, as also their chastitie, goods, and good names; to beare no malice nor hatred in our hearts; to keepe our bodies in temperance, sobernes, and chastitie; to be true and iust in all our

doings; not to couet other mens goodes, but labour truely to get our owne liuing, and to doe our dutie in that estate of life vnto which it pleaseth God to call us.

64. For the preseruation of the chastitie of mens persons, wed-locke is commaunded vnto all men that stand in need thereof. Neither is there any prohibition by the word of God, but that the ministers of the Church may enter into the state of Matrimony: they being no where commaunded by Gods Lawe either to vow the estate of single life, or to abstaine from marriage. Therefore it is lawfull also for them, as well as for all other Christian men, to marrie at their owne discretion, as they shall iudge the same to serue better to godlines.

65. The riches and goodes of Christians are not common, as touching the right, title, and possession of the same: as certaine Anabaptists falsely affirme. Notwithstanding euerie man ought of such things as hee possesseth liberally to giue alms to the poore according to his ability.

66. Faith giuen is to be kept, even with Hereticks and Infidells.

67. The Popish doctrine of Equiuocation & mentall Reseruation is most vngodly, and tendeth plainely to the subuersion of all humaine society.

Of the Church, and outward ministry of the Gospell.

68. There is but one Catholike Church (out of which there is no salutation) containing the uniuersall company of all the Saints that euer were, are, or shalbe gathered together in one body, vnder one head Christ Iesus: part whereof is already in heaven triumphant, part as yet militant heere vpon earth. And because this Church consisteth of all those, and those alone, which are elected by God vnto saluation, & regenerated by the power of his spirit, the number of whome is knowen only vnto God himselfe; therefore it is called Catholike or vniversall, and the Inuisible Church.

69. But particular and visible Churches (consisting of those who make profession of the faith of Christ, and liue vnder the outward means of saluation) be many in number: wherein the more or lesse sincerely according to Christs institution, the word of God is taught, the Sacraments are administered, and the authority of the Keyes is vsed, the more or lesse pure are such Churches to bee accounted.

70. Although in the visible Church the euill bee euer mingled wiht the good, and sometimes the euill haue chiefe authoritie in the ministration of the word & Sacraments: yet, for as much as they doe not the same in their owne name but in Christs, and minister by his commission and authority, we may vse their ministry both in hearing the word and in receiuing the Sacraments. Neither is the effect of Christs ordinance taken away by their wickednesse: nor the grace of Gods gifts diminished from such as by faith and rightly doe receaue the Sacraments ministred vnto them; which are effectuall, because of Christs institution and promise, although they be ministred by euill men. Neuerthelesse in appertaineth to the discipline of the Church that inquiry be made of euill ministers, and that they be accused by those that haue knowledge of their offences, and finally being found guiltie, by iust iudgement bee deposed.

71. It is not lawfull for any man to take vpon him the office of publike preaching or ministring the Sacraments in the Church vnless hee bee first lawfully called and sent to execute the same. And those we ought to iudge lawfully called and sent which bee chosen and called to this worke by men who haue publike authoritie giuen them in the Church, to call and send ministers into the Lords vineyard.

72. To haue publike prayer in the Church, or to administer the Sacraments in a tongue not vnderstood of the people, is a thing plainly repugnant to the word of God and the custome of the Primitiue Church.

73. That person which by publike denunciation of the Church is rightly cut off from the vnitie of the Church, and excommunicate, ought to bee taken of the whole multitude of the faithfull as a Heathen and Publican vntill by Repentance he be openly reconciled and receaued into the Church by the iudgement of such as haue authoritie in that behalfe.

74. God hath giuen power to his ministers not simply to forgiue sinnes (which prerogatiue he hath reserued onely to himselfe), but in his name to declare and pronounce vnto such as truely repent and vnfainedly beleeue his holy Gospell, the absolution and forgiuenesse of sinnes. Neither is it Gods pleasure that his people should be tied to make a particular confession of all their knowen sinnes vnto any mortall man: howsoeuer any person grieued in his conscience, vpon any speciall cause may well resorte vnto any godly and learned Minister to receaue aduise and comfort at his hands.

Of the authoritie of the Church, generall Councells, and Bishop of Rome.

75. It is not lawfull for the Church to ordaine any thing that is contrary to Gods word: neither may it so expound one place of Scripture that it be repugnant to another. Wherefore although the Church bee a witnesse and a keeper of holy writt: yet as it ought not to decree any thing against the same, so besides the same ought it not inforce any thing to be beleeued vpon necessitie of saluation.

76. Generall Councells may not be gathered together without the commaundement and will of Princes; and when they be gathered together (for as much as they be an assembly of men and not alwaies gouerned with the spirit and word of God) they may err, and sometimes haue erred, euen in things pertaining to the rule of pietie. Wherefore things ordained by them as necessary to saluation, haue neither strength nor authority vnlesse it may be shewn that they bee taken out of holy Scriptures.

77. Euery particular Church hath authority to institute, to change, and cleane to put away ceremonies and other Ecclesiasticall rites as they be superfluous or be abused; and to constitute other, makeing more to seemelynes, to order, or edification.

78. As the Churches in Ierusalem, Alexandria, and Antioch haue erred: so also the Church of Rome hath erred, not onely in those things which concerne matter of practice and point of ceremonies, but also in matters of faith.

79. The power which the Bishop of Rome now challengeth, to be Supreame head of the vniversall Church of Christ, and to be aboue all Emperours, Kings and Princes, is an usurped power, contrary to the Scriptures and word of God, and contrary to the example of the Primitiue Church: and therefore is for most iust causes taken away and abolished within the Kings Maiesties Realmes and Dominions.

80. The Bishop of Rome is so farre from being the supreame head of the vniuersall Church of Christ, that his workes and doctrine doe plainely discover him to bee that man of sinne, foretold in the holy Scriptures whome the Lord shall consume with the spirit of his mouth, and abolish with the brightnes of his coming.

Of the State of the old and new Testament.

81. In the Old Testament the Commaundements of the Law were more largely, and the promises of Christ more sparingly and darkely propounded, shaddowed with a multitude of types and figures, and so much the more generally and obscurely deliuered, as the manifesting of them was further off.

82. The Old Testament is not contrary to the New. For both in the Old and New Testament euerlasting life is offered to mankinde by Christ, who is the onely mediator betweene God and man, being both God and man. Wherefore they are not to be heard which faine that the old Fathers did looke onely for

transitory promises. For they looked for all benefits of God the Father through the merits of his Sonne Iesus Christ, as we now doe: onely they beleeued in Christ which should come, we in Christ already come.

83. The New Testament is full of grace and truth, bringing ioyfull tidings vnto mankinde, that whatsoeuer formerly was promised of Christ is now accomplished: and so in stead of the auncient types and ceremonies, exhibiteth the things themselues, with a large and cleere declaration of all the benefits of the Gospell. Neither is the ministery thereof restrained any longer to one circumcised nation, but is indifferently propounded vnto all people, whether they be Iewes or Gentils. So that there is now no Nation which can truly complaine that they be shut forth from the communion of Saints and the liberties of the people of God.

84. Although the Law giuen from God by Moses as touching ceremonies and rites be abolished, and the Ciuill precepts thereof be not of necessitie to be receaued in any Commonwealth: yet nothwithstanding no Christian man whatsoeuer is freed from the obedience of the Commaundements which are called Morall.

Of the Sacraments of the New Testament.

85. The Sacraments ordained by Christ be not onely badges or tokens of Christian mens profession: but rather certaine sure witnesses, and effectuall or powerfull signes of grace and Gods good will towards us, by which he doth worke inuisibly in vs, and not onely quicken but also strengthen and confirme our faith in him.

86. There bee two Sacraments ordained of Christ our Lord in the Gospell, that is to say, Baptisme and the Lords Supper.

87. Those fiue which by the Church of Rome are called Sacraments, to witt, Confirmation, Penance, Orders, Matrimony,

and Extreame vnction, are not to be accounted Sacraments of the Gospell: being such as haue partly growen from corrupt imitation of the Apostles, partly are states of life allowed in the Scriptures, but yet haue not like nature of Sacraments with Baptisme and the Lords Supper, for that they haue not any visible signe or ceremonie ordained of God, together with a promise of sauing grace annexed thereunto.

88. The Sacraments were not ordained of Christ to be gazed vpon, or to be carried about; but that we should duely vse them. And in such onely as worthyly receaue the same, they haue a wholesome effect and operation; but they that receaue them vnworthylie, thereby draw iudgement vpon themselues.

Of Baptisme.

89. Baptisme is not onely an outward signe of our profession, and a note of difference whereby Christians are discerned from such as are no Christians; but much more a Sacrament of our admission into the Church, sealing vnto vs our new birth (and consequently our Iustification, Adoption, and Sanctification) by the communion which we haue with Iesus Christ.

90. The Baptisme of Infants is to be retained in the Church as agreeable to the word of God.

91. In the administration of Baptisme, Exorcisme, Oile, Salte, Spittle, and superstitious hallowing of the water are for iust causes abolished: and without them the Sacrament is fully and perfectly administered to all intents and purposes agreeable to the institution of our Sauior Christ.

Of the Lords Supper.

92. The Lords supper is not onely a signe of the mutuall loue which Christians ought to beare one towards another, but much more a Sacrament of our preseruation in the Church, sealing vnto us ovr spirituall nourishment and continuall growth in Christ.

93. The change of the substance of bread and wine into the substance of the Body and Bloud of Christ, commonly called Transubstantiation, cannot be proued by Holy Writ; but is repugnant to plaine testimonies of the Scripture, ouerthroweth the nature of a Sacrament, and hath giuen occasion to most grosse Idolatry and manifold superstitions.

94. In the outward part of the Holy Communion, the Bodie and Bloud of Christ is in a most liuely manner represented: being no otherwise present with the visible elements than things signified and sealed are present with the signes and seales, that is to say, symbolically and relatiuely. But in the inward and spirituall part the same Body and Bloud is really and substantially presented vnto all those who haue grace to receaue the Sonne of God, euen to all those that beleeue in his name. And vnto such as in this manner doe worthylie and with faith repair vnto the Lords table, the Bodie and Bloud of Christ is not onely signified and offered, but also truly exhibited and communicated.

95. The Bodie of Christ is giuen, taken, and eaten in the Lords Supper, onely after an heauenly and spirituall manner; and the meane whereby the Body of Christ is thus receaued and eaten is Faith.

96. The wicked and such as want a liuely faith, although they doe carnally and visibly (as Saint Augustine speaketh) presse with their teeth the Sacrament of the body and bloud of Christ, yet in no wise are they made partakers of Christ; but rather to their condemnation doe eat and drincke the signe or Sacrament of so great a thing.

97. Both the parts of the Lords Sacrament, according to Christs institution and the practise of the auncient Church, ought to be ministred vnto Gods people; and it is plain sacriledge to rob them of the mysticall cup, for whom Christ hath shed his most precious bloud.

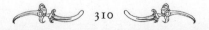